Treating Complex Trauma

In *Treating Complex Trauma*, renowned clinicians Mary Jo Barrett and Linda Stone Fish present the Collaborative Change Model (CCM), a clinically evaluated model that facilitates client and practitioner collaboration and provides invaluable tools for clients struggling with the impact and effects of complex trauma. A practical guide, *Treating Complex Trauma* organizes clinical theory, outcome research, and decades of experiential wisdom into a manageable blueprint for treatment. With an emphasis on relationships, the model helps clients move from survival mindstates to engaged mindstates, and as a sequential and organized model, the CCM can be used by helping professionals in a wide array of disciplines and settings. Utilization of the CCM in collaboration with clients and other trauma-informed practitioners helps prevent the re-traumatization of clients and the compassion fatigue of the practitioner so that they can work together to build a hopeful and meaningful vision of the future.

Mary Jo Barrett, MSW, is the executive director and founder of the Center for Contextual Change. She is currently adjunct faculty at the University of Chicago School of Social Service Administration, the Chicago Center for Family Health, and the Family Institute at Northwestern University. She has published numerous articles in the areas of family violence, compassion fatigue, child sexual abuse, and domestic violence. She has coauthored two books and numerous book chapters. Ms. Barrett has served as the director of Midwest Family Resource and has been working in the field of family violence since 1974.

Linda Stone Fish, MSW, PhD, is the David B. Falk Endowed Professor of Marriage and Family Therapy at Syracuse University. She is the author of numerous research and theoretical articles and is the coauthor of *Nurturing Queer Youth*. Dr. Stone Fish has been training couple and family therapists for over 25 years and has been working with clients with a history of complex trauma for more than 30 years.

ROUTLEDGE PSYCHOSOCIAL STRESS SERIES
Charles R. Figley, Ph.D., Series Editor

1. *Stress Disorders Among Vietnam Veterans*, Edited by Charles R. Figley, Ph.D.
2. *Stress and the Family Vol. 1: Coping with Normative Transitions*, Edited by Hamilton I. McCubbin, Ph.D., and Charles R. Figley, Ph.D.
3. *Stress and the Family Vol. 2: Coping with Catastrophe*, Edited by Charles R. Figley, Ph.D., and Hamilton I. McCubbin, Ph.D.
4. *Trauma and Its Wake: The Study and Treatment of Post-Traumatic Stress Disorder,* Edited by Charles R. Figley, Ph.D.
5. *Post-Traumatic Stress Disorder and the War Veteran Patient*, Edited by William E. Kelly, M.D.
6. *The Crime Victim's Book, Second Edition*, By Morton Bard, Ph.D., and Dawn Sangrey.
7. *Stress and Coping in Time of War: Generalizations from the Israeli Experience*, Edited by Norman A. Milgram, Ph.D.
8. *Trauma and Its Wake Vol. 2: Traumatic Stress Theory, Research, and Intervention*, Edited by Charles R. Figley, Ph.D.
9. *Stress and Addiction*, Edited by Edward Gottheil, M.D., Ph.D., Keith A. Druley, Ph.D., Steven Pashko, Ph.D., and Stephen P. Weinsteinn, Ph.D.
10. *Vietnam: A Casebook*, by Jacob D. Lindy, M.D., in collaboration with Bonnie L. Green, Ph.D., Mary C. Grace, M.Ed., M.S., John A. MacLeod, M.D., and Louis Spitz, M.D.
11. *Post-Traumatic Therapy and Victims of Violence*, Edited by Frank M. Ochberg, M.D.
12. *Mental Health Response to Mass Emergencies: Theory and Practice*, Edited by Mary Lystad, Ph.D.
13. *Treating Stress in Families*, Edited by Charles R. Figley, Ph.D.
14. *Trauma, Transformation, and Healing: An Integrative Approach to Theory, Research, and Post-Traumatic Therapy*, By John P. Wilson, Ph.D.
15. *Systemic Treatment of Incest: A Therapeutic Handbook*, By Terry Trepper, Ph.D., and Mary Jo Barrett, M.S.W.
16. *The Crisis of Competence: Transitional Stress and the Displaced Worker*, Edited by Carl A. Maida, Ph.D., Norma S. Gordon, M.A., and Norman L. Farberow, Ph.D.
17. *Stress Management: An Integrated Approach to Therapy*, by Dorothy H. G. Cotton, Ph.D.
18. *Trauma and the Vietnam War Generation: Report of the Findings from the National Vietnam Veterans Readjustment Study*, By Richard A. Kulka, Ph.D., William E. Schlenger, Ph.D., John A. Fairbank, Ph.D., Richard L. Hough, Ph.D., Kathleen Jordan, Ph.D., Charles R. Marmar, M.D., Daniel S. Weiss, Ph.D., and David A. Grady, Psy.D.
19. *Strangers at Home: Vietnam Veterans Since the War*, Edited by Charles R. Figley, Ph.D., and Seymour Leventman, Ph.D.
20. *The National Vietnam Veterans Readjustment Study: Tables of Findings and Technical Appendices*, By Richard A. Kulka, Ph.D., Kathleen Jordan, Ph.D., Charles R. Marmar, M.D., and Daniel S. Weiss, Ph.D.
21. *Psychological Trauma and the Adult Survivor: Theory, Therapy, and Transformation*, By I. Lisa McCann, Ph.D., and Laurie Anne Pearlman, Ph.D.
22. *Coping with Infant or Fetal Loss: The Couple's Healing Process*, By Kathleen R. Gilbert, Ph.D., and Laura S. Smart, Ph.D.
23. *Compassion Fatigue: Coping with Secondary Traumatic Stress Disorder in Those Who Treat the Traumatized*, Edited by Charles R. Figley, Ph.D.
24. *Treating Compassion Fatigue*, Edited by Charles R. Figley, Ph.D.
25. *Handbook of Stress, Trauma and the Family*, Edited by Don R. Catherall, Ph.D.
26. *The Pain of Helping: Psychological Injury of Helping Professionals*, By Patrick J. Morrissette, Ph.D., RMFT, NCC, CCC.
27. *Disaster Mental Health Services: A Primer for Practitioners*, By Diane Myers, R.N., M.S.N., and David Wee, M.S.S.W.
28. *Empathy in the Treatment of Trauma and PTSD*, By John P. Wilson, Ph.D., and Rhiannon B. Thomas, Ph.D.
29. *Family Stressors: Interventions for Stress and Trauma*, Edited by Don. R. Catherall, Ph. D.
30. *Handbook of Women, Stress and Trauma*, Edited by Kathleen Kendall-Tackett, Ph.D.
31. *Mapping Trauma and Its Wake*, Edited by Charles R. Figley, Ph.D.
32. *The Posttraumatic Self: Restoring Meaning and Wholeness to Personality*, Edited by John P. Wilson, Ph.D.
33. *Violent Death: Resilience and Intervention Beyond the Crisis*, Edited by Edward K. Rynearson, M.D.
34. *Combat Stress Injury: Theory, Research, and Management*, Edited by Charles R. Figley, Ph.D., and William P. Nash, M.D.
35. *MindBody Medicine: Foundations and Practical Applications*, By Leo W. Rotan, Ph.D., and Veronika Ospina-Kammerer, Ph.D.
36. *Understanding and Assessing Trauma in Children and Adolescents: Measures, Methods, and Youth in Context*, By Kathleen Nader, D.S.W.
37. *When the Past Is Always Present: Emotional Traumatization, Causes, and Cures*, By Ronald A. Ruden, M.D., Ph.D.
38. *Families Under Fire: Systemic Therapy with Military Families*, Edited by R. Blaine Everson, Ph.D., and Charles R. Figley, Ph.D.
39. *Dissociation in Traumatized Children and Adolescents: Theory and Clinical Interventions*, Edited by Sandra Wieland, Ph.D.
40. *Transcending Trauma: Survival, Resilience and Clinical Implications in Survivor Families*, By Bea Hollander-Goldfein, Ph.D., Nancy Isserman, Ph.D., and Jennifer Goldenberg, Ph.D., L.C.S.W.
41. *School Rampage Shootings and Other Youth Disturbances: Early Preventative Interventions*, By Kathleen Nader, D.S.W.

Editorial Board

Treating Complex Trauma

A Relational Blueprint for Collaboration and Change

MARY JO BARRETT AND LINDA STONE FISH

Routledge
Taylor & Francis Group

NEW YORK AND LONDON

First published 2014
by Routledge
711 Third Avenue, New York, NY 10017

and by Routledge
2 Park Square, Milton Park, Abingdon, Oxon, OX14 4RN

*Routledge is an imprint of the Taylor & Francis Group,
an informa business*

© 2014 Taylor & Francis

The right of Mary Jo Barrett and Linda Stone Fish to be identified as authors of this work has been asserted by them in accordance with sections 77 and 78 of the Copyright, Designs and Patents Act 1988.

Library of Congress Cataloging-in-Publication Data
Barrett, Mary Jo.
Treating complex trauma : a relational blueprint for collaboration
    and change / Mary Jo Barrett, Linda Stone Fish. — 1 Edition.
        pages cm. — (Routledge psychosocial stress series)
    Includes bibliographical references and index.
    1. Post-traumatic stress disorder—Treatment.   2. Psychic
trauma—Treatment.   3. Client-centered psychotherapy.
4. Brief psychotherapy.   I. Stone Fish, Linda.   II. Title.
    RC552.P67B372 2014
    616.85'21—dc23
    2013044842

ISBN: 978-0-415-51020-2 (hbk)
ISBN: 978-0-415-51021-9 (pbk)
ISBN: 978-0-203-12449-9 (ebk)

Typeset in Minion
by Apex CoVantage, LLC

MIX
Paper from
responsible sources
FSC
www.fsc.org   FSC® C014174

Printed and bound in the United States of America by Sheridan Books, Inc. (a Sheridan Group Company).

To our clients, our colleagues, our students, our friends, our enemies, and our families. Thank you for teaching us about the importance of collaboration.

This book could not have been written without the hard work, dedication, and collaboration of the staff at the Center for Contextual Change and Dennis O'Keefe and Ronald C. Fish.

Contents

Series Editor's Foreword

Sometimes those trying to help the traumatized—be they family or therapists—believe the traumatized are in need of direction; that all clients must somehow fit into the treatment protocol; the attitude that the doctor knows best. This client-centered approach was quite dominant from the 1950 to the 1980s, until practitioners themselves asked for more rigor in the assessment of treatment protocol.

Systemic Treatment of Incest: A Therapeutic Handbook, written by Terry Trepper and Mary Jo Barrett, was published in this book series in 1989. Trepper, the family psychology professor and expert on human sexuality, and Barrett, the pioneer practitioner who was the first to apply family-systems strategies to traumatized families, drew from her years of work with incest survivors and their families. Together they wrote a book that shook up the psychotherapy community.

The book was written by practitioners for practitioners who wanted to hear, in their own language, about clients struggling with sexual trauma and about ways in which practitioners could adopt systemic treatment approaches to fully engage and treat wounded families. *Systemic Treatment of Incest* was among the first books to do so, and it was published at a time when it was rare for trauma specialists to treat families at all, and when they treated them it was certainly not in a way recognized today as systemic or contextually.

In the late 1980s, there were efforts to professionalize psychotherapy, including family therapy, through state licensure, clinical membership standards of practice, and efforts to manualize treatment approaches to better establish evidence-based practice. At the same time, the art of psychotherapy flourished with important innovations to improve help for the traumatized. Most mental-health training now recognizes the importance of context, the therapeutic relationship, the importance of making sure our clients become customers to the change process, and self-care for the psychotherapist working in the trauma field.

Stated another way, in our rush to quantify our effectiveness in symptom reduction, we tended to blind ourselves to the humanity of our clients; separating us from their reality. We found that, though it sounds simple to listen to clients' stories and solutions before developing a treatment plan, it's clinically effective.

Barrett and Stone Fish take us back to our roots, completing what Trepper and Barrett started in the 1980s.

The Psychosocial Stress Series and its editorial board welcome Mary Jo Barrett and Linda Stone Fish's *Treating Complex Trauma*, a 25-year follow-up to Trepper and Barrett's book. This book is a gem. It expands the earlier book by incorporating what Barrett and Stone Fish have learned from both research and especially practice and by focusing on complex trauma. Most trauma treatment experts view the assessment and treatment of complex trauma to be the most difficult of clients. What these scholar-practitioners have discovered from toiling in the field of clinical practice not only provides a roadmap for treating complex trauma but also says a great deal about treating all forms of trauma inside and outside the family context.

This book draws from and extends this tried-and-true treatment approach with sexual trauma to traumatized families generally, though the focus here is on complex trauma. It is a very important and multi-systemic challenge.

Complex trauma—cases of relational abuse over an extended period of time—is the most difficult to correctly assess and treat, and this book provides a standard of practice for doing so. The key concept in the Barrett and Stone Fish approach to treating complex trauma is collaboration. Practitioners are guided on how best to collaborate with their clients, and through a flexible but clear clinical roadmap, they're presented with a clear and evidence-informed plan for treatment, one that leads to the clients' human development and self-care plan for the rest of their lives.

This book about treating complex trauma could have been titled the Collaborative Change Model (CCM). Because although Barrett and Stone Fish have written a remarkable book for practitioners working with clients with complex trauma, collaborative change is the key variable in their model and has far reaching implications for all therapists working with any traumatized client who wants to move forward after a traumatic event.

Complex trauma is about a multitude of issues that must be addressed. These authors have discovered that this should be done in a particular sequence. The multiple issues include but are not limited to violence and abuse at many levels: interpersonal, psychological, sexual, spiritual, and emotional. The authors point out that this type of trauma is complex and leaves deep wounds requiring a delicate operation and a close and positive working relationship between therapist and clients.

The authors' dynamic, phase-based model is a road map for practitioners. It guides the practitioner through three phases or stages of working with complex trauma clients: Creating a Context for Change (e.g., six activities including assessing vulnerabilities, setting goals); Collaborative Treatment Plan development (e.g., seven activities including exploring treatment options, challenging vulnerabilities, and the function of symptoms); and finally, the stage of Consolidation of Change and Moving Forward (e.g., six activities including engaging vulnerabilities and engaged acknowledgement).

Practitioners who want to do right by their traumatized families can use this book as a guide to understanding individuals, couples, and families from the inside out and collaborating on which treatment at what time under what conditions for how long with what kind of outcome works best for everyone.

Charles R. Figley
Series Editor

Introduction

> In the long history of humankind (and animal kind, too) those who
> learned to collaborate and improvise most effectively have prevailed.
>
> Charles Darwin

This book provides a practical and clinically evaluated model for treatment with
clients who have experienced complex trauma. The material presented and the
model it details is intended as a blueprint or meta framework that can be used by
mental health professionals from a wide array of disciplines working in various
settings. The model helps organize the treatment of all types of clients with a history of interpersonal trauma. It has been used to guide professionals with training
and expertise in specific therapeutic approaches in working with trauma, and used
by those with no formal training in trauma work. The model has been used by
professionals in the United States, Latin America, the Middle East, Asia, and parts
of Europe and by practitioners working with people from majority and minority
cultures around the world. The model is a collaborative construct, which means
that when working from it, practitioners are encouraged to engage professionals
in their communities and the clients themselves and their support systems to work
from the model to reach the most effective outcome. It is a model that generates
teams in order to create change and growth. As Helen Keller reminds us, "Alone
we can do so little; together we can do so much."

Many individuals who have a history of complex trauma are stuck and need
help. They may be living on their own, in families, in residential facilities, in jail, or
in communities. Many are merely surviving day to day while continually awaiting
the next unsettling crisis. Clients with complex trauma often begin the journey of

engaging in treatment with added emotional baggage from traumatization in foster homes, residential facilities, jails, and other therapeutic relationships, just like the ones they are entering into when they seek help. Professionals, on the other hand, come to the relationship with the explicit understanding that they are to be helpful. They may be adept in a variety of effective treatment modalities and have an open heart but lack an effective blueprint for optimizing their interventions and relational skills for those with complex trauma. Without a blueprint, when mental health professionals are in challenging relationships with their clients they may unintentionally re-traumatize clients who have been traumatized by people in positions of power that have done terrible things to them. Armed with a blueprint that is explained step-by-step to our clients, practitioners and clients collaborate so that, as many clients have said about our model, "we are in this together." A predictable, structured, goal-driven, stage model that is collaboratively created with the client creates a non-traumatic healing context. This is the model for treatment we detail in the book.

We suggest that you read this book in a deliberate fashion, slowly, thinking of the context in which you work, thinking of your clients, applying the concepts and interventions to your own work and style, and integrating the ideas so they become your own. In other words, we want you, the reader, to practice living in the model as you read about it.

Stage One: Creating a Context for Change	Stage Two: Challenging Patterns and Expanding Realities	Stage Three: Consolidation of Change and Moving Forward
Creating Refuge	Collaborative Exploration of Differential Trauma-Informed Interventions	Nurturing Environments
Assessing Vulnerabilities and the Function of the Symptom	Expanding the Refuge and Context for Change	Engaging Vulnerabilities
Assessing Resources	Challenging Vulnerabilities and the Function of the Symptoms	Integrating Resources
Exploring the Positive and Negative Consequences of Change	Expanding Resources	Choosing Engaged Mind
Understanding and Validating the Client's Denial, Availability, and Attachment	Challenging and Expanding Availability	Engaged Acknowledgement
Setting Goals	Accomplishing Goals	Incorporating Success
Introducing Acknowledgement	Ongoing Acknowledgement	

The Model

The Collaborative Change Model (CCM) is a recursive sequence model, which mirrors a natural cycle of change. The model divides the recursive sequence into three distinct stages. In the first stage of the sequence (Creating a Context for Change) the emphasis is on stabilizing therapeutic engagement with clients by focusing on safety and refuge. In Stage One, practitioners gather information about how client symptoms and behaviors are an adaptation to complex trauma, develop a common language about the survival cycle of trauma and how change occurs, and design a treatment plan together understanding how the client uniquely changes. Challenging Patterns and Expanding Realities (Stage Two) is the skill-building stage in which clients immerse themselves in new ways of thinking and behaving and expanding their worldviews to consider alternative patterns of living. Consolidation (Stage Three) focuses on highlighting the adaptive changes that the client is incorporating as well as looking into the future, whether it is the next day, the next week, or life after treatment, and planning how to stay focused on engaging constructively during times of stress. Although the model follows a very clear sequence of stages and steps, it is at the same time flexible and adaptive to individual therapist style, theoretical model, and clinical setting as well as client symptomatology. Practitioners can be creative in designing interventions that fit their particular talents. Helping others grow and change is a creative and sacred process. The CCM allows each and every client and therapist together to design the creative process of change that fits their strengths and styles. At the same time, the CCM holds that the natural cycle of change occurs in all good treatment for clients with a history of complex trauma. The beauty of the model is that, much like a blueprint organizes a creation, it organizes a journey toward healing for all involved in a simple recursive loop that is creative, respectful, practical, client-centered, and effective.

A Brief History of the Model

Barrett and Trepper (1986; Trepper and Barrett, 1989) first wrote about the model, at that time called the Multiple Systems Approach. The stages were first created to systematize treatment and help practitioners manage the anxiety involved when working with violence in the family. Barrett and Stone Fish have been working with the model since its inception, influencing each other with wisdom from their joint and respective scholarly pursuits (e.g., Barrett, Stone Fish, & Trepper, 1990; Stone Fish, 2000; Stone Fish & Harvey, 2005). As we have expanded our understanding and incorporated new information into our model, it has evolved into what we have now named the Collaborative Change Model (CCM).

We have used the model to train students, practitioners who work in outpatient psychotherapy practices, school settings, child welfare organizations, jails, hospital-based programs, and residential treatment centers. The model has been further expanded using feedback from over 500 process evaluation interviews with CCM clients who have given us feedback about what has been helpful. Over the past 30 years, we have gained a tremendous amount of wisdom from trauma-informed researchers, theorists, and scholars (e.g., Briere, 1995; Herman, 1992; Ford & Courtois, 2009; Siegel, 2010; Porges, 2001; Van der Kolk, 1987; Van der Kolk, McFarlane, & Weisaeth, 2006), from the clinicians at The Center for Contextual Change, and from thousands of clients about how complex trauma impacts individuals and families.

At the Center for Contextual Change in Chicago, Illinois, Mary Jo and her colleagues have been using the CCM as their therapeutic approach to treating clients who present with complex trauma, and victims and perpetrators of interpersonal maltreatment. Clients have an initial assessment at the Center, which may include the Trauma Symptom Inventory-2 (TSI-2) (Briere, 1995; Briere & Elliott, 2003) used both at the beginning of therapy, in the middle, and at termination, and many are interviewed after treatment is terminated. Periodically, clients who have terminated therapy over five years ago have also been contacted and asked what was helpful about therapy and how they have consolidated the changes that occurred. The CCM, which we will explore in great detail in the book, has integrated client feedback, which in turn helped sculpt the model. Therapeutic teams and client voices will be heard throughout the book sharing how the CCM navigates the complexity of each unique situation.

Terminology

Complex Trauma

We define complex trauma as a pervasive mindset that develops from historical and often ongoing relationships of violation, abuse, and neglect. Complex trauma, according to Briere and Lanktree (2012) "usually involves a combination of early and late-onset, sometimes highly invasive traumatic events, usually of an ongoing, interpersonal nature, frequently including exposure to repetitive childhood sexual, physical, and/or psychological abuse" (p. 1). Physical, sexual, psychological, and emotional violation perpetrated by and not handled supportively by caregivers and/or communities creates traumatization. A pervasive mindset of traumatization occurs when a vulnerable person is victimized, out of control, and unable to cope.

One of the key ingredients in complex trauma is that it is often embedded within relationships and larger systems and communities that are supposed to be protective. Vulnerable people are exposed to and harmed by violating events and are then re-traumatized when caregivers and communities deny, blame, or ignore those who are being violated. This betrayal trauma (DePrince & Freyd, 2007) occurs with victimized individuals when caregivers re-victimize them through further abuse or neglect, serving to compound the traumatic event and/or ongoing traumatic relationships.

Survival Mindstate

Individuals with complex trauma histories often develop survival mindstates. "If children are exposed to unmanageable stress, and if the caregiver does not take over the function of modulating the child's arousal, as occurs when children are exposed to family dysfunction or violence, they are unable to organize the experience in a coherent fashion" (Van der Kolk, 2005, p. 375). When we are unable to organize our experiences and make meaning of them in a way that makes predictable sense, our development, growth, and learning are impacted. Complex traumatic histories impair affect regulation, ego adaptive capacities, impulse control, and attachment patterns (Ford & Courtois, 2009). When individuals are unable to control their emotions, cognitions, behavior, and relationships, we suggest that they may be acting from a survival mindstate. They experience themselves as powerless, out of control, devalued, and disconnected. And they react to stress in fight, flight, and/or freeze responses that are wired for survival.

Engaged Mindstate

The goal of treatment is to help clients move from a survival mindstate to an engaged mindstate. In an engaged mindstate individuals have access to and incorporate tools that regulate their affect, cognitions, behavior, and relationships. They experience themselves as powerful, in control, valued, and connected to themselves, a support system, and to the world around them. They are aware of their strengths, their resources, and their vulnerabilities, and have developed a skill set to deal with stress. When people are acting from an engaged mindstate, they have self-awareness and other awareness, practice mindsight (Siegel, 2010), are engaged in supportive relationships, and have a meaningful vision of the future.

Overview of the Book

Blueprint to Awareness and Change

We will detail the blueprint of the CCM in a practical way so that mental health professionals are equipped with what they need to help clients with histories of complex trauma. The book is divided into two parts. Because we believe that growth and development are optimized in a reoccurring cyclical process, we have organized the book to mimic the cycle of change and demonstrate treatment using the CCM. We consciously repeat the essential concepts in every chapter, just as we recommend practitioners repeat when applying the model in order to facilitate change and growth. We believe that repetition is a practitioner's best intervention.

In the first part of the book, Creating a Context for the Journey of Change, we introduce the concepts that organize our thinking about complex trauma and about the process of change from a survival mindstate to an engaged mindstate. The first chapter reviews the literature and explores our understanding of how individuals respond and adapt to repeated traumatic experiences as they grow and develop. The first chapter also covers the attachment relationship and how caregivers' behavior impacts an individual's response to traumatic events. Chapter 2 begins with the goals of trauma-informed practice and what we have learned from our clients about the essential ingredients to effective treatment. The third chapter details the five foundational treatment elements that practitioners must attend to for treatment to be successful and the final chapter in the first part of the book details the specific essential practitioner variables for effective trauma-informed practice.

In the second part of the book, Expanding Realities: The Collaborative Change Model, we detail the three-stage model. Stage One: Creating a Context for Change, is detailed in chapter 5. In this chapter, we articulate how we create safety and assess individual, familial, and contextual variables that impact clients. In Chapter 6 we explore Stage Two: Challenging Patterns and Expanding Realities. This chapter is devoted to detailing interventions that we have found helpful in moving clients from survival mindstates to engaged mindstates. In the last chapter, we detail Stage Three: Consolidation. Consolidation is the stage in which we unify the treatment process in each therapy encounter and in treatment as a whole.

The CCM has been applied to almost any setting where there is trauma and the desire and need for change. Specifically it has been utilized in schools, hospital settings, inpatient, outpatient, and residential facilities for children, adolescents, and adults, in correctional facilities, in homes, and in business offices settings. The treatment model can be used for victims, perpetrators, and family members. Our belief is that violent behavior and other forms of maltreatment in the context of a relationship are often the result of complex trauma. Hence, the model can be used by psychotherapists, case managers, child care staff, nursing staff, physicians, lawyers, probation officers, police officers and police social workers, investigators, and administrators. The model is sequential in nature and so time periods are not relevant. Change can happen in moments and over years. Consequently, the CCM can be used to organize a three-hour CPS investigation, for an intake interview, in preparing a person to testify in court, to intervene in a crisis situation on a floor in a residential facility, and in a phone call with a client. The CCM can be used with children, adolescents, adults, couples, families, and groups. The CCM is also used with victims, offenders, and bystanders of violence and trauma. Because it is an organizational model to facilitate the natural cycle of change, it can be used in any setting during any interaction while furthering the process of recovery from trauma.

We have introduced pause and ponder sections (personal communication with Anita Mandley, 2011) that we hope you will use as a moment to think and integrate the material you have just read. The pause is actively utilized in the process of change, so we have integrated it into the writing of this book. This is an exercise designed for you to experience the three stages of the model as you read the book. Pause sections for Stage One will ask you to think of the following questions: How are you feeling? What are you thinking? Do you want to write anything down? Do you want to reread anything? How does it feel to integrate the material as a resource for you? How are you creating interventions as you read? Pause sections for Stage Two will suggest you ask yourself questions such as: Do the ideas you have just read make sense to you? Can you see how you can make these concepts applicable to your setting? How will you use the knowledge in your work with trauma? How does it expand your thinking and prepare you for your work? And pause sections for Stage Three will ask you questions such as: Are you ready to move on? Do you need to take a break, a rest, put the book down? Do you want to take some notes? Go for a walk? Share some ideas with others? Are you excited about the next pages? Are you motivated and encouraged and hopeful that the words contained in the next pages will help you be empowered, valued, and connected to yourself and your work? When you arrive at a pause and ponder section, please use it as an opportunity to experience the CCM and become familiar with your own process of change. Seriously, pause before you go on to the next step in your learning.

Our intention is to provide you with a resource that will expand your ability and capacity for working with individuals, families, couples, and group members who have experienced complex trauma, and all the array of symptoms that accompany being traumatized within a relationship. This will be a blueprint applicable to the setting in which you work. The book is filled with examples (names and details have been changed to assure confidentiality) of all types of practitioners, clients, and settings to use as stimulation for your own creative work with the CCM. The CCM is a blueprint for you to organize and build treatment so that the best possible outcome occurs for all involved.

> For an audio file that explains the Introduction of the book, please refer to the book's eResources site: www.routledgementalhealth.com/9780415510219.

References

Barrett, M. J., Stone Fish, L., & Trepper, T. (1990). Feminist-informed family therapy for the treatment of intra-family child sexual abuse. *Journal of Family Psychology, 4,* 151–166.

Barrett, M. J., & Trepper, T. (Eds.) (1986). *Treating incest: A multiple systems perspective.* Binghamton, NY: Haworth Press.

Briere, J. (1995). *Trauma Symptom Inventory professional manual.* Odessa, FL: Psychological Assessment Resources.

Briere, J., & Elliott, D. M. (2003). Prevalence and psychological sequelae of self-reported childhood physical and sexual abuse in a general population sample of men and women. *Child Abuse & Neglect, 27,* 1205–1222.

Briere, J. N., & Lanktree, C. B. (2012). *Treating complex trauma in adolescents and young adults.* Los Angeles, CA: Sage.

DePrince, A. P., & Freyd, J. J. (2007). Trauma-induced dissociation. In M. J. Friedman, T. M. Keane, & P. A. Resick (Eds.), *Handbook of PTSD: Science and practice* (pp. 135–150). New York: Guilford Press.

Ford, J. D., & Courtois, C. A. (2009). Defining and understanding complex trauma and complex traumatic stress disorders. In C. A. Courtois & J. D. Ford (Eds.) *Treating complex traumatic stress disorders: An evidence based guide.* New York: Guilford Press.

Herman, J. L. (1992). *Trauma and recovery: The aftermath of violence—from domestic abuse to political terror.* New York: Basic Books.

Porges, S. W. (2001). The polyvagal theory: Phylogenetic substrates of a social nervous system. *International Journal of Psychophysiology, 42,* 123–146.

Siegel, D. J. (2010). *Mindsight: The science of personal transformation.* New York: Bantam.

Stone Fish, L. (2000). Hierarchical relationship development: Parents and children. *Journal of Marital and Family Therapy, 4,* 501–510.

Stone Fish, L., & Harvey, R. (2005). *Nurturing queer youth: Family therapy transformed.* New York: W.W. Norton & Co.

Trepper, T., & Barrett, M. J. (1989). *Systemic treatment of incest: A therapeutic handbook.* New York: Routledge.

Van der Kolk, B. (1987). *Psychological trauma.* Washington, DC: American Psychiatric Press.

Van der Kolk, B. (2005). Editorial introduction: Child abuse and victimization. *Psychiatric Annals, 35,* 374–378.

Van der Kolk, B., McFarlane, A. C., & Weisaeth, L. (Eds.) (2006). *Traumatic stress: The effects of overwhelming experience on mind, body, and society.* New York: Guilford Press.

Part I

Creating a Context for the Journey of Change

one
Complex Trauma

The Individual

Humans are wired to anticipate and react to all of the various elements in our environment that pose a threat. This is a survival instinct and is stored in the part of the brain that we share with all animals. Our brain is triune—that is, it is divided into three sections, the brainstem, the limbic system, and the cortex. The part of the brain that we share with our reptilian cousins is the brainstem and it manages our impulses and controls our states of arousal. "Working in concert with the evaluative processes of both the limbic and the higher cortical regions, the brainstem is the arbiter of whether we respond to threats either by mobilizing our energy for combat or for flight, or by freezing in helplessness, collapsing in the face of an overwhelming situation" (Siegel, 2010a, pp. 16–17). When we experience threat or danger, our amygdala is activated, we are wired to fight the danger, flee from it, or freeze in a protective nature. This physiology is reactive and protective. When we react to threat from the brainstem, it is an automatic reaction that has survival functions.

Our autonomic nervous system has two branches, the sympathetic and the parasympathetic nervous systems. The sympathetic nervous system is activated under moments of threat and stress and helps to protect us from potential danger by getting us ready to fight or run. The amygdala, part of our sympathetic nervous system, remembers threat and responds. Our bodies are amazing instruments programmed for exquisite—survival—positive functioning. For example, our heart rates increase and blood flows toward the muscles to ready a protective response or a run for our lives. Our mouths feel dry because our saliva dries up, since our bodies know that we are probably not planning on eating anytime soon. Our skin temperature drops since we are using resources that we might normally use to keep our bodies warm and our pupils dilate so we can see our target more clearly. In other words, we are pumped. We are not thoughtful, we are not calm, nor are we relaxed. We are ready for danger. This survival physiology has kept the species alive for a very long time. The image of what danger looks like has changed over time and is different for every single individual. What is threatening to one person is absolutely not necessarily threatening to another. Consequently, all of our modes of fight, flight, and freeze are different and have evolved over time depending on the contexts in which we live.

Porges (2001) coined the term "neuroception" to explain how the nervous system detects threat and danger without our conscious awareness. His polyvagal theory (2001, 2003) explains that there are three basic stages that occur which are activated phylogenetically and subconsciously. Acute threat triggers the vagal nerve. When we feel safe, the evolved branch of the vagal nerve is activated and we are calm and able to engage socially and access support when we are threatened. When we feel threatened and unsafe, we are mobilized toward fight or flight. When both those branches fail, we rely on the unmyelinated visceral vagus, which renders us immobile (Porges, 2001).

Levine (2010) states: "When acutely threatened, we mobilize vast energies to protect and defend ourselves. We duck, dodge, twist, stiffen and retract. Our muscles contract to fight or flee. However, if our actions are ineffective, we freeze or collapse." This is very important in our understanding of trauma and the key to the trauma cycle. What Levine recognizes in this simple and brilliant statement is actually our phylogenetic response to complex trauma. The parasympathetic reaction drives the body toward action. When you are faced with a traumatic event that you cannot fight or escape from, your body enters lockdown mode. To observe this primitive response in action, watch a herd of animals being chased by a predator. The predator targets a vulnerable animal, stalks and then gives chase. When death is inevitable, the prey clearly drops into lockdown mode. This lockdown or locked in experience has been called tonic immobility or animal hypnosis by ethologists (e.g., Burghardt, 1990) and is starting to be studied in humans as well.

The primitive and protective reaction of freezing, collapsing, or playing dead (many names describing the same activity) is, for animals that face being eaten, apparently to reduce the experienced pain of their death, or perhaps to encourage the predator to leave without attacking. When we talk to clients who have been threatened and cannot escape, many describe this experience. This protective function is known as dissociation. Although the dissociative process may be an evolutionarily adaptive response to unmanageable stress, it becomes maladaptive when incorporated into a person's functioning as a result of the repeated assaults (and psychic escapes) inherent in complex trauma. An understanding of how this process functions maladaptively allows us to assist clients in transitioning from a survival mindstate to an engaged mindstate that is more aware, wiser, more present, and more attuned to self and other.

Disruptive, violent, stressful, and violating events that are not processed by the body and the mind become traumatic. When the body enters lockdown mode, the natural sympathetic nervous system response that activates reaction to danger is suppressed, and this activating urge is stored in the body (Levine, 2010). The body has a memory of its own and, when threatened by another perceived disruptive, violent, stressful, or violating event, will tend to act in ways that were protective at one time. The amygdala remembers. We refer to the result of this phylogenetic pattern of locking down as "acting from a survival mindstate" associated with a history of complex trauma. The survival mindstate is the result of a multitude of locking down reactions in the face of overwhelming persistent trauma. Van der Kolk, Van der Hart, and Marmar (1996) show that persistent trauma and the use of dissociation change the pathways between the amygdala and the hippocampus, disrupting the storage of memories and the individual's capacity to cope.

Complex trauma occurs in environments replete with unmanageable stress. A history of complex trauma inevitably involves relationships with caregivers who failed to model, teach, support, and encourage constructive adaptive responses to stressful situations. Unmanageable stress is stress that the developing human (and we are always developing) cannot manage. A stressful event that we can manage is mediated by the sympathetic nervous system so that our body is mobilized to flee or fight and by our neocortex so that we are thoughtful about the best response. When an event is unmanageable, the unmyelinated dorsal vagal branch is activated (Porges, 2001), we go into lockdown mode, we are immobile, and we survive. The ways we survive in these unmanageable situations become our ways of coping. In this manner, over time, these immobilizing coping mechanisms become our typical survival skills.

Stan, for example, was repeatedly sexually abused by his older brother when he was a child. The abuse hurt him physically and when he complained of discomfort his brother told Stan he would tell their mother that Stan made him do it if he yelled out in pain. Stan coped with years of physical and psychic pain by numbing the pain, shutting down from his body, and not feeling any physical sensation. By adolescence he had perfected this coping style and felt dead inside. In moments of stress, for instance, when he fought with his parents and felt as though they were inflexible and he had no control, he found that he needed to burn himself and feel the pain of physical injury to cope with the stressful event in the present. Stan could not cope with discomfort and knew if he created physical pain, he could numb the discomfort because had had been doing it all his life. The coping mechanism of his childhood trauma became his survival skill when under stress.

Survival skills are fueled by the limbic area of our triune brain. The limbic system regulates the autonomic nervous system. So, when stressed and ready to fight or flight, the adrenal glands release cortisol, which puts our body on high alert. Unfortunately, in overwhelming stress, again, that stress that we cannot cope with, the cortisol levels can become toxic. "These high cortisol levels can also be toxic to the growing brain and interfere with proper growth and function of the neural tissue" (Siegel, 2010a, p. 18). While the limbic system helps us survive in dangerous situations, when we are no longer in danger we may be in overdrive and unable to turn off the high levels of cortisol distribution in our bodies. Porges (2003) and Badenoch (2011) state that when the vagal branch that connects us to calm and engaged states of mind or to fight or flight reactions are not functioning because of this overdrive situation, our immobility, trauma mindstate sets in and we survive.

Ledoux (1998) calls this the fear reaction system. As a result of relational trauma, our brains see threat when it is not there. The trauma creates a hyperactivation of the amygdala and impairs parts of the brain that help with inhibition and the capacity to integrate complex information. In other words, as a result of complex trauma, the brain has difficulty communicating with itself and actually perceiving complex information. The amygdala continually detects threat. Ledoux (1998) suggests that a traumatic response is one in which a stick always looks like a snake. Of course, it is adaptive for the brain to perceive danger in a situation that is dangerous, but complex trauma makes it difficult for someone to differentiate whether danger actually lurks. Complex trauma triggers a hyperaroused, hyperactive state that overperceives threat and hinders accurate integration of information. Without the ability to effectively perceive and process threatening stimuli, hyperaroused and hyperactive reactions are not helpful. They tend to be simplistic and rigid and isolative as opposed to integrative and complex. Furthermore, these survival mindstates may encourage behaviors which sabotage the development of constructive responses, including and especially the ability to use social support.

For example, when people offend others physically, sexually, emotionally, or verbally, this offending behavior may be conceptualized as emerging from people who are acting from a survival mindstate. A hyperaroused and hyperactive reaction to discomfort has the tendency to alert people to fight, flight, or freeze. The offenders are reacting to stressful events as if something about them is in danger. Their power, sense of control, and/or self-worth feel threatened. They are powerless, out of control, and they are in danger. Their fear is triggered and their traumatic history has not taught them to respond in an engaged mindstate to stressful events. Instead, stress is overgeneralized as danger, resulting in a misguided attempt to survive the perceived threat through aggressive behaviors supposed to address control and self-esteem needs.

In another example, a child who is sexually abused by an uncle protectively reacts with freezing and tonic immobility because she is too small and vulnerable and therefore unable to fight or run. This tonic immobility decreases her physical and emotional pain as she psychically disconnects and is no longer consciously present. She may or may not remember the event but her body remembers this state. With no one to help her cope with experiences that are too much for her to cope with alone, she develops trauma mindstate coping. Cortisol levels continue to rise and become toxic. This survival skill that helped her cope as a child, however, becomes maladaptive when she is under stress later on in life. Whenever in a stressful situation, then, even though she is no longer actually as vulnerable and incapable as she used to be, she perceives it as if it is a threat to her life and still reacts as if she is incapable of fighting or fleeing.

Take this same child as a young adult woman and married to a young man with a temper. He has had too much to drink one night and wants to have sex. She is tired and is aware that she would prefer not to have sexual relations at that time. He pushes himself onto her and she collapses, limp, and in lockdown. She cannot move. She cannot tell him to stop and she cannot assert her position because her survival skill is activated and she is immobile. Her early reaction to imminent danger, useful when she was a child, is no longer useful and it ends up perpetuating her survival mindstate. If she were not in a trauma state of mind, her sympathetic nervous system would be activated and she could fight or flee. She would sense danger, recognize she was in a dangerous situation, have been taught how to modulate her arousal so she could thoughtfully respond, and/or remove herself from the situation. She could clearly and assertively tell her husband she was not going to have sex with him. If he persists and aggresses against her, she recognizes that she is in a dangerous relationship and has the cognitive and emotional resources to generate constructive alternatives.

Complex trauma changes the way our brains are organized (Perry, 1994, 2001). The brain reacts to persistent traumatic experiences in childhood and individual brain chemistry is altered because of these experiences. When children are in constant states of hyperarousal and/or dissociation, it alters their brain chemistry. There is some evidence that boys are more likely to use hyperarousal and girls to use dissociation (Perry, Pollard, Blakely, Baker, & Vigilante, 1995) and that these lead to externalizing and internalizing behaviors respectively in adulthood. Either way, the complex trauma response which may have previously assisted survival becomes a maladaptive state of being in adulthood. This is the survival mindstate.

People in a survival mindstate tend to react to signs of stress or discomfort as if each experience is traumatic; their coping response is thereby informed from a reactive state as opposed to a calm and engaged perspective. In other words, we use the two most basic parts of the triune brain, the brainstem and the limbic regions, and fail to include the cortex, which is the part of the brain that is useful in higher-level decision-making. Our understanding of interpersonal neurobiology (Cozolino, 2006, 2010; Schore, 2003; Siegel, 2007, 2010a) is helpful here. To make intelligent decisions, we require strong connections to the prefrontal region of our cortex. When in a trauma/survival mindstate, the neurons connected to that region are not firing. The prefrontal cortex is responsible for sophisticated, complicated functioning such as paying attention and managing our relationship with self and with others. It is what allows mindsight (Siegel, 2010a). When in a trauma mindstate, we are not engaging the cortex that helps us accurately map and engage the world and our responses to it.

Surviving dominated by a trauma mindstate prohibits us from optimal functioning in our daily lives. We have learned to react impulsively rather than respond thoughtfully. This concept is key to understanding the goals of trauma treatment. We want to help clients to respond to their own internal cues and to the cues of others. Frantic reactivity does not serve us well in most situations. Reactivity leads us to abuse ourselves and others, maintaining the cycle of complex trauma, re-traumatizing ourselves and/or others. Responding utilizing the amazing resources of an integrated, interconnected brain and body serves us much better. When we are reacting, we are not using all of our brain but only that part that experiences threat. Mindsight (Siegel, 2010a) is the term for a part of our brain function that we are not using when we are in a survival mindstate. As we stated above, our triune brain's three regions are the brainstem, the limbic area, and the cortex. The cortex is the part of the brain that we share only with primates and is more evolved in humans; the prefrontal cortex only functions in humans. Mindsight, then, is the capacity to pay attention, to be in an engaged state of mind that is not possible to access if we rely only on reacting to threatening situations and our survival skills (see the user-friendly diagram of the brain in Appendix 1).

Pause and Ponder: Does the neurobiology summary make sense? Is it clear how our clients are homeostatic and in a trauma/survival mindstate? Do the "mindstate" concepts seem applicable to self and others? To produce change it is important that we believe that all humans are created with the capacity to grow and change. It is important, no matter what age or learning capacity of our clients, that we create methods of how to communicate these concepts. Take some time to explore and generate ideas of how to utilize and communicate these concepts to clients in our day-to-day practice.

Attachment and Complex Trauma

Children who experience trauma may be more dramatically affected by chronic hyperarousal than adults. Trauma in childhood occurs before the brain has developed normal modulation of arousal. One of the most essential functions of parenting is to provide children with external modulation for their internal states. To develop optimally, children require exposure to environmental stress sufficient to promote skills development and mastery experiences combined with sufficient buffering to prevent them from becoming overwhelmed. Only gradually and with the responsive care of adults do children develop the ability to modulate their own level of emotional response to both events that come from outside and events that originate within their own bodies. Children cannot always soothe themselves and therefore the capacity of adults to soothe frightened, angry, or shamed children is essential to their development. Without such help, children may become chronically hyperaroused and will develop a panoply of destructive symptoms and behaviors in attempts to diminish this insupportable state (Bloom, 1997, pp. 20–21).

Since Bowlby's (1969, 1973, 1980, 1988) groundbreaking attachment theory and Ainsworth, Blehar, Waters, and Wall's (1978) Strange Situation Classification (SSC) work, researchers have continued to validate the importance of early secure attachments to caregivers and their significance to a child's development. Family researchers (e.g., Doane & Diamond, 1994; Byng-Hall, 1991; Reiss, 1981) have added to the child development research by showing how attachment and family typology work together to secure attachment between caregivers and children and also how attachment disorders negatively impact on a child's development. With the advent of neuroscience, we are now able to understand more completely how attachment relationships impact children's growing brains and why complex trauma in attachment relationships can be so devastating.

Intersubjectivity (Stern, 2004; Trevarthan & Aitken, 2001) is a concept used to describe how children make meaning. Children learn about themselves and about the world around them by interpreting it through the lenses of their caregivers. Aitken and Trevarthan (1997) have shown that the infant is an active participant in attempting to create this meaning through wiring of the brain that is present at birth. When caregivers and infants are attuned, attached, and communicative, infants learn that the world is a safe and predictable place. This idea is crucial to understanding how children develop and bears repeating. Parents lend their view of the world to infants and children and this is how humans begin to make meaning of themselves and the world around them. In relationship with their responsive parents, children learn that they are significant as they learn to modulate their intense emotions by being soothed. The borrowed view of themselves and the world then gets incorporated through intersubjectivity into their worldview of self and other. The neural circuits of the infant's brain are being wired for resilience, flexibility, and a solid sense of coherence (Badenoch, 2011).

Responsive caregivers help children self-regulate (Koenen, 2006). These are caregivers who are responding, not reacting, and are giving care from an engaged mindstate. When children feel safe and they and their world are predictable and regulated, they can explore their inner and outer world and develop a brain and body that is focused on learning (Ford, 2009). When children have a responsive caregiver who engages them in life and protects them from overwhelming stress and violation that they cannot manage, then the children's triune brain fires toward maximum growth and development. In childhood and early adolescence, the neural pathways in the brain are being developed and structured and tend to be the ones that we use throughout life (Lewis, 2005). One of the reasons that complex trauma is so complex is because it often occurs during vulnerable times in the brain's development. The pathways that are established (but not irreversibly) in childhood become developmental trajectories for wiring and firing and serve to maintain a stable sense of self.

This stable sense of self is problematic for children who have not had relationships that provided a safe, protected, and engaged view of themselves and the outside world. When children are not given the opportunity to thrive in relationships that are positively attuned to their well-being, their brains may develop differently. When children are not provided with the opportunity to be frustrated, to have difficulties, and to learn constructive problem-solving and adaptational skills, they may be mired in repetitive patterns of fight, flight, and freeze. The neural pathways in the brain that are being developed and structured by manageable stress and reasonable challenges are those that help children survive. Conversely, their repeated experiences of fear without escape leave them unable to cope with their distress (Hesse & Main, 2000). Danger lurks internally and externally and their sense of self in relation to the world reflects their unsettling internal reality. When caregivers do not create safe havens for children or encourage them to learn from their mistakes, the children do not feel safe exploring intersubjectivity (Hughes, 2006). Their experiences of the world are negative and incoherent and so is their sense of self. Because their developing brains and bodies are focused on surviving unmanageable stress, their neural pathways are wiring toward fight, flight, or freeze, and they cope the best way they know how.

Raven was 4 years old when her mother lost custody of her because of drug addiction and neglect. Raven was sent to live with her grandparents who lived in another state and all three attempted to cope as best as they could. Raven was quiet and self-sufficient and never complained. She spent her days sitting on her grandmother's lap and following her around the house when she did her chores. One snowy day, Raven's grandmother bundled her up to go outside to sled. Raven went outside while her grandmother put her own boots and coat on. When grandmother came outside, she found Raven lying face down in the snow and Raven was not moving. Her grandmother watched her for a long time and then became concerned enough to pick her up, bring her inside, and call her primary care doctor for help. Through psychoeducation, Raven's grandmother learned that Raven's behavior was a sign of early deprivation from inadequate caregiving. Raven had no way of comforting herself when left to her own devices. Her inner world was as silent as her outer world had been when she lived with her mother. Once Raven's grandmother understood what was happening, she worked with many helping professionals to get Raven and her family the help they needed.

Research is beginning to corroborate what trauma-informed clinicians have known for many years, that attachment relationships that are not secure make it difficult for children to tolerate traumatic experiences (Sroufe, Egeland, Carlson, & Collins, 2005). Furthermore, early disorganized attachment relationships coupled with traumatic experiences throughout childhood are predictive of coping styles that match the survival mindstate. Brown (2009) completed a retrospective study on children living in a residential home for boys and an orphanage who were physically and sexually abused by caregivers on site. He found that those who came from families with responsive caregivers were less likely to exhibit severe dissociative processes as adults than those who were also abused but had early disorganized attachment relationships. In other words, securely attached caregivers helped children mediate terribly traumatic events. On the other hand, those lacking adequate caregivers seemed to continue to deteriorate following the same traumatic events.

Disorganized attachment relationships can set the stage for chronic hyperarousal. The difficulties inherent in a child developing in a state of instability, disruption, and unpredictability are seen in emotional regulation and information processing (Ford, 2009). For some children this may manifest itself as a lack of frustration tolerance. Waiting in line for a drink of water in an elementary school cafeteria when you are thirsty is tolerable if you can comfort yourself with the knowledge that your turn will come and your thirst will go away. If you have not learned to manage your frustration with this information, you may have to push your way through the line to quench your thirst. When children who have attentive caregivers experience unmanageable discomfort, they are helped to manage it by their caregivers. These parents validate their children's internal experience of discomfort and soothe them, distract them, and/or teach them how to soothe themselves. When children are left on their own to manage unmanageable discomfort, it appears that the main survival skill they develop is avoidance. This response is seen in young children whose caregivers are not responsive (Bowlby, 1988; Main, 1977).

Muller's (2010) attachment work with avoidant clients who have a history of trauma conceptualizes the development of avoidance as a logical, goal-driven reaction to a withholding environment. He suggests that, in order for children to get their basic needs met by parents who are unavailable, they must avoid emotional expression and curiosity for the sake of proximity to the caregiver without whom they could not survive. Ford (2009) suggests that a posttraumatic survival brain leaves children primarily attempting to avoid harm rather than doing what children who have not been traumatized do, which is to be open to new experiences.

Ford's (2009) survival brain describes the hyperaroused survival mindstate we have been discussing. When we react to stress in a survival mindstate, we are not engaged in the world around us, nor are we connected to our own thoughts, feelings, relationships, and options. Stress and discomfort trigger our survival brain and our only options are to impulsively fight, flee, or freeze. Notice that each of these reactions serve as a way to avoid the internal discomfort. We lose access to internal resources, which could assist us in making a calculated and mature response instead of reacting. We feel powerless, out of control, devalued, and disconnected. We react as if we are in danger and thus perpetuate the cycle by making life decisions with impaired judgment. Some of the symptomatic behaviors and effects of this survival mindstate are detailed in the worksheet on page 12.

Pause and Ponder: Does the terminology make sense? Do the concepts of neurobiology and attachment theory fit together in creating an understanding of the trauma cycle? Is the natural cycle of change apparent in the treatment modalities you utilize? Do you see how your own attachment style and the attachment style of your clients create a good working model? When you imagine your work, do you see how you create attachment and what impinges on your ability to attach with your clients? If needed, reread this chapter to create your answers to the questions. Is there anything you want to reread or apply to your work setting before you continue your reading?

THE EFFECTS OF TRAUMA WORKSHEET

Survival Mindstate Activity

Examples of Survival Mindstate Skills:

Fight, Flight, and Freeze

Powerless, Out of Control, Devalued, and Disconnected

- Mistrust of others
- Flashbacks
- Anxiety, fear, and terror
- Hyper-vigilance
- Shame, guilt, self-hatred
- Anger and aggressive behavior
- Cognitive distortions
- Depression, passivity
- Disassociation
- Detachment, numbing, or withdrawal
- Disturbed relatedness
- Sexual promiscuity or aversion to sex
- Sexual aggression
- Physical health issues
- Personality disorders and mental illness
- Suicide, self-mutilation
- Denial
- Unavailable to ourselves
- Eating disorders
- Drug or alcohol abuse

The Change Process: From Survival Mindstate to Engaged Mindstate

Humans are wired to survive traumatic events and they are wired to evolve, grow, and change. Therapists working with the Collaborative Change Model (CCM) know that in order to help clients move from a survival mindstate to an engaged mindstate, we need to understand how both mindstates work and perpetuate themselves as cycles. A survival mindstate can be triggered by an internal and/or external event. A stressful, threatening, or dangerous situation triggers the beginning of the cycle; we often attempt to cope but cannot find the skills to do so, then we move into a fright, fight, or freeze zone, where the brain and body recalibrates to react and respond as if we are threatened and endangered. We then react by using our survival skills that actually keep us in a survival mindstate.

The survival cycle and the change cycle are natural processes that are available to all of us interpersonally and interactionally. Stress, traumatic stress, and survival mindstates follow similar patterns. When under stress, we react to a challenge that disturbs our equilibrium. This reaction is formulated in the part of the brain that triggers survival patterns of fight, flight, and/or freeze. The change process from survival mindstate to engaged mindstate mirrors a similar process whether we have a history of complex trauma or are reacting to stress in a way that triggers the brain toward fight, flight, or freeze. The difference is often one of degree. Most people access, when triggered, a survival mindstate and most people can access, when safe, an engaged mindstate. Practitioner and client alike can get triggered into a survival cycle of interaction. While we are focusing on clients with a history of complex trauma, this knowledge that practitioners can also get caught in interactional cycles of survival helps us work the model.

A cycle of survival mindstate with someone with a history of complex trauma may look something like this: Jamie was a recent graduate from college with a history of physical, sexual, and emotional abuse in her family of origin. She decided to seek therapy because she was on the verge of losing her job. When she described her work environment, it became obvious that her history of complex trauma was triggered in relationship with her direct boss and interfering with her job performance. He was sexually suggestive with her and Jamie had no idea how to handle his inappropriate behavior. Instead of being able to deal with it in a way that was productive, she reacted from a trauma mindstate. Following each interaction with him she found it necessary to flee into her office, close the door and try and calm herself down. She was unable to access internal mechanisms to soothe herself, so she became immobile. Hours would pass and she would remain unproductive. The further behind she fell in her work, the more panicked and anxious she became. The cycle worsened as she began to miss deadlines, avoid colleagues, and forget to attend meetings. Her boss would then take it upon himself to try and boost her morale by being extra solicitous, which triggered her danger signal and Jamie's survival cycle would perpetuate itself. She decided to seek therapy because she was starting to feel so anxious and depressed she was afraid she was going to do something dramatically hurtful to herself if she lost this job.

Caught in this cycle of reacting to stimulus as dangerous, whether it is truly dangerous or not, we assimilate to all situations using the same tools that helped us cope with traumatic events in our past. When Jamie was a teenager, for example, she isolated herself from friendships and social situations that could potentially feel threatening in their intimacy. This isolation had adaptive elements. She excelled in school and read and wrote voraciously. This survival skill kept her safe from dangerous situations and afforded her a certain stability. This is a homeostatic process, a natural part of all cycles, which maintains stability and protects against change.

Like the survival cycle, the cycle toward change and evolution is also part of human nature. Herman (1992), in her groundbreaking book on trauma and recovery, articulated the power of the change process in healing the wounds of trauma, and evidence-based practice (e.g., McMackin, Newman, Fogler, & Keane, 2012) on trauma therapy has confirmed that which we have been helping our clients understand for over 30 years. Humans evolve, and we believe that most each and every one of us is capable of doing this. Simply put, when we are open to the change process, we accommodate to a new environment, and we grow and develop and become more complex. When we are closed to the natural cycle of change and assimilate all new information into our well-developed and constricted survival schemas, we stay stuck in the freeze, flight, and fight way of reacting. Both cycles are at our disposal.

The evolving cycle begins with a pause, a contraction, which then expands into ever increasing complexity and change and then evolution occurs when the change is consolidated. In this contraction our minds, our brains, our bodies, create a space and it is in this space that growth and change are created. Nature is a useful metaphor that helps therapists and clients visualize the change cycle. We can look to nature to see this cycle of growth. A tree or plant begins with a seed, buried in the ground. This seed, in fact, decomposes. It might look as if it no longer exists during the first phase of growth, yet it is becoming many forms before it is a full-formed tree or plant or flower. The seed relies on resources—earth, sun, and water—to change and grow, and it is in the gathering of resources that the expansion happens from the contraction; pieces of the seed are put back together in an evolved manner.

This cycle of change is more visually apparent in the caterpillar to butterfly transformation. A caterpillar is born and when it is time for it to change into a butterfly, it pauses, and through a process of contraction, the caterpillar creates a cocoon that is strategically placed for safety and refuge from danger. Similar to the seed, the caterpillar decomposes as it changes. While this may seem like an end, it is actually the process of evolving. While it might look like something different when it emerges, it still has all of the components and resources that were always there, just in a new form.

Families evolve and have their own cycles of contracting, expanding, and consolidating as well. The family life cycle is an example. One person leaves home and the family contracts, only to expand when that same person partners. The new in-law is consolidated into an evolved family dynamic. A baby is born and the family expands again. Then a grandparent dies and the family contracts and consolidates into another unit. Relational development occurs the same way. Each stage of individual development can be characterized by its function and that function is either to individuate, i.e., contract, or to be relational, i.e., expand (Kegan, 1982). As children grow into adults, they pass through a series of developmental stages and these stages are balanced in their interpersonal and individuating results. In early adolescence, for example, youths may want to fit in and expand themselves by being part of a peer group. They may identify as athletes, musicians, drama kids, the smart ones, etc. By late adolescence, however, they may want to contract and be seen as the only one of their friends who is an athlete or a star in the school musical. They are not interested in expanding their social circle and their relationships, but interested instead in pursuing their own interests. They are in a stage of contraction, which is as much a part of their growth and development as is their stage of expansion.

Each of these stages of development consolidates into the people they are at present, who continue to evolve if they are not impeded by survival cycles as a result of complex trauma. Within the survival cycle, this natural evolution is derailed when the person finds it impossible to believe that change will in fact protect them better than the thoughts and behaviors they currently use. The CCM is metaphorically the cocoon and the earth, sun, and water for the evolving cycle of change. The therapeutic community, in collaboration with clients, helps clients pause and contract in the first stage of our model. In the second stage, clients learn how to engage old and new resources toward cycles of change, and in the third stage they learn to consolidate those changes. The CCM mirrors the natural cycles of growth.

Clients engage in treatment when they are stressed and stuck and are looking for ways to de-stress and change. Those who have a history of complex trauma are often mired in survival cycles of fight, flight, or freeze because these are the only ways they know how to handle stress. The effects of complex trauma make it difficult for them to cope productively with and react to stressful events in their everyday lives. The clients' brittle reactivity is their best way to protect themselves from the danger they fear.

When Jamie first came to see her CCM therapist, she was isolated, avoidant, and anxious. She was still going to work but barely functioning. She lacked a coherent picture of her past or present life circumstances. When asked about her childhood, as is the case with many clients in Stage One, she could not articulate that she had a history of complex trauma. She was able to talk about a chaotic family life filled with parents and stepparents who were in and out of her life and not able to care for her in ways that felt loving and engaged. She also was able to acknowledge that her present work environment felt hostile and unwelcome, but she wasn't sure why. She was uncertain whether she had ever been in an environment that was supportive, except for one class in undergraduate school. It was a small seminar and the professor was consistent, warm, and engaging, yet kept strict boundaries around himself and the class. He was very encouraging to Jamie and appreciated her work ethic and productivity. She said that this was the first and only class in which she experienced herself as having value. When she spoke of this class, she was fully engaged. The CCM therapist used this opportunity to introduce the model.

The therapist talked with Jamie about her survival and her engaged mindstates. When he asked Jamie how she made sense of her situation at work, she said, "I just don't understand how I got myself in the same situation I was in at home. It's like the universe hates me or forgot about me or something. It's always this way with me and it is never going to change. First they put me in a vicious family and then they put me in a vicious job. I just don't understand how so many people can be so cruel." The therapist asked her how she responded in both situations and Jamie said that she did the same thing, she shut down, sometimes she fought back, but mostly she tried to distance herself from it. With a bit of empathy, but not too much, remembering the strict boundaries around the professor that made Jamie feel safe, the therapist talked about how exhausting it must be to have to protect herself all the time from mean people, then immediately moved toward how Jamie responded in the undergraduate class when she was in an engaged mindstate. Once Jamie was able to experience the different ways of being, the therapist suggested that the goal of therapy was to help Jamie move from responding to stressful situations like she adaptively did as a child toward an engaged mindstate similar to how she felt in the undergraduate class.

The CCM therapist was planting the seed of change. It was a moment of pause or contraction. Like the seed that is planted in the soil and the caterpillar in the cocoon, Jamie's ability to experience a different way of responding to stress was already part of her being that she was not able to access. When clients with histories of complex trauma enter therapy, many are stuck in cycles of survival that are homeostatic and stable. They may not feel stable to the people who are encased in them, but in fact, trauma mindstates are often predictable and stable enough that people have a difficult time believing that things can be different. Jamie saw her current situation as a constant and had no hope that life would be better in the future. The therapist's gentle challenge of an exception to the otherwise bleak narrative of her life story (White & Epston, 1990) was an attempt to suggest that change was possible. With the help of a therapeutic team that understands the importance of the pause, expand, and consolidating stages of the process of evolution, Jamie was able to access an engaged mindstate and reach her destination.

Pause and Ponder: The trauma cycle and the change cycle both begin with a state of contraction. Therapy is the process of helping clients to use their engaged mind to create pathways in the change cycle. Both the trauma/survival cycles and the change cycle are natural processes that we are wired to perform. The more repetitive and complex our trauma, the more well-worn are the pathways that exist for homeostasis in the trauma mindstate. Can you see this every day in your life and the life of your clients? Can you identify how your own theory of change and/or theoretical models you subscribe to mirror the natural cycle of change?

References

Ainsworth, M., Blehar, M., Waters, E., & Wall, S. (1978). *Patterns of attachment.* Hillsdale, NJ: Erlbaum.

Aitken, K. J. & Trevarthan, C. (1997). Self/other organization in human psychological development. *Development and Psychopathology, 9,* 653–677.

Badenoch, B. (2011). *The brain-savvy therapists workbook: A companion to being a brain-wise therapist.* New York: W.W. Norton & Co.

Bloom S. (1997). *Creating sanctuary: Toward the evolution of sane societies.* New York: Routledge.

Bowlby, J. (1969). *Attachment and loss, Vol. 1: Attachment.* New York: Basic Books.

Bowlby, J. (1973). *Attachment and loss, Vol. 2: Separation.* New York: Basic Books.

Bowlby, J. (1980). *Attachment and loss, Vol. 3: Loss, sadness and depression.* New York: Basic Books.

Bowlby, J. (1988). *A secure base: Parent–child attachment and healthy human development.* New York: Basic Books.

Brown, D. (2009). Attachment and abuse history. In C. A. Courtois & J. D. Ford (Eds.) *Treating complex traumatic stress disorders: An evidence-based guide.* New York: Guilford Press.

Burghardt, G. M. (1990). Cognitive ethology and critical anthropomorphism: A snake with two heads and hog-nose snakes that play dead. In P. Marler & C. A. Ristau (Eds.) *Cognitive ethology: Essays in honor of Donald R. Griffin* (pp. 53–90). New York: Psychology Press.

Byng-Hall, J. (1991). The application of attachment theory to understanding and treatment in family therapy. In C. M. Parkes, J. Stevenson-Hinde, & P. Marris (Eds.) *Attachment across the life cycle* (pp. 199–215). New York: Routledge.

Cozolino, L. (2006). *The neuroscience of human relationships: Attachment and the developing social brain.* New York: W. W. Norton & Co.

Cozolino, L. (2010). *The neuroscience of psychotherapy: Healing the social brain.* New York: W.W. Norton & Co.

Doane, J. A., & Diamond, D. (1994). *Affect and attachment in the family: A family based treatment of major psychiatric disorder.* New York: Basic Books.

Ford, J. D. (2009). Neurobiological and developmental research: Clinical implications. In C. A. Courtois and J. D. Ford (Eds.) *Treating complex traumatic stress disorders: Evidence-based guide.* New York: Guilford Press.

Herman, J. L. (1992). *Trauma and recovery: The aftermath of violence—from domestic abuse to political terror.* New York: Basic Books.

Hesse, E., & Main, M. B. (2000). Disorganized infant, child, and adult attachment: Collapse in behavioral and attentional strategies. *Journal of the American Psychoanalytic Association, 48,* 1097–1127.

Hughes, D. A. (2006). *Building the bonds of attachment: Awakening love in deeply troubled children.* New York: Jason Aronson.

Kegan, R. (1982). *The evolving self: Problem and process in human development.* Cambridge, MA: Harvard University Press.

Koenen, K. (2006). Developmental epidemiology of PTSD: Self-regulation as a core mechanism. *Annals of the New York Academy of Sciences, 1071,* 255–266.

Ledoux, J. (1998). *The emotional brain: The mysterious underpinnings of emotional life.* New York: Simon & Schuster.

Levine, P. A. (2010). *In an unspoken voice: How the body releases trauma and restores goodness.* Berkeley, CA: North Atlantic Books.

Lewis, M. D. (2005). Self-organizing individual differences in brain development. *Developmental Review, 25,* 252–277.

Main, M. B. (1977). Analysis of a peculiar form of reunion behaviour in some day-care children: Its history and sequelae in children who are home-reared. In R. Webb (Ed.) *Social development in childhood: Day-care programs and research* (pp. 33–78). Baltimore, MD: Johns Hopkins University Press.

McMackin, R. A., Newman, E., Fogler, J. M., & Keane, T. M. (Eds.) (2012). *Trauma therapy in context: The science and craft of evidence-based practice.* Washington, DC: American Psychological Association.

Muller, R. T. (2010). *Trauma and the avoidant client: Attachment-based strategies for healing.* New York: W.W. Norton & Co.

Perry, B. D. (1994). Neurobiological sequelae of childhood trauma: Posttraumatic stress disorders in children. In M. M. Murburg (Ed.) *Catecholamine function in posttraumatic stress disorder: Emerging concepts* (pp. 253–276). Washington, DC: American Psychiatric Press.

Perry, B. D. (2001). The neurodevelopmental impact of violence in childhood. In D. Schetky & E. P. Benedek (Eds.) *Textbook of Child and Adolescent Forensic Psychiatry* (pp. 221–238). Washington, DC: American Psychiatric Press.

Perry, B. D., Pollard, R., Blakely, T., Baker, W., & Vigilante, D. (1995). Childhood trauma, the neurobiology of adaptation and "use-dependent" development of the brain: How "states" become "traits". *Infant Mental Health Journal, 6*(4), 271–291.

Porges, S. W. (2001). The polyvagal theory: Phylogenetic substrates of a social nervous system. *International Journal of Psychophysiology, 42,* 123–146.

Porges, S. W. (2003). Social engagement and attachment: A phylogenetic perspective. *Roots of Mental Illness in Children, Annals of the New York Academy of Sciences, 1008,* 31–47.

Reiss, D. (1981). *The family's construction of reality.* Cambridge, MA: Harvard University Press.

Schore, A. N. (2003). *Affect regulation and the repair of the self.* New York: W.W. Norton & Co.

Siegel, D. J. (2007). *The mindful brain: Reflection and attunement in the cultivation of well-being.* New York: W.W. Norton & Co.

Siegel, D. J. (2010a). *Mindsight: The science of personal transformation.* New York: Bantam.

Siegel, D. J. (2010b). *The mindful therapist: A clinician's guide to mindsight and neural integration.* New York: W. W. Norton & Co.

Sroufe, L. A., Egeland, B., Carlson, E. A., & Collins, W. A. (2005). *The development of the person: The Minnesota Study of Risk and Adaptation from Birth to Adulthood.* New York: Guilford Press.

Stern, D. (2004). *The present moment in psychotherapy and everyday life.* New York: W.W. Norton & Co.

Trevarthan, C., & Aitken, K. J. (2001). Infant intersubjectivity: Research, theory, and clinical applications. *Journal of Child Psychology and Psychiatry, 42,* 3–48.

Van der Kolk, B., Van der Hart, O., & Marmar, C. R. (1996). Dissociation and information processing in posttraumatic stress disorder. In B. van der Kolk, A. C. McFarlane, & L. Weisaeth (Eds.) *Traumatic stress: The effects of overwhelming experience on mind, body, and society* (pp. 303–327). New York: Guilford Press.

White, M., & Epston, D. (1990). *Narrative means to therapeutic ends.* New York: W.W. Norton & Co.

two
Engaged
Mindstate

Clients who enter therapy with a history of complex trauma are often mired in survival mindstates that perpetuate cycles of feeling powerless, devalued, and out of control. The goal of treatment then is to help clients move from survival mindstates to engaged mindstates. People who are working in an engaged mindstate feel powerful, in control, and of value. They have access to inner and outer resources and are collaborative and flexible. They practice mindfulness and are engaged in supportive relationships.

Individuals acting from an engaged mindstate have access to and incorporate tools that regulate their affect, cognitions, behavior, and relationships. They are able to access their strengths, their resources, and their vulnerabilities, and have developed a skill set to deal with stress. Furthermore, an engaged mindstate incorporates hope and a meaningful vision of the future.

While each individual is unique and each therapeutic encounter different, there are some core ingredients that facilitate the process of change toward engaged mindstates. For over 20 years and in different treatment settings, we have been conducting assessment and consolidation interviews with clients who have experienced complex trauma. These clients come from differing age groups, genders, and treatment contexts. They are court mandated, referred by child abuse organizations, trauma centers, inpatient and outpatient facilities, other therapists, agencies, friends, physicians, and self-referred. Some are specifically referred because of current and/or past experiences with trauma and others present with unspecified or different problems. Some are currently perpetrators of violence and some are currently victims of violence. All of their successes and struggles, however, have informed our model and the way we work. In our assessment and consolidation interviews, clients are asked to think about what happened in the therapeutic context that helped them to change. Their responses have taught us about the process of therapy from their perspective. They have shared what successful therapy is and what it takes.

When we reviewed the development of survival mindstates, we discussed the ways in which responsive caregivers help children develop a coherent sense of self, experience themselves as important, and have a secure base from which to explore. Responsive caregivers share experiences with children that implicitly teach that relationships are supportive and that their experiences are valid. Responsive caregivers help children's brains develop to their full capacities, so that they can engage in their inner and outer worlds, exploring both, and readily adapt to and integrate their inner and outer experiences.

The responsive caregiver mirrors the engaged mindstate, one that incorporates a continuum of disassociation (Carlson, Yates, & Sroufe, 2009). Dissociative processes are different from categorical dissociative states. From a developmental perspective, dissociative processes are typical and can be seen in all age groups. The process that allows children to have superpowers when they dress in caped pajamas is the same process that shows up when you exit the shower not remembering if you shaved. While dissociation experiences usually decrease with age, dissociative processes continue to be adaptive, and can be helpful in times of unmanageable stress. Many of us have experienced a certain numbness in a crisis, or an altered state experience, only to break down and cry when we see a loved one who we know will take care of us. This process is adaptive and helpful in times of unmanageable stress.

A history of complex trauma, on the other hand, elicits a categorical dissociation, which is more like a mindstate. The chronic use of dissociation is actually one of the most important indicators of a history of complex trauma (Van der Kolk, Weisaeth, & Van Der Hart (1996). Putnam (1988, 1997) carefully articulates the emergence of states as organizational ways in which we develop consciousness. He suggests that responsive caregivers help infants transition across states with flexibility so that this process becomes homeostatic and stable. He then suggests that unresponsive caregivers and a history of complex trauma create what he identifies as state-change disorders. "Certain psychiatric disorders can be conceptualized as 'state change' disorders, in that a major pathophysiological component of the disorder comes from dysregulation of the state transition process" (1988, p. 26). He uses depression as an example of a state change disorder. Individuals who can more flexibly change states might experience a depressing period and be able to pull themselves out of it using idiosyncratic techniques (shopping, food, entertainment, calling a friend). Clinical depression is diagnosed when someone is in a state of depression for more than two weeks. This is an example of inflexibility in changing states and has similar characteristics to a trauma mindstate. Clinical depression may not be preceded by a history of complex trauma and complex trauma need not manifest as clinical depression, but people in a trauma mindstate are homeostatically stuck in a mindstate of hyperarousal and danger. The smooth state shifting (Putnam, 1997) that occurs in an engaged mindstate is not as easily accessible to someone in a depressive mindstate, an anxious mindstate, or a trauma mindstate.

The Collaborative Change Model (CCM) organizes treatment, which essentially is a process of helping clients move from a mindstate that is categorical and repetitive to an engaged mindstate, which is collaborative and flexible and uses inner and outer resources. The CCM is an organizational meta-model based on years of treatment of clients with a history of complex trauma, an integration of client feedback, and wisdom from research and treatment protocols in neuroscience, attachment, and trauma-informed treatment practices. The journey from survival mindstate to engaged mindstate must include clients' idiosyncratic voices that speak to their needs and a structure for how those needs are going to be met. One client said, "I needed structure and order to put my life back in order." Another said, "My therapist and her team held hope for my family that we never had. We all hated ourselves and what we were doing to each other and they cared for us despite our behavior. It made a world of difference." Based on client feedback, we have organized the five essential ingredients needed to help clients move from survival to engaged mindstates.

The Clients' Perspective: Five Essential Ingredients of Effective Therapy

For over 20 years and in different treatment settings, we have been conducting assessment and consolidation interviews with clients who have experienced complex trauma. Clients are asked to think about what happened in the therapeutic context that helped them to change. Their responses have taught us about the process of therapy from their perspective. They have shared what successful therapy is and what it takes. We have integrated their wisdom into the five essential ingredients or themes for trauma treatment.

First, clients told us that they were helped to change because they felt valued. This experience of feeling valued empowered them to change (Value and Empowerment). Second, clients told us that actually learning specific skills which they could use in their present contexts enabled the change process (Skills). Third, clients told us that therapy helped them find access to their own resources (Resources). The fourth theme centers on an understanding of contextual variables needed to be in an engaged mindstate (Context) and the last theme focuses on workable realities and a hopeful vision of the future (Workable Reality). These five ingredients are missing in a traumatic environment. People need to feel they have value, power, control, and connection as opposed to the experience of powerlessness, the sense of being out of control, and the experience of being devalued and disconnected to self and others that occurs as a result of traumatic violation. Our model organizes these ingredients or themes in the natural cycle of evolution to help clients move from survival mind to engaged mind.

Our interviews with clients are enhanced by the ideas embedded in interpersonal neurobiology, particularly as defined by child psychiatrist Daniel Siegel (e.g., Siegel, 2010a, 2010b) and integrated into practice by Bonnie Badenoch (2008, 2011). Siegel's groundbreaking book on mindsight (2010a) explains the interpersonal relationship between the embodied and the relational brain, which we discussed in our definition of complex trauma. Siegel (2012) posits four S's as the four essential ingredients for successful therapy: Seen, Safe, Soothe, and Secure. Siegel states that clients need to be seen by therapists; to feel safe in the therapeutic environment; to feel soothed by the process of therapy; and to feel secure with the therapist's skills and competence. These four S's cohere with our five essential ingredients.

Badenoch (2008, 2011), a student of Siegel's, reviews the brain basics in a way that is accessible for therapists to teach to clients. Much of what she reports is exactly what our clients have taught us and she explains their wisdom from an interpersonal neurobiology perspective. Her workbook (2011) instructs therapists in the practice of techniques to fully engage their embodied and relational brains, and practice mindfulness when in the presence of clients. We have incorporated some of Badenoch's techniques in our training with therapists using the CCM because they fit so well into our model. We have also incorporated Kabat-Zinn's (2005) mindfulness-based practice in our model and encourage therapists and clients to find which techniques work best for them to develop mindful awareness in their lives.

We believe that the body needs to be brought into therapy as well as the brain, and we have integrated many different body sensitive theories into the model. For example, many CCM therapists are greatly influenced by the somatic experiencing approach (Levine & Frederick, 1997; Levine, 2010) which helps explain how the body holds trauma and how the body can release it. CCM therapists collaborate with clients by sharing with them current research and theory in trauma studies. For example, a CCM therapist worked with a 9-year-old boy who had endured multiple medical treatments for cancer as a toddler, in which he was restrained so that doctors and nurses could provide medical care. He had no memory of the medical treatments and had developed gripping anxiety and panic in so many areas that he could hardly function. Whenever he was bumped into at school, he fell down and cried and could not be consoled. He wanted to play sports but was deathly afraid of getting hurt or having any physical contact. He screamed uncontrollably when his mother washed his hair and cried hysterically when anyone mentioned giving him a hug. The CCM therapist worked with the family by educating them on the immobilizing effect of his medical traumas and together they found a way for him to release some of the stored body experiences so he could tolerate touch.

The experiences of being seen, safe, soothed, and secure that interpersonal neurobiologists discuss are also the essential ingredients of securely attached relationships in families. Therapists are practicing using attachment-related concepts with clients with a history of complex trauma (e.g., Hughes, 2006; Johnson, 2005;

Muller, 2010) and we have incorporated their work as well, since it fits with our clients' descriptions of the essential ingredients of successful therapy. Hughes' (2006) work focuses on helping caregivers to create loving environments for children who have attachment disorders. His work is significant because he addresses the caregiver's attachment style as well, which fits into our model of collaborating with the context in which our clients are embedded. Johnson (2005) has expanded her extensive evidence-based Emotionally Focused Couple Therapy to work with clients with a history of complex trauma, which resounds with client feedback we have incorporated into our work. Muller's (2010) excellent clinical work integrates interpersonal neurobiology and attachment styles for clients with a history of complex trauma and utilizes both concepts in his therapeutic work with avoidant clients.

Since Trepper and Barrett's (1986) book on systemic treatment of incest, in which some foundational elements of our model were first introduced, much has been written on trauma-informed psychotherapy practice. There are a few that have informed our work because they resonate with our model and with feedback from the exit interviews we have conducted. The trauma-informed practices that have significantly influenced CCM focus on ways to create healing environments for clients (e.g., Bloom, 1997; Briere & Scott, 2012; Courtois & Ford, 2009; Herman, 1992; Van der Kolk, 1987). This practice gives voice to the client with a history of complex trauma, understands the dynamic interplay between trauma mindstates and resiliency, and helps therapists create environments in which the natural cycle of growth can be accessed. The CCM has integrated colleagues' work with our own experience and hundreds of process evaluation interviews to help develop our organizational model, which rests on the five essential ingredients for successful therapy with clients who have a history of complex trauma.

Pause and Ponder: Can you see examples of the natural cycle of change repeated daily in your life and the lives of your clients? Witness the contraction and the expansion cycle. Using our natural resources to change means using our brain, our mind, and our body. Humans are born with the natural capacity to grow and evolve. Once we understand the innate survival processes and the natural processes for change, we can understand how to help our clients change states. Attempt to increase your awareness of this natural cycle in your daily life.

Five Essential Ingredients

We recommend that you use the five essential ingredients as a checklist at the end of each and every session. A successful and change-oriented session will involve all five ingredients. When treatment as a whole and each individual session incorporates the five essential concepts, we are creating contexts that embody the natural cycle of change and help to elicit engaged mindstates.

1. Value and Empowerment

An attached collaborative relationship with clients facilitates the development of feeling valued and empowered. We have long known that social support ameliorates the emotional consequences of a traumatic event. Interpersonal neurobiologists are now studying how the brain develops in the absence of social support, or warmth, and when undervalued in relationships. To be fully integrated into an engaged mindstate, both parts of our top brain, or the cortex, have to be activated. The cortex is divided into two parts, the right and the left hemisphere. The right side of our brain, which is more connected to the limbic system and the brainstem, is that part of the brain that is activated when we are younger. It is the nonverbal, feeling part of the brain, the part that is social and relational. If the right part of the brain has not developed, we may tend to use the left part of our brain more. Engaged mindstates integrate all parts of the brain so while leaning to the left may be helpful for many activities, we want to be able to integrate all parts of our brain to get out of the survival state of trauma mind. Attached collaborative and therapeutic relationships feed the right part of the brain.

We feel we are of value when we are treated as such by the people who care for us or are in intimate relationships with us. This is one of the essential ingredients to attachment and fuels activation on the right side of the brain. Hughes (2006) describes affect attunement in the attachment relationship. When a child has not bonded securely to a caregiver, this affect attunement, so essential to self-esteem, is absent. Lack of the core experience of having fully engaged a loved one results in a sense of self as uninteresting and of having little value. Optimal emotional development requires children to have the incorporated idea that they have had a positive impact on the key people in their intimate life. While a child may not be able to articulate this exact experience, it is internalized.

A CCM practitioner was treating a mother, Pam, who was having difficulty bonding with her infant daughter Stephanie. Pam complained that Stephanie hated her. "She calms down when my husband picks her up and when my mother feeds her, but she just gets so agitated whenever I am around. And I am the one around all the time. My husband works late and my mother lives out of town. It's like she's mad at me, the little piss ant. I can't calm her down so I end up screaming at her and when it gets so I can't take it anymore, I lock myself in my closet so I can't hear her." There are many children like Stephanie whose primary caretakers are unable to engage themselves in responsive caretaking. While Stephanie may not remember the specifics of being left to fend for herself when in distress, she does learn that a relationship with her mother is not soothing. When Stephanie is agitated, her mother is even more agitated or absents herself. Stephanie learns that that she has no power to influence her environment and she learns that she has no value.

When we are traumatized by the people we love or by outsiders and then fail to be comforted within loving relationships, we may enter therapy with the experience of distrust of ourselves and of relationships. We may not experience social support as positive and are wary of anyone trying to help us. When talking about this experience with our clients, we may compare it to mountain climbing. Say, for example, you took a hike up a mountain and fell off a cliff when you were young. The rescue workers were piloting a broken helicopter, arrived at the wrong mountain, and were too drunk to land anyway, with the end result that you and your pain were not attended to. You experience yourself as having little value. The longer you wait to be rescued, the more mishaps occur, and you grow even more wary of taking another hike.

Many of the stories we hear of difficult psychotherapy journeys occur because clients come into treatment with a history of feeling devalued, are hyper-alert to any and all attempts to perpetuate this experience, and clinicians have been unable to forge a productive psychotherapeutic alliance. In our assessment and consolidation interviews, many clients talk about the healing value of relatively minor interactions that helped them believe they were valuable. A receptionist who noticed in the waiting room that you were having a hard time and gave you a smile, a member of your psychotherapy group who acknowledged learning something from you, a therapist whose tears flowed from joy when you were sharing an accomplishment, are moments in which clients acknowledge feeling valued.

The importance of believing that you have value cannot be overstated. A father who had been referred from the state social service department for child abuse anxiously attended a meeting with his family and four professionals from three different agencies who all worked collaboratively and had been trained in the CCM. He sat in the corner of the room with a hat pulled over his head and his face in his hands. He became engaged when we asked for his opinions about what was going on in his family and what he thought the family needed to be able to reconnect and function as a loving family again. As he was leaving the room, he said: "Having you all take the time, care enough about our family, and really hear us and make sure we understood you, makes me feel like we are all on the same team and that my opinion is as important as yours."

Furthermore, the more relationships clients have where they feel valued, the better it is for them. As therapists, we often forget that being a part of a treatment team that works together is more valuable than going solo. The CCM includes the ingredients of a caring community, which reminds clients over and over again that they can be in relationships that are responsive and supportive. The more relationships clients can be involved with in which they feel valued, the faster they will reach their destination. Helping empower clients by helping them feel valued is the safe and soothing healing environment that organizes our model and fertilizes the soil of growth.

Mary spoke for many of our clients when she discussed the importance of multiple responsive relationships as the key to her successful therapy experience with the CCM. She had been sexually abused as a child and physically abused in her marriage and until working with us had only felt blamed and attacked in relationships. When asked, during her consolidation interview, what was helpful in therapy, she said: "I never realized that there could be so many people who could understand me and help me make sense of how I was living my life. I never realized that some of the things I did that I always thought were crazy because everyone told me I was crazy were in fact survival techniques that simply needed tweaking. It was so helpful to have more than one therapist sending me the same message of my potential. And they were all on the same page about how to get to my potential; completely the opposite of my family. There was a method to my madness, in fact, and once a few people explained this to me, without blaming me, I realized I could change."

Clients shared that they felt empowered and valued as a result of being taught the CCM and the fundamentals of how change occurs. Survival mindstate is often a result of action or inaction being perpetrated upon people in ways that they do not understand. Clients often remark that they would say to themselves, "Why is this happening to me? Why are they doing this? What did I do to deserve this? Why am I being treated this way, etc.?" Insights gleaned from being taught the CCM assist clients in not experiencing a further continuation of this devalued and helpless position. Clients report that having practitioners explain the process, overtly explore their relationships, mentor their own natural cycles of change in the therapy room, in other words have the therapy experience be "the practice that is preached," creates a powerful and empowering psychotherapy.

An adolescent seen by a CCM practitioner shared an experience that she credits with helping her form a positive therapeutic alliance, when she had been unable to in the past. Michelle was 16 when she and her family came to therapy. She had been sent to a succession of school counselors, psychiatrists, and social workers since she was 8 years old, but she had not connected to any of them. She was initially seen following her disclosing to her mother that her uncle was taking nude photos of "her doing bad things to him." The night her mother confronted her brother-in-law about the abuse he hung himself in his upstairs bathroom. No one in the family ever talked about it and Michelle was the only one sent to therapy even though she had a brother who was present while her uncle was abusing her. Her parents argued constantly, blaming each other for the abuse and the suicide, and their fights would periodically get violent. Michelle was haunted by the conviction that someone else in her family was going to commit suicide, and it would be her fault, but she could never bring herself to discuss this fear with anyone. By the time she was 16, she was running away from home to flee from a chaotic and angry family whose members hadn't a clue what to do with her or what had gone so terribly wrong.

Michelle credits her CCM team for keeping her in therapy and she told one story that stood out for her that made her feel empowered and valued. It occurred in one of the first family sessions as her mother and father were fighting viciously. What Michelle remembers is the therapist getting out of her chair and standing in between her parents and saying something like this: "I need to stop you two for a moment and gather my thoughts." Then, according to Michelle, the therapist sat down, took a very deep breath and blew it out and then did it again a few more times. Then she said, "When the two of you fight like this, I want to run away. I think I am beginning to understand what happens to Michelle. I am a seasoned therapist with 20 years of experience and when you fight, I become immobilized and scared that something is going to go terribly wrong. Before we can move forward, I must teach you all some ways to talk with each other so that this does not happen again. This is part of our model. But in Stage One, which we are in now, most important is that we all feel safe and it seems to me when the two of you go after each other like this, that no one feels safe. Am I right?"

Michelle said this moment was important for a number of reasons, some of which she was not able to understand or articulate at the time, but given the opportunity to talk about it, she gained some clarity about why it was such a pivotal moment for her. Firstly, she remembers that it was the first time that she felt seen and understood. Here was an adult and an expert on human behavior who could not function when her parents attacked each other. It validated what she had been experiencing for a very long time that no one had ever validated before. Secondly, it was the first time that she recognized that her parents also did not feel safe. When the therapist asked about safety and both parents acknowledged that they did not feel safe in their family, it was a profound moment for the entire system. She credits this experience as the first time she thought about her parents as people outside of their role as mother and father and she had a sense that they were functioning poorly as parents not because she was a bad child but because they had problems of their own. Michelle then felt empowered to share some of the ways she thought everyone could create safety together.

2. Skills

Clients are very clear that therapy must be informative to be helpful and that learning skills is an essential ingredient to moving from a trauma mindstate to an engaged mindstate. When therapy is successful, clients have learned self-regulation/mindfulness skills and relationship/communication skills (see Appendix 2). In Stage One, for example, we might notice that a client has difficulty with frustration tolerance. While complaining about the bus never being on time or her daughter's friends, we might ask her if, when frustrated, she has difficulty calming herself down enough to thoughtfully engage in problem-solving. We inform her that she will learn how to better manage this frustration in therapy. We will teach her what we know about the brain (some of us have pictures in our offices) and we will practice mindfulness techniques together as part of therapy. If, as another example, we discover together that a lack of good and effective communication skills keep certain families from problem-solving because they have never been used or taught in their families of origin, we not only assist families to communicate more effectively, we explain what we are doing and how it is working. The following statement occurs often in therapy:

> So we have agreed that you would like to work on communicating more effectively with each other so that your conversations are more helpful and less hurtful. Remember in the first session, when I explained to you that

change happens in stages? Well, learning happens in the same three stages. So first we will explore some reasons behind why you talk with each other this way. And then you will learn skills that will help you both feel seen, heard, and understood. I am going to teach you a communication skill that will help you listen better to each other which will in turn make your conversations go more smoothly and lead to less miscommunication and hurtfulness.

Communication skills are often discussed and taught within the first sessions of Stage One when working with couples and/or families. It seems that most clients can benefit from more thoughtful discussion of a skill that we often take for granted. In discussing communication skills, we share the importance of practicing new communication patterns when having the difficult conversations necessary in therapy.

Alternative forms of healing are introduced in the first few sessions of therapy as skills that clients may want to incorporate. Working from the mindset of a collaborative model, we believe that clients are often more successful if they are engaged with numerous helpful people. Our experience and our perspective teach us that in most situations, we are never enough. The problem in many psychotherapy practices, however, is that, by the time clients are referred to other helping professionals, they tend to experience the referral as a failure of some sort. If a therapist asks a client in the fourth session to see a psychiatrist for an evaluation for psychotropic medication, the client may experience this request as an indication of deteriorated mental health and a failure of the current therapy to produce positive change. If, on the other hand, the therapist explicitly states in the first session that she often uses a particular psychiatrist in the collaborative model of practice, this same client may be more likely to be receptive to a referral for a psychiatric evaluation. The same is true for referrals to cognitive behavioral therapy (CBT) (e.g., Beck, 2011; Newman, Leahy, Beck, Reilly-Harrington, & Gyulai, 2001; Rothbaum, Meadows, Resick, & Foy, 2000), dialectical behavior therapy (DBT) (e.g., Linehan, 1993a, 1993b; Decker & Naugle, 2008; Miller, Rathus, & Linehan, 2006), eye movement desensitization and reprocessing (EMDR) (Greenwald, 2007; Shapiro, 1998), internal family systems (IFS) therapy (Schwartz, 1997) and individual, couple, family, and group sessions, psychoeducational groups, alcohol and drug evaluations, yoga, mind/body interventions, nutritional and alternative medical referrals.

We were told by one client, "having therapy be a combination of a class and a delving into my life made it easier to handle. The skills gave me relief and made me feel less crazy. They also gave me confidence in myself and the therapist and therapy in general." Another client reported, "when I was taught the importance of pausing before I reacted and looked at my life as a series of choices that I did have some control over, I felt empowered and then of course the logical next step was to learn skills so that I would have a choice about how to respond and not just impulsively react."

We believe that effective trauma-informed therapy is skill based. We are not advocating a certain set of skills or a particularly type of therapy model which teaches skills. This is an opportunity for the therapist and client to collaboratively determine what skills are necessary for change and for the client to move from a trauma mindstate to an engaged mindstate. This is also an opportunity for therapists to use their own creative and idiosyncratic style, model, and contexts to help clients.

3. Resources

Clients come to treatment endowed with resources that they are not using. We define resources as the capabilities that we have already utilized when under stress. We actively and openly work with our clients to identify and name individual resources such as creativity, humor, faith, courage, and self-awareness, and relationship resources such as friendships, colleagues, and family relationships. Many clients, in their exit interviews, reported that learning, not only about their vulnerabilities, but about their resources, helped them move from a survival mindstate to an engaged mindstate. In traditional therapy, therapists assess clients to help determine which technique(s) within their methodology may be most helpful. The CCM intentionally and vigorously promotes client self-awareness. Therapists serve as tour guides for their client travelers. As clients set out on their journeys, they are filled with doubts about whether they will safely and successfully arrive at their destination. They know their lives are out of control, that they do not feel valued, and that they feel powerless to effect meaningful change. Therapy helps them connect with the resources they do have; resources within themselves, within their families, and within their communities, so that they can use these resources to help them have influence, and feel valued and empowered.

Our clients have reported that part of what they discovered during the therapeutic process was that in fact they have what is necessary to grow and change. The process of therapy helped them identify their resources and then develop ways to access their resources. After they become acquainted and then familiar with the neuro pathways they utilize in their survival mindstate—the repetitious thoughts and behaviors of "fight, flight, and freeze"—they create new pathways utilizing their engaged mindstate and their own resources to create pathways of resilience.

Knowing your own strengths and resources differs from skill-based learning, which also occurs in our model. Both are extremely important but they are different facets of the model. So, for example, on the journey of psychotherapy, if your client has no sense of direction, skill-based learning would entail directing the client to become familiar with the use of a GPS, which has become a necessary tool on complicated trips and will help your client arrive at her next destination. A strength-based perspective takes that lack of sense of direction and finds a way to harvest its strength. In WWII, for example, those with a poor sense of direction were used as navigators on airplanes because they wanted navigators who would rely solely on maps. This hyper-alertness is an asset in a crisis, in fog, or in other demanding situations. We also use the client's strengths to determine both which skills will be most effective to create change and the best way to teach the skills.

Clients universally appreciate the CCM's emphasis on identifying and utilizing their existing resources and let us know that they value our strength-based perspective. A CCM therapist was treating a very bright survivor of complex trauma. She taught physics to doctoral students, and clearly possessed an exceptional intellectual level and capacity, but had no access to her emotions. Her ability to use the left side of the brain was a great resource that helped her survive a chaotic childhood filled with unstable relationships and abuse, but her emotional, right side of her brain was underdeveloped. She had been in numerous failed therapies and experienced herself as a "therapy moron" who frustrated therapists and couldn't do feelings the right way.

Instead of criticizing or becoming impatient, her CCM therapist carefully matched her pacing and assigned reading to do between sessions, suggesting that she highlight parts she wanted to talk about in therapy. Her intellect was her strength and her therapist taught her to use it to help heal. The client eventually was able to talk about what she was feeling as she read. She was able to take risks and share her current and past emotional experiences in conjunction with the utilization and validation of her intellectual resource.

To summarize, when working with clients during Stage One, we identify resources: that is, we are curious when, how, and with whom in their current life they experience safety, are seen, and feel secure and soothed (Siegel, 2012). The identification of these resources is a critical foundation for the skill-building and relational aspects of the treatment. For example, if we identify that clients have a strong relationship with music, we might explore with them whether music is a resource. We may introduce music in session and encourage them to use music in their lives more deliberately as a way to soothe themselves when they feel tense. Identifying clients' resources may also help us identify alternative healing practices which we can incorporate into our treatment. For example, one CCM therapist referred a couple to a ballroom dance class after discovering that music was the only thing the couple believed they had in common. Ballroom dancing was then used metaphorically as guidance throughout the treatment.

For therapy to be successful, therapists must work together with clients to find their resources. A CCM supervisor consulted with a therapist who could say nothing nice about one of the clients with whom she was working. The therapist expressed active vociferous dislike of the client, Dana, relating story after story about how mean Dana was to her family. The therapist had a concretized negative impression of Dana and conceptualized her as characterologically impaired. Neither the therapist nor her colleagues could imagine a positive outcome for this case, and the therapist wanted badly to pass Dana on to someone else in the agency. The supervisor recommended, before she transferred her, to try to find something she liked about her before the next consultation. "The goal is not to make her nice," the supervisor said, "your goal will be to try to find ways to like her." When the supervisor came back, the therapist reported the following: "I was quite skeptical of your assignment, thinking it simplistic. However, I figured

I had nothing to lose so I went into the next session with Dana and asked her about her cats. It turns out that Dana has made it her mission to save feral cats in her community from euthanasia. She methodically and seriously talked for 15 minutes about her mission and she enthusiastically shared a tremendous amount of knowledge with me. I was fascinated and saw a completely different side of Dana. As a matter of fact, I began using her mission to help plan treatment with her and for the very first time, she thanked me for a good session. I guess I don't really need to transfer her anymore." Searching for and finding strengths is of great assistance in designing interventions for dealing with stressful situations that are bound to arise between sessions and after termination. The identification and incorporation of skills based on strengths helps clients feel valued by their therapists and secure in their own ability to change. It also reinforces them feeling seen and understood.

4. Context

In our exit interviews, clients reported that our attention to maintaining a safe context in their lives with clear boundaries, less chaos, and more predictability was an essential component of treatment. Clients experienced clear structure and secure boundaries as a means to create safety. Most treatment models emphasize creating safety or refuge when exploring therapeutic space and the therapeutic relationship. Our model adds to this dynamic by making it overt in the first few sessions and continuously throughout treatment. We discuss with clients the necessity of transparency in the therapy process and model this by making certain they are always fully aware and in agreement with what we are doing, why we are doing it, and the potential impact on them. This transparency in the therapeutic milieu is a stark contrast to the contexts in which they were violated.

We ask our clients to think about what makes them feel safe, about what would make them feel safe in the office, how together we can create a relationship in which they feel safe, and how they can create a sense of safety outside the treatment setting. In future sessions, then, when they come in agitated, angry, anxious, or off balance, we collaborate in discovering this as a symptom of some trigger that occurred in or out of therapy that made them feel unsafe. We have already discussed how to create safety and are then able to prompt them to use those skills to promote safety in and out of therapy.

Together we develop an understanding of how the unknown creates chaos, which is triggering to their brain, and ignites their survival mindstate. Chaos and the accompanying feeling of being out of control can feel dangerous to hyperaroused people. When the chaos is self-generated, there might be some comfort in the familiar patterns, and they might even feel soothed and feel an illusory sense of control, yet it is still chaotic and perpetuates a survival mindstate. Either way, it is the unknown that contributes to the trauma mindstate. Treatment, then, should not be an unknown. A thorough exploration of the clients' perception of safety, the variables that contribute to a safe context for them, and how we can make therapy a safe place, are all explored at the beginning of therapy.

Through years of experience working with clients with complex trauma and from interviews conducted with clients who have benefited from our change model, many have come to recognize that clear boundaries and reasonable structure help them feel safe. We know that children feel safe when boundaries are respected and structure is in place to ensure that they and others do not lose control and while we assume that adults will have the same knowledge, many do not. Children's optimal development occurs when they are raised with predictable rules and roles. They are free to explore and expand their world when held with appropriate limits. In fact, many clients do not recognize that they can help create environments for themselves where they feel safe, where there is predictable structure and boundaries. Giving clients an opportunity to discuss this idea in the first session and then throughout therapy has been an essential component for clients achieving their therapeutic goals.

Therapists can inquire about safety directly or they can create an experiential exercise for individuals and families that help clients remember about safety. For example, Sally was interviewed about her experiences in family therapy 20 years after treatment had terminated (Barrett, 2011). Sally had been seen in family therapy when she was 15 years old (Barrett, 2011). She had been sexually abused by her stepfather and at the time of family therapy he was being reunited with the family after having been in prison for five years. When Sally returned to be interviewed, she proudly displayed a laminated card that she had kept in her wallet since terminating family therapy. The card contained an old recipe card that her therapist had laminated for her. The exercise entails giving clients recipe cards and asking them to put the ingredients of safety on the cards. Sally's ingredients included 1 cup of no alcohol, 2 tablespoons of patience, 3 teaspoons of humor, 2 cups of belief in God and that things were going to work out. She told the interviewer that she used this card whenever she needed to make a decision that scared her and was ever grateful for the knowledge of what helped her feel safe, secure, and soothed.

Another session we often use is what we have named "The Structural Session," fondly named after Structural Family Therapy (Minuchin, 1974; Minuchin & Fishman, 1981). This session will be described in more detail later in the book when we detail Stage One, but briefly it is a session that outlines the importance of benevolent hierarchies and boundaries in families. During the follow-up interview, a client shared that he used the image of the picture he created during the structural session repeatedly, to make sure the boundaries continued to be healthy between himself and his children. In fact, he kept the newsprint he had drawn in the structural session on the wall until his last child left home.

5. Creating Workable Realities and Meaningful Visions of the Future

When clients come to therapy, they are trapped in negative cycles of homeostatic thinking in which their vision of the future is filled with thoughts that life will always be this way, they can't get out, they have no control or ability to improve their situation, they have no influence, and their relationships are painful. They often live their lives waiting for the other shoe to drop. They experience themselves, their lives, and their place in the world as hopeless and helpless. When therapy is successful, clients report that they have a meaningful vision of the future that is more fluid and optimistic. They believe that positive change can happen and that they can be agents of this change. When stressed, they can remember that things are not always going to be this way, they have some influence and control, and they have a recognition that being in a relationship can be healing. In therapy language, they have reframed their lives from limited to full of possibility.

Clients reported that successful treatment provided hope throughout the process and that the belief that their life can improve if they work to change is an essential ingredient in successful therapy outcomes. Reframing is change that occurs by thinking differently about a situation rather than the situation changing (Minuchin and Fishman, 1981). Therapists helped clients find ways to reframe their problems and current life situations to a more workable and hopeful reality and then to effectively work toward those new potentialities.

For example, a CCM practitioner was working with a family in which the mother, Darlene, was furious and verbally abusive toward her daughter, Sharon, because Sharon had not told her that, for over eight years, she had been sexually abused by her father. When the therapist asked Darlene about her understanding about why Sharon had not told her, Darlene said it obviously meant that her daughter must have wanted the sexual relationship with her father. While this explanation is inaccurate and disturbing, it also provides little hope for change to occur. The therapist instead helped the family create a more workable reality so that a context for change was in place. The CCM therapist reframed the daughter's silence by explaining trauma mindstate. The therapist said that Sharon could not tell her mother the truth because the trauma itself and the chaotic and violent atmosphere at home that they had been describing made it impossible for her to share the truth. Sharon was in a state of immobility and this state was explained to the family. Secondly, the daughter did not tell her mother because "her mother was not there" emotionally: the mother was in flight and freeze throughout the marriage due to her own abuse history and the physical abuse she experienced in the marriage. The CCM therapist said, "Sharon would have told you, Darlene, there are many examples of her turning to you and confiding in you. She didn't tell the traumatized person who was there, that person was really not present. When you are present Darlene, Sharon turns to you for guidance. When you were not present, Sharon had no one to go to, so she told no one. In therapy we will help you find ways to come back into the relationship with your children; we will work together for you to be present."

In the winter of 2011 Palestinians, Israelis, and Jews from around the world were learning about and using the CCM. Sam, an Israeli living in Jerusalem, and Nassim, a Palestinian living in the West Bank, were both agitated and reacting from a trauma mindstate. As they compared stories, the CCM trainer saw a shift occur in Nassim. As the conversation intensified, the trainer experienced him withdraw into himself for a moment, she watched his breathing slow down and his body become calm. He glanced down, paused, and then he looked at Sam and said, "Sam, you and I could out victimize each other forever and how will that lead to peace? We can compete forever over who is the most damaged and who is the most aggressive, but we have to work together to make something different happen." Nassim was experiencing a meaningful vision of the future and using skills to change himself and his interaction with Sam. This meaningful vision of the future reminds us of the brilliance of Nelson Mandela as he made the decision not to fight but to love for South Africa. He wrote: "If there are dreams about a beautiful South Africa, there are also roads that lead to their goal. Two of these roads could be named Goodness and Forgiveness."

When clients have experienced the process of therapy as successful, they are left with a meaningful vision of the future, which incorporates hope. People have hope in themselves, despite an accurate assessment of their own limitations and capabilities, and the limits and capabilities of those in their lives. They have created what we call "workable realities," meaning that they, together with their friends, family, and therapeutic communities, have found ways to make their lives work for them. They believe in themselves and the process of growth and change. Linehan (1993a) calls this state a life worth living.

The idea of instilling hope, while also a successful presidential running slogan, comes directly from clients interviewed following treatment. Clients who sensed that their treatment team thought they would improve tended to believe it as well. Most clients with complex trauma have been told that their diagnosis prevents healing and growth and it also makes them difficult clients. Clients tell us how valuable it is to feel their therapeutic team never gives up hope that things will work out for them. They do not feel blamed, clinicians are confident in their treatment approach and its utility, and everyone holds the hope that things will work out. This does not mean, certainly, that life will be problem-free, but that when problems occur, they believe they have what it takes to work things through.

We conceptualize hope as a necessary ingredient in creating a workable reality. When therapists are overwhelmed, decentered, and reactive, clients often interpret their frustration as hopelessness about their lives. The ethically attuned therapist working with the CCM has clear treatment plans organized with achievable treatment goals, and confidence in the collaborative treatment relationship. These antidotes for therapist burnout help to maintain a hopeful atmosphere and a workable reality for the client.

Many therapists who work with traumatized populations tell stories of remarkable human beings who have overcome great tragedies. Some people with histories of complex trauma have channeled energies from their horrific experiences into creativity, adaptability, and being able to see tremendous possibilities in the world. As a result of adverse, overwhelming, and threatening life experiences, clients have developed capacities that allow them to create realities of possibility. One of the results of complex trauma can be a belief that a person can and will survive.

It is quite significant that the five essential ingredients to successful therapy experiences emerged from our clients' own words. Many of the clients we see in therapy have experienced past helping relationships as re-traumatic experiences. The very institutions that are supposed to help them have violated them. A client may feel powerless as a result of a mandate to receive services from social service agencies, courts, the military, or a family member who insisted upon their involvement. This is an unintended consequence of a service delivery system. The trauma of treatment might simply develop as a person in a position of power (the practitioner) is telling them what to do in what appears as a means to meet the practitioner's ends; a replication of the client's experience of abuse. Re-traumatization can also be triggered because practitioners are the same gender, race, or other social location as the perpetrator of their abuse.

Treatment can trigger survival mindstates because clients do not know what is ahead of them. It is safe inside the cave of homeostasis and the outside world is dangerous because of the unknown. It is also dangerous to not understand what is happening and to feel once again the context is chaotic. Treatment can also be dangerous because it is a relationship that encourages intimate conversation and thus creates vulnerability for clients.

Unfortunately, clinicians who are not mindful of survival mindstates can replicate and stimulate the basic themes of trauma: powerlessness, feeling out of control, devaluing self and/or other, and experiencing disconnection to self and/or other. The five essential guidelines of the CCM are the antidote to triggering a traumatic reaction in the client. These five essential themes, taken directly from clients' experiences, help each and every one of our clients make as smooth as possible the transition from trauma mindstate to engaged mindstate. Each session is a day in the journey.

Practitioners wanting to work from the CCM can ask themselves the following questions, before, during, and/or after each and every therapy session. These questions can help the practitioners work the model themselves. We are recommending the therapist pause and ask the following questions to ensure the therapy is constructed to not reenact trauma relationships and instead help clients engage in the natural cycle of change.

1. **Value and Empowerment:** Did my clients feel that I valued them? Did my clients experience the therapeutic relationship as collaborative and validating? Was there any indication that this experience empowered them? What were the therapeutic interventions utilized and my style that communicated value and collaboration? How did it look? Did I check in with them throughout the session, no matter what my intervention, and see if the technique felt hopeful and helpful?

2. **Skills:** Did my clients learn new skills today that they can use to help with daily living? Did those skills include mindfulness and communication? Will those skills help them move from survival mind to engaged mind? Did I demonstrate the use of engaged mindstate skills in my behavior and interaction with the client? Do my clients understand the importance of "practice" of skills? Did I reinforce the necessity and importance of daily practice of a variety of skills?

3. **Strengths:** Did I explore strengths with my client? Did I validate my clients' resources, resilience, energy, and strengths today? Are they able to find ways to use those strengths to help them move from survival mindstates to engaged mindstates?

4. **Context:** Was therapy a safe place today? Did I overtly discuss or ask about safety? Did I ensure that clients felt safe and that they had the resources to move into safety if and when it felt dangerous? Did I follow the structure of the session, making sure I began the session connecting to the last session, checking on homework, teaching, and mentoring, and consolidating the session by talking with the client about how they are feeling, summarizing the work we did today, and what they are taking with them for their work during the week?

5. **Workable Reality and Meaningful Vision of the Future:** Did I instill hope today in any way? Did my clients leave therapy more hopeful than when they came in? If not, are they able to hold on to the meaningful vision of the future we have worked on so that they can be more hopeful? Do they have a new way of looking at themselves, at others, and their symptoms? Was our session and time together motivating?

Pause and Ponder: These five essential ingredients described are necessary to create productive cycles of change. These concepts came directly from our interviews with clients. Listing them hopefully provides an affirmation and confirmation of what you already do that works. When therapy is working, the ingredients are present. And when we feel stuck or homeostatic with a client, we need to see how we are not integrating effectively all the ingredients necessary for change. Effective therapists integrate these ingredients naturally and are often unaware that the ingredients are present. We are offering the idea to make treatment more consistently effective; be aware that all these ingredients are present in every session and throughout the relationship that is being built. We are suggesting that one mindfully, before and after every session, go through a checklist or list of questions to assure that all our available resources and ingredients essential to create change are being utilized.

References

Badenoch, B. (2008). *Being a brain-wise therapist: A practical guide to interpersonal neurobiology.* New York: W.W. Norton & Co.

Badenoch, B. (2011). *The brain-savvy therapist's workbook: A companion to being a brain-wise therapist.* New York: W.W. Norton & Co.

Barrett, M. J. (2011). Therapy in the danger zone: Breaking the cycle of family trauma. *Psychotherapy Networker, 34.*

Beck, J. S. (2011). *Cognitive behavior therapy.* New York: Guilford Press.

Bloom, S. (1997). *Creating sanctuary: Toward the evolution of sane societies.* New York: Routledge.

Briere, J. N., & Scott, C. (2012). *Principles of trauma therapy: A guide to symptoms, evaluation, and treatment.* New York: Sage.

Carlson, E. A., Yates, T. M., & Sroufe, L. A. (2009). Dissociation and development of the self. In P. F. Dell, J. O'Neill, & E. Somer (Eds.) *Dissociation and the dissociative disorders: DSM V and beyond* (pp. 39–52). New York: Routledge.

Courtois, C. A., & Ford, J. D. (Eds.) (2009). *Treating complex traumatic stress disorders: An evidence based guide.* New York: Guilford Press.

Decker, S. E., & Naugle, A. E. (2008). DBT for sexual abuse survivors: Current status and future directions. *Journal of Behavior Analysis of Offender and Victim: Treatment and Prevention, 1*(4), 52–69.

Greenwald, R. (2007). *EMDR within a phase model of trauma-informed treatment.* New York: Routledge.

Herman, J. L. (1992). *Trauma and recovery: The aftermath of violence—from domestic abuse to political terror.* New York: Basic Books.

Hughes, D. A. (2006). *Building the bonds of attachment: Awakening love in deeply troubled children.* New York: Jason Aronson.

Johnson, S. (2005). *Emotionally focused couple therapy with trauma survivors: Strengthening attachment bonds.* New York: Guilford Press.

Kabat-Zinn, J. (2005). *Coming to our senses: Healing ourselves and the world through mindfulness.* New York: Hyperion.

Levine, P. A. (2010). *In an unspoken voice: How the body releases trauma and restores goodness.* Berkeley, CA: North Atlantic Books.

Levine, P. A., & Frederick, A. (1997). *Waking the tiger: Healing trauma: The innate capacity to transform overwhelming experiences.* Berkeley, CA: North Atlantic Books.

Linehan, M. (1993a). *Cognitive-behavioral treatment of borderline personality disorder.* New York: Guilford Press.

Linehan, M. (1993b). *Skill training manual for treating borderline personality disorder.* New York: Guilford Press.

Miller, A. L., Rathus, J. H., & Linehan, M. M. (2006). *Dialectical behavior therapy with suicidal adolescents*. New York: Guilford Press.

Minuchin, S. (1974). *Families and family therapy*. Cambridge, MA: Harvard University Press.

Minuchin, S., & Fishman, C. (1981). *Family therapy techniques*. Cambridge, MA: Harvard University Press.

Muller, R. T. (2010). *Trauma and the avoidant client: Attachment-based strategies for healing*. New York: W.W. Norton & Co.

Newman, C. F., Leahy, R. L., Beck, A. T., Reilly-Harrington, N. A., & Gyulai, L. (2001). *Bipolar disorder: A cognitive therapy approach*. Washington, DC: American Psychological Association.

Putnam, F. W. (1988). The switch process in multiple personality disorder and other state-change disorders. *Dissociation, 1*(1), 24–32.

Putnam, F. W. (1997). *Dissociation in children and adolescents: A developmental approach*. New York: Guilford Press.

Rothbaum, B., Meadows, E. A., Resick, P., & Foy, D. W. (2000). Cognitive-behavioral therapy. In E. B. Foa, T. M. Keane, & M. J. Friedman (Eds.) *Effective treatments for PTSD: Practice guidelines from the International Society for Traumatic Stress Studies* (pp. 320–325). New York: Guilford Press.

Schwartz, R. C. (1997). *Internal family systems therapy*. New York: Guilford Press.

Shapiro, F. (1998). *EMDR: The breakthrough "eye movement" therapy for overcoming anxiety, stress, and trauma*. New York: Basic Books.

Siegel, D. J. (2010a). *Mindsight: The science of personal transformation*. New York: Bantam.

Siegel, D. J. (2010b). *The mindful therapist: A clinician's guide to mindsight and neural integration*. New York: W.W. Norton & Co.

Siegel, D. J. (2012). Keynote address: The attuned therapist. *Psychotherapy Networker Conference*, March.

Trepper, T., & Barrett, M. J. (Eds.) (1986). *Treating incest: A multiple systems perspective*. Binghamton, NY: Haworth Press.

Van der Kolk, B. A. (1987). *Psychological trauma*. Washington, DC: American Psychiatric Press.

Van der Kolk, B. A., Weisaeth, L., & Van Der Hart, O. (1996). History of trauma in psychiatry. In B. van der Kolk, A. C. McFarlane, & L. Weisaeth (Eds.) *Traumatic stress: The effects of overwhelming experience on mind, body, and society* (pp. 47–74). New York: Guilford Press.

three
Treatment
Guidelines

Clients shared what helped them change and we have incorporated their ideas into the Collaborative Change Model (CCM). Best practices in trauma-informed care have also influenced the model. A comprehensive review of the literature coupled with decades of clinical practice have shown us there are certain consistent structures and functions present when therapy is successful. So while the five essential ingredients spring specifically from the clients' reporting of their experiences, the foundational elements of effective treatment permeate the observation and study of effective trauma treatment models. In fact, clients have reported to us what makes therapy work for them, and we have observed this in action by attending to the vast array of theoretical models. Together this is an affirmation of good treatment. There are five foundational treatment elements that organize guidelines for good care and these elements parallel the five essential ingredients reported by clients and are similar to what Linehan (1993) has described. We have found the following five foundational elements. The first element is to augment and amplify the client's natural capacity and capabilities, expanding their repertoire of thought and action. The second is to provide inspiration, motivation, and incentive to work away from survival mindstates toward engaged mindstates. The third is to provide predictability, order, and structure for treatment and for the treatment team. The fourth element is ensuring generalizability of learning outside the therapy encounter, and the fifth and final is to enhance therapeutic confidence and competence.

The Practitioner's Perspective: Five Foundational Treatment Elements

Whenever practitioners walk away from a meeting with clients feeling good about their work, or a client reports satisfaction and change in the therapeutic process, we will argue that the treatment included the client-centered ingredients and the foundational elements and guidelines for treatment. Conscientious, talented practitioners who have honed their craft, studied their treatment models, availed themselves of supervision, and elicited feedback from their clients are probably using the ingredients and elements that we describe here. We are suggesting that instead of thinking about these as inherent in sound therapeutic practice, we deliberately place the five ingredients and five elements front and center so as to inform the therapeutic journey and each and every session of our time together. We look at these as the necessary tools when creating and implementing the blueprint for change. These guidelines are embedded in the CCM and are designed to be utilized with all theoretical and treatment modes and models.

The first element is to strengthen and amplify our clients' capacities and capabilities and expand their repertoire of thought and action. The second is to provide motivation to work away from survival and towards evolving. The third is to provide order and structure for the treatment team. The fourth is to ensure generalizability of learning outside the therapy encounter, and the fifth and final element of a sound relational trauma-informed model is to enhance therapeutic confidence and competence. The five essential ingredients clients have shared with us that have promoted success will be accomplished if the therapist pays attention to the five foundational treatment elements. Once again, as we suggested for the essential ingredients, use these elements as a checklist in preparing for sessions, as a way to pause and recalibrate when off balance during sessions, and as a method of consolidating at the end of the session. Guidelines for treatment include both the clients' perspectives, which were summarized in the essential ingredients and the practitioners' foundational elements, which are detailed below.

Five Treatment Elements

1. Augment and Amplify Clients' Natural Capacity and Capabilities

All trauma-informed treatment models enhance clients' capabilities and resources. Any successful therapeutic intervention or therapy model includes a skill-building component, which enhances the clients' capability to navigate life more successfully. Collaboratively, practitioners and clients determine what skills are necessary to move the clients from survival mindstates to engaged mindstates and to diminish symptomatic behavior. While the list of capabilities we discuss below is not exhaustive, we know that these are some of the essential capabilities we find ourselves working on over and over again in our work with clients stuck in survival mindstates.

a. Interactional Cycles of Survival

Clients who have experienced complex trauma often find themselves mirroring past relationships in some very profound, disturbing, and complex ways. They often feel unable to extricate themselves from the cycles that end up perpetuating their traumatic experiences. We call these patterns interactional cycles of survival. In previous work, Barrett and Trepper (1991) have labeled these patterns the vulnerability/survivor cycles, and they are similar to Duhl's (1975) Velcro loop cycles. Interactional cycles of survival are cycles with no beginning and no end in which people spark each other toward their trauma mindstate ways of being. The amygdalas are firing and the engaged minds are nonfunctional. Person A's amygdala or fear center is triggered by a survival behavior of Person B. When Person A's fear center is triggered, a trauma response follows. That trauma response triggers Person B's amygdala, which then ignites Person B's trauma response that is going to trigger Person A and the cycle continues until someone is in too much pain or exhausted to continue, or the situation escalates and others become involved and/or someone gets hurt. Neither person has any idea how to escape the cycle. In therapy, together, we map these cycles and help clients learn skills to respond differently and stop the cycles from reoccurring and escalating.

Interactional cycles of survival occur in the intimate relationships of people with a history of complex trauma because intimate relationships have the potential to feel threatening. They often trigger survival mindstates because traumatic events have occurred in intimate relationships that make the relationships feel dangerous. Using a water metaphor, intimate relationships are the equivalent of a warm bath. Often, however, when stressed, relational dynamics appear more like boiling water or ice cubes. When the water boils or freezes, we recognize that people are responding from interactional cycles of survival and we work to help each partner respond differently so that change cycles can occur instead (see Appendix 3).

An unfortunate and common interactional cycle of survival is a violence cycle that may go something like this: Jake was physically abused and berated by his hostile and withholding father. In his adult couple relationship, whenever he believes that his partner Joyce is not paying enough attention to him, he experiences her other-than-him preoccupation as rejecting and withholding. He becomes furious and confused and feels like he is being victimized all over again. Joyce's behavior triggers Jake's fear and frustration and he becomes caught in a trauma mindstate, focusing exclusively on his survival. Jake has physically shaken Joyce with frustration, threatened worse, and then pushed her out of the way so he can exit the situation and calm himself. His anger, violence, and threat of violence preoccupy Joyce, causing feelings of vulnerability, and she responds self-protectively by withholding more and more. She is clearly triggered by his threatening and dangerous behavior and she retreats into flight and/or freeze. He experiences these cycles and his behavior as complete survival and self-defense and she experiences them as violent, which they are. We are very clear in therapy that Jake must hold himself accountable for his own behavior and that his behavior has to change. We explore the cycle with him so that he understands it completely. His anger, a self-defense fight response from childhood trauma, triggers his partner's fear, which triggers her self-defense flight response and she withdraws from him, which further angers him. The cycle is recursive and both experience it as never ending and out of control. They are in an interactional cycle of survival and both are in survival mind. Neither Jake nor Joyce have any idea how to transform this punishing interactional cycle into more satisfying relationship patterns.

The CCM therapist helped enhance Jake's capabilities by increasing his knowledge of his own responses and behaviors as they constituted and perpetuated the interactional cycle of survival. As Jake gained systemic insight, he developed hope that he could change and this reinforced his already powerful motivation to change. The therapist helped him find alternatives to his self-defense behaviors that were not self-sabotaging and abusive to Joyce. The skills Jake learned that were helpful to him in increasing his capacity to engage in more evolved cycles were not only cognitive and behavioral skills, but were also body sensitive, assisting Jake to recognize and cope differently with the familiar physical signals of escalation. He learned where he was experiencing the fear and the rage in his body and how to pay attention to it and change its color from a deep red to a burnt orange. Cognitively, Jake learned that his partner's behavior, concretely, might trigger his memory of his father's behavior, but in fact, his partner was not his father. When she was not paying attention to him, it was often because she was preoccupied with something that was going on in her own life. This preoccupation was not, in fact, a message about him but it was a message about what was going on for her. He learned to be more curious about her state of mind. Behaviorally, Jake learned to manage his anger through self-soothing techniques. He made a commitment to never touch his partner when angry and stuck to it. When angry, he reminded himself that he was okay, that he could control himself, and that he was bigger than the momentary anger he was feeling. Jake's enhanced capacities challenged this interactional cycle of survival. He had choices and hope.

Family, couple, and/or group treatment are often good venues to help clients move away from interactional cycles of survival. The timing of family, couple, and group treatment is collaboratively decided upon depending on the vulnerabilities and resources of the client and the hierarchy of the symptoms; in other words, in which areas of their lives they are experiencing the most distress. As relational beings, clients' most significant relationships offer the best opportunities to practice new skills. As Jake progressed in his couple relationship, he asked his father to join him in therapy and spent a few sessions developing a new relationship with him.

Interactional cycles of survival are also triggered in relationships between clients and practitioners. For example, a school counselor, Elizabeth, requested supervision after being triggered into survival mindstate during a meeting with a parent and her adolescent son. The son had been thrown against a locker by a couple of basketball players and needed stitches, so his mother was called out of work to take her son to emergency care. The mother stormed into the guidance office where the son was waiting and said, "Damn it Adam, I told you not to dress like an f-ing fag." Elizabeth had a traumatic stress reaction and she stood up and yelled at the mother, "How can you blame Adam for this?" In CCM-informed supervision Elizabeth said, "I went right to fight. I was not mindful, I was not engaged, I was totally caught in survival brain. I was able to calm myself down and apologize but the damage was already done." Supervision then focused on helping Elizabeth understand what had been triggered in this relationship and what work she needed to do so that she was working from an engaged mindstate when she was triggered in her work environment.

Elizabeth learned to cognitively monitor her triggers before, during, and after her meetings with parents and youth. She knew what some of them were: for example, she had not felt seen by her parents and had been the target of bullying in middle school, but also knew that there might be more that she was unaware of and made a commitment to monitor her reactivity before each session. Behaviorally, she made a decision to not engage any parent unless they were both sitting, because she felt more settled and calm in her chair. She also realized that she had become tightly wound and felt stress in her shoulders and back that concerned her and made a commitment to go back to a weekly yoga class she had stopped attending.

b. Self-Regulation Skills

When stuck in survival mindstates, with the amygdala reacting, regulating self is inherently difficult. People whose lives are informed by complex trauma often respond in extreme ways to everyday stressful events that they experience as dangerous. Although these events are stressful and difficult, the majority of these situations are not physically or psychically dangerous. People who have not experienced complex trauma may have learned to cope with these difficult situations in productive rather than reactive ways. Those who have experienced complex trauma may not have learned those coping skills. Perry (2001) states: "if the neurobiology of a specific response, hyperarousal or dissociation, is activated long enough, there will be molecular, structural and functional changes in those systems" (p. 229). Hyperarousal may encourage overreaction to an emotionally charged event, whereas dissociation may cause an underreaction to the same event. Trauma-informed treatment teaches clients how to regulate their own emotional states so that they are able to thoughtfully respond to emotionally charged events.

Mary Jo, while teaching the model in Rio de Janeiro, Brazil, had a moment to practice self-regulation under an emotionally charged event. Her hosts and everyone she encountered in Rio were warm and engaging. They all also warned Mary Jo about the dangers of their city. Multiple kidnappings had occurred recently and the threat of violent crime seemed to permeate their concerns. While Mary Jo was presenting to a crowd of about 100 people, she heard loud male voices in the hallway and then noticed her host aggressively stand up and rush out of the room. Mary Jo could hear sounds but no words as the host was talking to the men outside. The host then rushed back into the conference room and hurried towards the front where Mary Jo was presenting. As she was walking toward Mary Jo she gathered a few of her colleagues from the audience and seemed to be strategizing to take over the stage and stop the conference. Mary Jo experienced herself in the middle of a stressful situation and her thoughts went something like this: something is occurring that is impacting my workshop. I am aware that my host is anxious about the men in the hallway and I am aware that everyone has been telling me that Rio is dangerous. Is this a dangerous situation? Then Mary Jo noticed that her host was applying lipstick as she strode toward the podium. Mary Jo's engaged mindstate was able to process this external stimulus to determine that this was not a dangerous situation, and she self-regulated. The host then announced that the photographer and journalist from the local paper had five minutes to interview Mary Jo and her, so they needed to take a break.

Some of us are born with an inherent and hardy ability to regulate our emotional states, but most of us learn this through interactions with responsive caregivers. When we have traumatic experiences and our caregivers fail to be responsive and supportive, we respond self-protectively as well as possible, but only with the natural resources available to us. Without engaged adult wisdom and guidance in negotiating complex situations, there is a failure in the development of our ability to process the experience and regulate our emotional responses. Trauma-informed treatment helps rewire our brains toward coping skills that are useful and help regulate our emotional states.

Mindfulness techniques based in meditation and neuroscience research help clients regulate their thoughts and emotions. Linehan (1993) created dialectical behavior therapy (DBT), an effective treatment protocol for work with clients who have difficulty self-regulating. We teach mindfulness, we refer clients to DBT groups, and we teach many DBT skills in our own therapy sessions. We explore these interventions further in the book when we discuss Stage Two of our treatment model.

An example of successful implementation of self-regulating techniques is our experience with a client named Alex. A CCM therapist saw Alex in therapy for a number of years. Alex had two alcoholic parents who often left her alone for long periods of time or with caregivers who paid little attention to her. She was a fearful child who overcompensated with extreme and risky behavior as an adolescent. Smart and resourceful, she put herself through college, became a teacher, and married a computer programmer. She sought therapy when her husband started traveling for work. She found herself frightened to be alone at night. She started meeting friends from work for drinks every night he was gone, and then having a nightcap at home afterwards. She found herself awakening at night and not being able to fall asleep again without more alcohol. She was often too hungover to go to work and started taking so many days off that her Principal gave her the choice of attending therapy or take a leave of absence.

One of the skills Alex needed to learn was self-regulation when she was left alone and experienced a sense of isolation. As a young child, Alex was often left alone and exposed to fearful situations that she was too young to tolerate. She was defenseless, she was incapable of protecting herself if something dangerous were to happen, and she had no one to talk to about these fears or to teach her how to cope with them. As an adult, Alex was in fact capable of protecting herself if something dangerous were to happen when her husband was traveling, but was stuck in a survival mind-state and felt incapable. Instead, she reacted to being left alone by numbing the fear through alcohol, which was the dominant coping mechanism she was taught. She had learned how to survive when she was fearful of being isolated, but she did not have access to her engaged mindstate at those times.

In therapy, Alex learned to regulate her fear reaction from an engaged mind-state rather than to numb it through alcohol. She learned how to do this in a number of different ways and through many discussions of her experiences in and out of therapy. She remembered the little girl she used to be and thought about what she would have wanted if she had a responsive adult by her side. As a responsive adult now herself, when she was frightened, she soothed the reactive frightened child inside by reminding her that she was capable of protecting herself now if something dangerous were to happen. She recruited her husband to call more often when he traveled. She found that reading and praying before she fell asleep helped and she rescued a dog from the pound who had been neglected by his owners. "We are both frightened little creatures who are protecting each other," she told her therapist, "We calm each other down."

CCM clinicians instruct clients how to use self-regulating skills early on in treatment and throughout subsequent sessions. As a way to build collaboration, we repeatedly tell clients the purpose of these exercises. We communicate that change is within their power and their responsibility. The practitioner is there to mentor and facilitate the change; we cannot make it happen. Mindfulness practices are taught within the first few sessions. These can be as simple as reminding clients to sit up straight and breathe. Practitioners who have a mindfulness practice themselves help remind clients to do the same. In an exit interview, for example, one client stated that she learned self-regulating skills by discussing them with her therapist, but she really believed that she learned them through the modeling from many mental health providers who she watched remain calm and directed when she and her family were under duress. She said, "Growing up, whenever there was conflict, it was total chaos, I never ever saw anyone be reasonable when anything intense was going on so it was a blessing to be in the room with people who remained calm when we were going at it with each other. I actually learned I could do the same thing by watching other people do it. One time when it got really intense, I watched Michael (a CCM therapist) take a stress ball out of the toy box and squeeze it. He saw me looking at him and found another ball and handed it over to me. It really helped. I squeezed it rather than scream at my mother and felt so much better afterwards. How awesome is that?"

There are many treatment methods and techniques that can be used to enhance self-regulation. We encourage clients to use what is available in their communities. Some of the most efficacious body/mind-oriented approaches that are currently available are yoga trauma-sensitive sessions, mindfulness practices, expressive arts, and imagery. There are many trauma-informed practices in which practitioners receive specialized training and that are well received by clients we have seen (e.g., internal family systems therapy (Schwartz, 1997), eye movement desensitization and reprocessing (EMDR) (Shapiro, 1995, 2013), mindfulness based stress reduction (MBSR) (Kabat-Zinn, 2005), life force yoga (Weintraub, 2004, 2012), trauma sensitive yoga (Emerson, 2011), sensorimotor psychotherapy (Ogden, 2006), somatic experiencing (Levine, 1997, 2013), transformative insight therapy (Underwood, 2013)). While certainly different in appearance and application, the common thread in these approaches is that they utilize methods that intervene at the level of self-regulation. No single intervention or therapeutic model is effective for every client and not every practitioner can be trained in a body-centered approach. Working with clients who have experienced complex trauma does demand the clinician to have a working understanding of the mind/brain/body connection and self-regulating skills must be introduced to the client. The learning of these skills creates an opportunity for teamwork with clinicians that specialize in any of these modalities mentioned. Self-regulation is an integration of cognitive and body awareness and the interventions must mirror this integration.

c. Understanding the Process of Evolving

A comprehensive treatment plan is most functional and effective when everyone involved understands how therapy works, and how the process of evolving occurs. Therapists may inadvertently trigger traumatized clients into a survival mindstate when the clients are not informed specifically about the therapy process. One of the most important functions of good therapy is to carefully avoid situations that replicate the abuse, the invalidation, and other memories of the trauma. Trauma occurring within the context of an abusive and/or neglectful relationship is the most common form of complex trauma presentation we see. In other words, our clients are often abused by people in a position of both power and intimacy. Their powerlessness may be related to differences in their age, gender, economic status, respective roles in the relationship, and the context of the relationship. The people violating them satisfy their own needs and without being deterred by a consideration of the impact of their behavior on the well-being of the victim. Practitioners may be perceived by our clients as potentially dangerous until proven otherwise, since we are in a position of both power and intimacy, potentially interacting with them to meet our own needs and to the extent we behave in ways they do not understand.

A CCM therapist was referred a 60-year-old mother (Sharlene) who said that she had been verbally abused by her previous therapist, a well-respected individual who was not known for being trauma-informed. Sharlene did not wish to press charges, she just wanted to talk about and process her experience because she knew she needed therapy but was frightened of being verbally abused again. Sharlene stated that her adult daughter brought her to therapy with Dr. C to facilitate discussion of a difficult time in their lives. According to Sharlene, her daughter, in front of Dr. C, "ripped into me, tore me to pieces, and manipulated Dr. C into thinking everything was my fault." When Sharlene tried to defend herself by stating that she would leave not only the therapy office but the country if this continued, Dr. C asked her to calm down, which enraged Sharlene. She did not remember events clearly afterwards, but does remember throwing the Kleenex box at the wall, screaming and crying, and running out of the room. Had Dr. C taken some time at the beginning of the session to explain the process of therapy and the importance of safety before change is going to occur, Sharlene may have left the session feeling less abused and reactive.

A true collaborative relationship creates a partnership in the process of change. Transparency is crucial in creating safety and collaboration. This transparent partnership is ongoing and overt throughout the treatment process. It is established first by sharing the CCM's philosophical underpinnings at the beginning of the relationship. At each stage of the model, our philosophy of the change process is articulated and we are constantly eliciting feedback from clients about the effectiveness of the process. This metacommunication about what is occurring between us is imperative in order to create the context necessary for change and to work with clients to move from a survival mindstate to an engaged mindstate. Mental health treatment itself is stressful under all circumstances. When the stress is acknowledged and the process is discussed, we are engaging mindfulness and beginning the process of rewiring the interpersonal neurobiology of the brain.

We help clients understand the stages of evolution as well as the process of "state of mind changes" moving from a traumatic, depressed, anxious, survival mindstate to an engaged mindstate. We are transparent about all the processes of treatment—what we are doing, what is happening, and why we are doing what we are doing. We explain the process of pausing and pondering that occurs in creating a context for change. We give examples of how challenging patterns works and repeatedly review the process of consolidation. We also explore what specific skills are necessary for clients to change and when, where, and how they will utilize these skills. We help clients understand the difference between reacting and responding and how to recognize what their bodies feel and their minds think when they are reacting and likewise what they feel and think while they are responding. We also help them understand that these skills are internal as well as interactional.

Changing long-standing survival patterns that have served to cement people in the world takes a great deal of effort and some discomfort. We teach our clients that both the capability and the responsibility of evolving from a survival cycle of interaction to a growth cycle is theirs. A recurring challenge of all therapies is due to the fact that the symptoms most difficult to give up are symptoms that manifest because resolution involves enduring situational tolerance of uncomfortable feelings of distress. Discomfort often triggers survival symptoms. Let us repeat this statement, because each therapist must help clients understand this. *Discomfort often triggers survival symptoms.* The survival actions triggered by the desire to escape from the uncomfortable symptoms may often be self-sabotaging, keep them stuck in a survival mindstate, and isolated from intimate and healing relationships. In the short run, these symptoms may make them feel empowered, valued, and relievingly disconnected. Importantly, however, the symptoms are intended to keep people from experiencing feared pain and discomfort. Because these symptoms are not responses from an engaged mindstate, they tend to not be thoughtful or carefully planned and well-executed responses to complicated situations and do not work in the long run. To expect someone to give up their symptoms, however, without also teaching them how to tolerate discomfort is unrealistic. We explain all this to clients.

When working with couples, families, and individuals in distress, discussing their interactional survival cycles and how to escape them is often one of the first items of dialogue. It helps bond the clients to the therapeutic process in that it instills hope that the work will produce results and their lives really can change. For example, Chris and Nora were both in their early thirties and had been a couple for over seven years when they initiated therapy. They were both survivors of childhood sexual abuse and had dealt with their traumatic experiences by contracting to never hurt each other sexually. In theory this is a lovely idea motivated by the best of intentions practically, however, the contract manifested itself through avoidance. Neither could tolerate the possibility that their sexual needs might make their partner uncomfortable, so they denied having them. When Nora discovered that Chris was thinking of having a sexual encounter with a co-worker, they came into therapy to try and save their marriage.

The CCM therapist explored with the couple and with Chris and Nora separately how they understood their interactional cycle of survival and also what each would need to understand about the change process and about each other for their cycle to be different. They discussed ways to soothe themselves and ways to soothe each other so that they could safely explore the possibility of having a different relationship. The therapist and clients set goals together about each stage of communicating differently with each other and they worked together to set the pace of treatment.

2. Provide Inspiration, Motivation, and Incentive

Change is hard work and it is as natural as survival. Trauma-informed treatment models must address how to assist clients with maintaining or improving their motivation to change. We as therapists are marketers for change. We need to inspire and motivate clients to work hard in therapy and to endure the challenges that accompany an ongoing self-examination and change process. Clients stuck in survival mindstates enter therapy with very little hope. They experience the world as physically and emotionally dangerous and feel powerless, devalued, and out of control. Interventions should help empower clients, and encourage their value and their control. When clients find themselves feeling safe and using new skills that are successful, it motivates them to continue the therapeutic relationship and to do the difficult work necessary to reach their engaged mindstate destinations.

What helps a client feel motivated? First, clients tell us that the transparent collaboration between the clients and practitioners is very motivating. Greater client involvement in decision-making seems to produce more investment in the outcome. From the very beginning of therapy the CCM therapist finds ways to involve clients in the process. Our clients have also shared with us that group therapies increase motivation. Experiencing and witnessing another's change is motivating. Seeing other people utilizing engaged mindstate skills and achieving significant life improvements is an important motivating source.

A practitioner's own enthusiasm for the model of treatment can be motivating to clients. In our exit interviews one client explained what helped him to change. "We were working with a new therapist right out of school. I know because she told us a lot about how new and exciting this model was for her. She had a supervisor behind a one-way mirror who would call her up and tell her what to do and she was so eager to please the supervisor and do it right. It helped us, my mother and me, want to do it right too. I know that sounds weird, but my mother and I actually talked about it afterwards. She was so enthusiastic about the model that it just sort of became contagious."

Another way to motivate clients is to design interventions and teach skills that work quickly. Small successes, repetitive relief, and steady progress instill hope and help inspire clients to want to practice and return to the next session for more. Clearly, discovering through Stage One the best way clients learn and how they experience relief and self-soothing and then practicing those skills during sessions will be motivating.

We use Prochaska, Norcross, and DiClemente's (1994) Stages of Change Model in thinking about motivation. The model reminds us that readiness to change is a continuum. The six stages of the change model, pre-contemplation, contemplation, preparation, action, maintenance, and relapse, are explored and often taught to clients. The model also serves as a guide to assess where clients are in the change process. So, for example, a CCM therapist was seeing an individual young woman in therapy, Maria, who had a history of complex trauma and was having casual sexual encounters with multiple male acquaintances. Maria was discussing a goal they had made for their work together which she was having a difficult time imagining. At one point Maria asked the therapist, "how do I know I will be happier if I am engaged and intimate with a partner? Maybe I feel happier if I feel safe and the only way I can feel safe is by protecting myself." This statement is a well-articulated sentiment that many of our clients experience in many different forms, and the therapist and Maria determined she was in the stage of contemplating change. Certainly, this explains why there might be ambivalence about change. The CCM therapist's response to Maria was to acknowledge and validate her reality and to help her examine both the positive and negative consequences to change and the positive and negative consequences to staying the same. For Maria, the positive consequences to change were that she might someday have a real relationship that had a future, but the negative consequences were that she might open her heart to someone who would hurt her. The positive consequences to staying the same were to avoid pain and the negative consequences were to be stuck in fear for the rest of her life. Having all her options explored in this way helped Maria consider moving forward and risking discomfort.

Some therapists use worksheets and motivational interviewing techniques (Miller & Rollnick, 2012) to motivate clients and some just have these stages in their minds as they interview. Again, all trauma-informed treatment protocols must help motivate clients to change and successful ones, whether articulated or not, probably use some form of motivational interviewing. Therapists must also remember to continually point out the change they observe the clients making. Small changes certainly add up to create large change. Therapists tend to focus on what needs to change rather than what has changed. Particularly in Stage Two of treatment, after we have created a strong bond with the client, we tend to take liberty at focusing on what needs to change and the existing patterns. As we fervently work toward change, we forget to punctuate regularly the changes already made.

Practitioners need to be clear how they motivate, and what interventions, talents, and skills they utilize to insure they can market their therapy and motivate the client to work toward change. Motivating our clients is a conscious and crucial step in creating successful treatment.

3. Create Predictability, Order, and Structure

Having a model that is structured with a standardized and flexible protocol helps provide a safe context for clients, which is an essential guideline for structured treatment protocols. Clients who experience complex trauma do so in an interpersonal context in which people in a position of power violate their boundaries and integrity of self. These violations are often not predictable and leave people feeling out of control. The environment is often chaotic and rigid. Predictable structure provides flexibility and adaptability. A therapy without a structure, where no one is clear what, how, and why certain therapeutic actions are being taken, runs the risk of reproducing a traumatic relationship. A predictable structured therapy provides safety, through establishing boundaries within the therapy and between the client and therapist.

A predictable, structured, goal-driven stage model that is collaboratively modeled with the client creates a non-traumatic therapeutic context. Even though it is a stage model, just like in the brain, the predictable repetition provides change.

The brain has neuroplasticity, and the repetitions are sculpting new reactions that become healthy behaviors. An individual and a family system also have forms of plasticity. Therapy can sculpt new interactions internally and interactionally by repetitions of the same predictable healthy sequences. Thus we also recommend that every session have a predictable structure. With order and structure, both client and therapist feel powerful, in control, creative, confident, and have more faith in the outcome.

Many clients told us in the exit interviews that structured sessions were helpful. Jack, a 25-year-old survivor of clergy abuse, said, "For someone like me, who came from a chaotic home, two divorces, an autistic brother, and then the reason I was in therapy to begin with, I think one of the things that helped me the most was knowing exactly what to expect in therapy. I mean, things came up that I wasn't aware of, but we always seemed to start therapy the same way and we always spent the last five minutes summing up the session. There is something incredibly comforting about this type of structure for someone like me. I learned how to put some of that in my own life as well because I realized how important it is to my mental health."

Boundaries are part of order and structure. Often when complex trauma is distilled, the essence of the traumatic interactions is a series of boundary violations. Boundaries that are undefined, inappropriately loose, hierarchically violated, and/or too rigid leave a person anxiously anticipating the next violation. Successful and non-traumatic therapy defines boundaries from the beginning. A series of conversations occur which discuss boundaries inside the office, outside the office, during sessions, and in between sessions. It is helpful for the client to have these conversations before any violation occurs, so it is essential to discuss boundaries right away.

In Stage One, we discuss the length of sessions, phone calls and emails in between sessions, texting, safety plans (including suicide, homicide, violence, child abuse), asking personal questions of the practitioner, and self-disclosure. Clients are also asked to share any boundaries that they might want to create within the therapy. Usually at some point in therapy we discuss boundary violations that could occur outside of therapy: Sightings on the street, knowing people in common, etc. (for more detailed discussions around boundaries, refer to Barrett & Butler, 2002; Barrett, 2012). The conversations about boundaries contribute to the order of treatment and the structure of the treatment plan.

4. Assure Generalizability of Learning and Practice

Excellent treatment models inform effective therapies that assist clients' learning to enhance their lives and relationships outside of the therapy office. Skills learned in therapy and relational experiences that clients encounter in their therapeutic contacts are effective to the extent they are generalizable to the clients' natural environment. Successful therapy makes therapeutic learning applicable to clients' lives outside of therapy in at least three ways. First, "firing creates wiring" is an expression of the recursive loop that occurs when clients try a new behavior which produces a positive result and thereby encourages the next attempt, and so on.

Second, we deliberately and repeatedly discuss ways to use new skills outside of therapy and third, we concretize new skills with homework assignments.

Assigning homework for purposes of practice and skill generalizability is a common therapeutic intervention in many therapeutic models. Unfortunately, this process is eroded when therapists forget to ask their clients about the homework when conducting the next session. Therapists may forget they have given homework or a new crisis draws the focus away from the previous session's assignment. In the CCM, it is imperative that there be follow-up on the homework. Forgetting or becoming distracted by crisis is more similar to an atmosphere of chaos and neglect and survival mindstates than an evolution to engagement.

We have found that the attentive therapist can make a connection between homework that is meaningful and directly related to clients' lives no matter what has happened during the week. For example, if the homework was to practice a particular skill and the client comes into the session in a crisis or reports a crisis during the week, the therapist can either practice the skill immediately in the session or can ask if the client practiced the skill in order to manage the crisis. If the client failed to practice the homework, then there is always something to learn from that as well. Was the skill not meaningful to the client's life, was the skill not suited for the learning style or resources, was it a poor assignment? At what point did the client decide not to do the assignment, and how was that decision made? Did the client know during the session that the assignment wouldn't work, and what prevented an open discussion at that point? There is always something to learn from an assignment done or not done.

Generalizability to the natural environment can also be practiced during couple, family, and group therapy. In fact, we believe that good trauma treatment involving multiple theoretical approaches, offering a variety of perspectives and a wide array of skills in order to interrupt a multitude of traumatic cycles, provides greater generalizability when offered in a variety of different treatment modalities. Each venue provides different and at the same time complementary contexts for the clients to practice new relationship skills. The problems and symptoms are complex, hence the interventions must mirror the complexities. For example, limits may be easier for a client to set with a therapist than with a spouse who may challenge a boundary that most therapists would naturally validate. Communication skills are another example of what can be taught in session, practiced in session, and then used daily outside of the office. In couple, family, and group therapy, clients can practice new communication skills while therapists can coach clients in these new behaviors in real time. The therapist can prompt when necessary and observe how the client delivered the skill. The therapist's perception of the client's use of the skill is based on first-hand observation rather than client report. The therapist may provide immediate skill-shaping feedback and reinforcement, and observe how the client's new behavior was received by others, and be able to process those reactions either at the time or in the next individual session.

Essentially every skill that is taught in a session needs to be practiced throughout therapy, both within sessions and between sessions. Clients understand this from the beginning of therapy and are reminded throughout the process: "firing makes wiring."

> I believe that we learn by practice. Whether it means to learn to dance by practicing dancing or to learn to live by practicing living, the principles are the same. In each, it is the performance of a dedicated precise set of acts, physical or intellectual, from which comes shape of achievement, a sense of one's being, a satisfaction of spirit. One becomes, in some area, an athlete of God. Practice means to perform, over and over again in the face of all obstacles, some act of vision, of faith, of desire. Practice is a means of inviting the perfection desired.
>
> Martha Graham (http://thisibelieve.org/essay/16583/)

5. Enhance Practitioners' Competence and Confidence

A comprehensive treatment model enhances therapists' personal and professional capabilities and an organization's ability to deliver services. Without a comprehensive model, professionals may find themselves in the middle of a long treacherous journey responsible for the lives of others with no map to guide them. This challenging situation often leaves therapists experiencing themselves as powerless, devalued, and out of control, and may lead them to unintentionally re-traumatize those in their care. An organized treatment plan, which informs the therapy, mediates therapist burnout and helps in preventing compassion fatigue (e.g., Barrett, 2010; Figley, 1995, 2002) and secondary posttraumatic stress disorder (e.g., Figley, 1995).

Compassion fatigue is a practitioner's survival mindstate. When practitioners are suffering from compassion fatigue, they have similar reactions to their clients, experience stress as dangerous, and avoid discomfort and connection. Hopelessness and a survival mindstate are not conducive to good treatment outcomes. Having guidelines for treatment helps build a therapist's competence and confidence, and enhances creativity. It also provides clients with the ability to pause and harness their particular cycles of change and recovery. This leads toward a sense of optimism and enthusiasm for the therapist, which is contagious, infecting clients with a heightened sense that they will be able to change, grow, and heal.

In the CCM, we conceptualize the presence of compassion fatigue and secondary posttraumatic stress disorder as indicative of an energy crisis. Symptoms materialize when a therapist passionately and compassionately gives more energy out to the therapeutic process than is replenished. Guidelines for good trauma treatment must include a methodology that helps a clinician maintain energetic balance. The replenishment does not necessarily come from the process of therapy itself, although it can. The energy comes from a plan of in session and out of session energy replenishment. As Loehr and Schwartz state in their 2003 book, *The Power of Full Engagement:* "Performance, health, and happiness are grounded in the skillful management of energy" (p. 5).

The CCM builds into the therapy session, the therapeutic process, and the process of supervision, a plan on how to manage energy effectively. For example, a practitioner was engaged with many clients with a history of complex trauma when she found out she was pregnant. She found herself exhausted and compassion-depleted. She worked with her supervisor on ways to manage her energy. With some clients the practitioner brought in co-therapists so that when she took maternity leave there would be continuity and she found herself less exhausted. She realized that with certain clients and certain content she had to use her time between sessions to meditate or nap, creating effective methods of taking care of herself. She also collaborated with the clients about ways to be as effective while taking good care of herself.

Therapists fully engaged with a finely tuned internal experience of their own energy are said to be working from an engaged mindstate. With practice that follows logically from the idea of ethical attunement (which we discuss in detail in the next chapter), practitioners are not only attuned to their clients but also to themselves and their own energy. Practitioners use the skills they teach to others for their own self-care.

In training, we refer to this as "working the model" or "self of the therapist" work. The CCM becomes a template for the emotional management of therapists' professional and personal lives. Ongoing supervision and consultation help personalize the treatment model to therapists' particular strengths and vulnerabilities, and fine-tunes the model so that it fits their personal and contextual variables. For example, a therapist who finds herself anxious before a particular client session or modality discovers that a 10-minute meditative practice calms and settles her before she begins these sessions. Another therapist finds himself triggered by a couple dynamic he repeatedly encounters and discovers he needs to engage mindfully in a more intimate way with his own partner before being able to be fully present for his clients with complex trauma. Any and all of the ways in which therapists work the model create opportunities for them to enhance their competence and confidence.

At the end of each and every session or the end of therapy, use the checklist on page 55.

1. **Augment and Amplify Clients' Natural Capacity and Capabilities:** Have I made clients aware of any interactional cycles of survival that occurred in the therapy room or while someone was explaining a pattern? Have I taught self-regulation skills? Have I focused on my own breathing? Have I focused on the process of evolving in a way that made clear how change occurs? Have I been a responsive therapist who mirrored and helped my clients self-regulate? Did I continue to create a partnership in the process of change? Did I talk about the process of therapy? Did we discuss discomfort and the importance of tolerating it in the process of change? Did I identify or continue to identify the client's natural ability to change?

2. **Provide Inspiration, Motivation, and Incentive:** Did I remind clients that change is hard work? Did I help clients feel understood, powerful, and in control? Did I collaborate in decision-making? Did I highlight small successes? Did I use interpretations that provided relief? Was my interviewing based on the client's stage of change? Did I provide some relief during the session? Could they imagine possibility? How did I provide hope?

3. **Create Predictability, Order, and Structure:** Did the session follow a predictable structure? Did I follow the stages of the model in a natural progression from the previous session? Did I create a context for change, then look at or challenge patterns based on which stage we were in, and did I spend time at the end of the session consolidating the session? Did I talk about the importance of order and structure and how they balance with flexibility? Was I respectful of boundaries? Was I punctual starting and did we end the session on time? Was I centered, structured, and flexible as a model for the model?

4. **Assure Generalizability of Learning and Practice:** Did I ask about ways clients were incorporating what they learned outside of therapy? Did I make sure to review homework from the last session and did I assign new homework for next week? Did we use the homework assignments in a way that was helpful? Did we practice skills in session that could be used in clients' lives outside of session?

5. **Enhance Practitioners' Competence and Confidence:** Did I experience myself as powerful, valued, and in control? Did I perceive myself as competent, confident, and creative? Did I experience optimism for the clients and for treatment? Did I feel hopeful about the therapy process? Did I pay attention to and manage my energy effectively? Was I attuned to energy depletion and have I made sure to practice self-care? Am I working the model in my own life? If I wonder if I could use help with this case, do I trust myself to utilize my existing contacts or develop new resources and will I make sure to use them? Did I recognize my survival cycle of interaction and pause to move myself into a growth cycle?

Pause and Ponder: *When designing treatment and thinking about the standard of care when treating complex trauma, it is imperative to follow the guidelines. These guidelines will help keep the client engaged and help client and professional stay grounded. It will provide a baseline to rely upon if and when we become confused about what we are doing. The guidelines also help us design the treatment plan, but also plan for consultation and supervision.*

References

Barrett, M. J. (2010). Healing from relational trauma: The quest for spirituality. In F. Walsh (Ed.) *Spiritual resources in family therapy,* 2nd Edition. New York: Guilford Press.

Barrett, M. J. (2012). Yesterday's ethics vs. today's realities: Boundaries in an age of informality. *Psychotherapy Networker,* July/August.

Barrett, M. J., & Butler, K. (2002). "Can we talk?": Let's end our conspiracy of silence about our ambiguous boundaries. *Psychotherapy Networker,* March/April.

Barrett, M. J., & Trepper, T. S. (1991). Treating women drug abusers who were victims of childhood sexual abuse. In C. Bepko (Ed.) *Feminism and addiction* (pp. 127–146). New York: Haworth Press.

Duhl, B. (1975). *Unhooking a negative Velcro loop.* Visual Publication.

Emerson, D. (2011). *Overcoming trauma through yoga.* Berkeley, CA: North Atlantic Books.

Figley, C. (Ed.) (1995). *Compassion fatigue: Coping with secondary traumatic stress disorder in those who treat the traumatized.* New York: Routledge.

Figley, C. (2002). *Compassion fatigue.* New York: Routledge.

Kabat-Zinn, J. (2005). *Coming to our senses: Healing ourselves and the world through mindfulness.* New York: Hyperion.

Levine, P. (1997). *Waking the tiger: Healing trauma.* Berkeley, CA: North Atlantic Books.

Levine, P. (2013). *Creating safety in practice: How the right tools can speed healing and reduce symptoms for even the most traumatized clients.* NICABM Webinar.

Linehan, M. (1993). *Skill training manual for treating borderline personality disorder.* New York: Guilford Press.

Loehr, P., & Schwartz, T. (2003). *The power of full engagement.* New York: Simon and Schuster.

Miller, W. R., & Rollnick, S. (2012). *Motivational interviewing: Helping people change,* 3rd Edition. New York: Guilford Press.

Ogden, P. (2006). *Trauma and the body: A sensorimotor approach to psychotherapy.* New York: W.W. Norton & Co.

Perry, B. D. (2001). The neurodevelopmental impact of violence in childhood. In D. Schetky & E. P. Benedek (Eds.) *Textbook of child and adolescent forensic psychiatry* (pp. 221–238). Washington, DC: American Psychiatric Press.

Prochaska, J. O., Norcross, J. C., & DiClemente, C. C. (1994). *Changing for good: The revolutionary program that explains the six stages of change and teaches you how to free yourself from bad habits.* New York: William Morrow & Co.

Schwartz, R. C. (1997). *Internal family systems therapy.* New York: Guilford Press.

Shapiro, F. (1995). *Eye movement desensitization and reprocessing.* New York: Guilford Press.

Shapiro, F. (2013). *The power of EMDR to treat trauma: Identifying, reprocessing, and integrating traumatic memories.* NICABM Webinar.

Underwood, K. (2013). Transformative insight therapy, personal communication.

Weintraub, A. (2004). *Yoga for depression.* New York: Broadway Books.

Weintraub, A. (2012). *Yoga skills for therapists.* New York: W.W. Norton and Co.

four
Ethical
Attunement

The range of what we think and do is limited by what we fail to notice. And because we fail to notice that we fail to notice, there is little we can do to change; until we notice how failing to notice shapes our thoughts and deeds.

R. D. Laing

Wilson and Thomas defined empathic attunement as: "The psychobiological capacity to experience, understand and communicate knowledge of the internal psychological state of being of another person" (2004, p. 20). Interpreting research on treatment with those who have experienced trauma, Wilson and his colleagues (Wilson & Lindy, 1994; Wilson, Friedman, & Lindy, 2001) developed the concept of empathic attunement and articulate therapist's reactive styles which interfere with being empathetically attuned. Siegel (2012) suggests that attuned therapists "feel the feelings, not merely understand them conceptually." He states that the most important element in an attachment-based, neurobiologically-informed psychotherapeutic approach is the clinician's ability to regulate his/her own emotions. This is, in a sense, a hands-on, body-on, mind-on therapy in that the therapist's whole self, while remaining emotionally stable, vibrates like a tuning fork to every quiver of emotion that the client experiences. Our concept of ethical attunement stands on Wilson's and Siegel's shoulders and adds the necessary components included in our Collaborative Change Model (CCM) of practitioner energy, reactivity, and relational components of complex trauma.

Ethical attunement is a full, clear, non-anxious, and warm validating observation of our clients. This occurs in conjunction with a full, clear, non-anxious warm, validating observation of oneself and a clear observation of our interactions with our clients. Ethical attunement is a fully engaged mindstate. It also includes wisdom of the CCM and how and when to use it with complex trauma. Many clients, particularly those with traumatic experiences in intimate relationships, are hypervigilantly attuned to a therapist's energy. As a reaction to a history of dangerousness in intimate relationships, many clients enter therapy with strong energy fields that repel others, maintaining a "safe" distance that does not allow challenges to homeostatic patterns of managing the anxiety generated by closeness. This energy, while often not intentional, keeps therapists at arm's length and thereby limits their potential therapeutic impact. Therapists, by nature and by training, sensitive to this energy, may react to this distancing. Without adequate training and guidance, the therapist's sensitivity may become a negative reactivity which may include becoming openly irritated, withdrawing, identifying the client as "an unworkable borderline," or a lost cause, etc. This reactivity has the potential to re-traumatize clients. Therapists who practice our CCM (what we call, working the model) recognize the importance of aiming for full, clear, non-anxious warm energy when guiding therapy and have a model for how to achieve this. Ethical attunement involves working from an engaged mindstate, which also includes tools for recognizing and altering self when one is not engaged.

We understand that it is a lack of ethical attunement that often creates a context for traumatic experiences. The community, the family, and the relationships that our clients are embedded in by definition have failed to hold their members' physical, psychological, emotional, spiritual, and sexual needs. Our work then is to offer an alternative through our collaborative practice of responding from an ethically attuned place. We introduce this concept in the beginning of therapy when we discuss safety and creating a context for change. Often CCM practitioners discuss use of self and are transparent about working the model to guide treatment from an ethically attuned place. A clinician may say something like, "I take five minutes between clients for a guided imagery where I think about how I hope the session goes. I tell you this because I want you to know how mindfulness helps me so when I am teaching it to you, you will know that I practice it as well and it is helpful."

CCM practitioners, actually, are in constant training and preparation. This preparation, like all parts of the model we will describe, occurs minute by minute in the session, week by week out of session, and year by year in the psychotherapist's life. Because of the recursive nature of our model, some have recommended that we call it a fractal model. A fractal involves a pattern, like a snowflake, that when dissected, has all parts of itself in all of its parts. The therapist works the model while she works with clients to do the same. Everything we teach in the book we teach our clients and practice ourselves.

Practitioner Energy

Preparation for guiding the journey of therapy begins with monitoring our own energy. Ethical attunement is a clear and open access to the energy of mind, body, and spirit. We strive to be as equally attuned to our thoughts, our emotions, our body experiences, and our autonomic arousal as we are to those of our clients. Being completely therapeutically available to our clients also means being there for ourselves. By welcoming challenging responses as opportunities to self-regulate, we assist clients in learning to self-regulate by fostering an environment of responsiveness. When we are ethically attuned to our clients, we enjoy being with them. In an exit interview a client spoke on behalf of her family when she said, "We were mandated to be in therapy because of the sexual abuse. We hated each other and loathed ourselves. Our therapist seemed to like us however, and she knew the truth. If she liked us, we couldn't have been all that bad. It made a difference."

We believe that compassion fatigue (e.g., Barrett, 2010; Figley, 1995, 2002) results from passionately and compassionately giving care, giving of ourselves, literally giving our energy to others. When we are fatigued in this way, symptoms permeate every area of our lives. The more depleted we are, the more we may become distracted, judgmental, critical, dissociative, anxious, depressed, aggressive, and prone to mistakes, sleeplessness, and illness. We think about the human machine as running on psychic energy. This energy is divided into five domains: emotional, physical, spiritual, intellectual, and sensual. In order to be fully present and engaged in our lives, we need energetic reserves in all of these areas.

Considering humans' marvelous genetic and environmental complexities, it can be assumed that there are a multitude of similarities and differences in how each human creates energy and expends energy. Yet we all expend energy continually in many areas of our lives. For people in the helping and caring professions, we are often expending energy from all five domains, all day long, in both our personal and professional lives. Mary Jo likes to say, "My husband the engineer goes to work and basically uses energy from the intellectual and physical domains, sometimes on the emotional domains. He comes home from work and when he engages with the kids and me, he then taps into his emotional, spiritual, and sensual energy. I, on the other hand, listen and witness all day long to stories of trauma, distress, physical, emotional, and sexual violence. I am using energy in all five domains throughout my professional day. I am emotionally and spiritually holding my clients' narratives and their interactions. I am intellectually using my knowledge and my skills to create interventions. When I come home I feel like saying, 'Sorry, guys, I gave at the office.' I am spent and at times there is nothing left for anyone, including myself."

To avoid compassion fatigue, we believe it is important to attempt to live a balanced life. We have to learn to monitor our energy level throughout the day and plan how to replenish the energy that has been expended. If you give emotionally at the office, you may have to take time to "recharge" emotionally at home. We need to have a plan that enables us to observe our energy expenditures and practice energy replenishment, throughout our day. We must monitor our tank at all times to assure that we do not run out of the necessary energy to function both at home and at work. Part of functioning with clients is our ability to stay ethically attuned; we cannot stay ethically attuned if we are energy-depleted.

Practitioner Reactivity

Energy depletion often is a major contributing factor to practitioner reactivity. Rather than responding with engagement, the clinician may react in a way that may interfere with therapeutic goals. Wilson and Lindy (1994) found that therapists working with clients with complex trauma developed reactive styles that prove unhelpful to the therapy process. Our experience suggests that these reactive styles are likely to occur when therapists are not energetically aligned and working the CCM. When therapists are not aligned, they will have a number of different experiences and these experiences, when they are working the model, can alert CCM therapists to their lack of alignment.

So, for example, when practitioners find themselves mentally preparing their grocery-shopping list when a client is emotionally expressing, they are not ethically attuned in session. Wilson and Lindy (1994) have labeled this empathic withdrawal. In empathic withdrawal our hearts are unbalanced: we are physically present while someone is in pain but we are emotionally, cognitively, and spiritually withdrawn. If practitioners, on the other hand, either during session, or between sessions, think they are the only people in the world who can help their clients, they are equally off balance. Wilson and Lindy (1994) label this imbalance empathic enmeshment. Empathic disequilibrium (Wilson and Lindy, 1994) occurs when clinicians find themselves feeling helpless, incompetent, and out of control for more than one to two minutes at a time. In times of empathic disequilibrium, we are spiritually unbalanced, our client's pain shakes us, and we are unable to respond in therapeutic ways. Empathic repression (Wilson and Lindy, 1994) manifests itself when practitioners have no affective connection to client's pain expressions, where curiosity is nowhere to be found, and our hearts are closed. If we find ourselves hoping clients cancel or terminate therapy, our empathic responses are probably lacking and we may be frustrated with or disappointed in our therapeutic road map.

In the CCM, we conceptualize empathic withdrawal, enmeshment, disequilibrium, and repression as survival mindstate responses to therapeutic stress. While practicing the CCM helps alleviate a great deal of unpredictability and unmanageable stress when working with clients, it is a given that some therapeutic encounters will trigger our reactive survival responses. At these times, the attuned therapist will recognize being reactive rather than engaged and responsive. Using the model, practitioners begin to recognize that when they feel powerless, devalued, or out of control, they may react in ways that are less than helpful to their clients. Paying attention in a mindful way to ourselves, our clients, and our relationships with them, helps us ease back into ethical attunement.

Ethical attunement is a non-reactive therapeutic stance in which practitioners are open and responsive to their own internal processes and to those of their clients. When clients express pain and we are ethically attuned, our triune brain is firing, we are thoughtfully engaged, compassionately empathizing with our hearts, have a road map of the model in our minds, and are spiritually grounded. Energetically, we are in a full and completely engaged mindstate. Lack of ethical attunement indicates a deficiency of access to the mind, body, or spirit when in therapy. To be fully observant about what clients need, therapists need to be working the model themselves. The model includes working toward mind, body, and spiritual attunement, in other words, engaged mindstate.

Ethical attunement is a non-reactive, responsive stance and it is an assessment instrument. Siegel's (2010, 2012) ideas of mindfulness are helpful in understanding ethical attunement as an assessment instrument. He has shown that when you are mindful, your mind is observant, objective, and open to both your inner world and to others' inner worlds around you. Ethical attunement is an empathic response coupled with knowledge of what response is in the best interests of the client at the particular time. Ethical attunement becomes an assessment instrument because therapists use their attuned selves to gather data about their questions and interventions. With the details of the map at hand, attunement is focused on the terrain.

Have you ever been lucky enough to witness a brilliant kindergarten teacher? She is masterfully attuned to the dignity and the vulnerability of 5-year-old children. When a child tries really hard to do something right, fails miserably, and her upper lip trembles with fright at the mistake she just made, the teacher's heart goes out to the student. An empathic response might be for the teacher to give the student a hug and to tell her how proud she was of her trying, and that everything was going to be okay. An ethically attuned response would be to be aware of both the vulnerability and the dignity of the 5-year-old. The ethically attuned teacher knows exactly what to do and sometimes that is to do nothing, to not acknowledge what happened but to be beside the child as she struggles, awaiting the child's asking for help. While this may look, to the untrained eye, as if the teacher is ignoring the child, the teacher is in fact intently focused in a calm way on the student and her needs and developmental process.

A CCM therapist was ethically attuned during the break she took before a particularly difficult session at the end of her clinical day. She paused and turned her attention to the couple scheduled as her next appointment. She had only seen the couple twice before. Their 16-year-old son had been arrested for prostitution. As the therapist thought about the couple, both professionals with two other successful children, she was reminded that she had been troubled by the seemingly blasé attitude they had expressed in the initial meetings. By taking this pause, the therapist realized that she needed to understand how their shallow affect and seeming unconcern made sense to them within their context so that she could honor its protective quality. As a consummate teacher honors a child's dignity as he learns, the therapist had to honor the obtuse non-affective expression while her heart stayed warmly engaged with her clients. Recognizing her own feelings of outrage at their apparent lack of concern allowed her to recognize that her reactions would interfere with her ability to connect, understand, and ultimately be useful to them. Reminding herself of this throughout the following sessions allowed her to stay connected and curious with the clients, and to gently and persistently assist the clients in understanding their reactions in their full complexity.

The wisdom to do nothing while staying fully engaged and curious can be taught. We want to be helpful and sometimes the best way to be helpful is to watch an interaction unfold without questioning it or intervening in any way. Working the model, the CCM therapist was fully attuned to her own negative reactions about the parents' stunted responses to their son's prostitution. The therapist was aware of the extent of her frustration with them and knew that she had to understand and manage her reactivity before she could be helpful to the couple. She had received feedback that her own anxiety when her children had difficulties manifested itself sometimes to others as her appearing to withdraw or distance. She also knew, from previous clinical experiences, that asking them directly about their emotional fugue would alienate the family and impede progress.

Instead the CCM therapist respected the dignity of the parents and engaged them quickly in therapy because their son was in great crisis. This meant internally acknowledging her reactivity and honoring the protective quality of their lack of affect while engaging them in the collaborative process of change. She was aware that in Stage One much of attunement is observation and awareness, with much more subtle action. It is not only being aware of countertransference; it means understanding how these experiences are impacting us in the moment with our clients, in the room, and knowing how to manage both the thoughts and body sensations, in order to stay present, professional, and a keen guide in the process.

Clinicians may have mistakenly learned in previous training settings that they should ignore or suppress uncomfortable reactions to clients rather than embracing these reactions and examining them and learning how to work with them constructively. Leaving your thoughts and feelings about self outside the therapy room so you can be objectively and fully intellectually engaged is an unfortunate part of many training protocols. This is akin to being an expert tour guide in a destination you have never visited. Ethically attuned practitioners who are working the model are fully and mindfully engaged in internal processes and what is occurring interactionally. In the above situation with the family that the CCM therapist was worried about, if she had ignored or tried to suppress her reactions a number of potentially re-traumatizing and harmful interactions could have occurred. If she had been taught to ignore her reactions, she might not only have missed a therapeutic opportunity but may have done damage. So, for example, experiencing their obtuse affective expression, and subconsciously judging it as bad parenting, she could have blamed the parents for their son's problems. The therapist's negative judgment could have been experienced as a lack of understanding or even hostility, with the result that the parents probably would not have engaged in what turned out to be a very productive treatment.

Ethical Attunement and Complex Trauma

Ethically attuned practitioners are involved with their minds, their hearts, and their spirits. Our five domains (emotional, spiritual, intellectual, physical, and sensual) are open, our energy is centered, and we are working from an engaged mindstate. We would venture to say that most clinicians are drawn to the field because we desire to be helpful. When we succeed in being helpful, a positive feedback loop is reinforced: our minds are active and engaged, we have an experience of worthiness, and the knowledge that our interventions were influential. When we are helpful, our hearts are open, and we feel lovingly connected with our clients who value the time we spend together. When we are helpful, we are spiritually engaged, and we have a sense of purpose, agency, and power. We experience the fulfillment that results from being fully engaged in an emotionally, spiritually, intellectually, physically, and sensually satisfying and meaningful profession.

We find ourselves challenged by those clients who do not naturally elicit our helpfulness. The "goodness of fit" between client and therapist that works behind the scenes to assist the therapeutic process fails to occur. We need more than just our openness to be helpful. We need a model. The issue at hand is that untreated complex trauma challenges clients' minds, hearts, and spirits. Without adequate intervention, complex trauma typically results in a loss of the experience of themselves as having influence (mind), feeling valued (heart), and having power (spirit). Mindfulness eludes them, their hearts are not filled with love and contentment in relationships, and their spirits do not feel powerful. They are stuck in trauma/survival mindstates and engaged in interactional cycles of surviving.

There are some clients who are not open to our support and our willingness to be helpful. They may not be literally or figuratively available to us and the process of therapy. This is particularly difficult for practitioners who are accustomed to experiencing validation when they give to others. Our gifts of listening, being compassionately present for others, and being helpful are often received with gratitude. When we perceive ourselves as being helpful and our gifts are not received, we may become reactive. We leave our space of being responsive.

When we find ourselves reacting and experiencing ourselves as powerless, devalued, or out of control, we too are stuck in survival mindstates and engaged in interactional cycles of surviving. Remember, unmanageable stress triggers flight, fight, or freeze reactions and practitioners, though trained to be responsive, still function like human beings when under overwhelming stress. In flight, we may find it difficult to attend to our clients and difficult to go to work on the days we know we are scheduled to see the clients that trigger us. In fight, we may become irritable, tense, or defensive and resentful, in and outside the office. In freeze, we may find ourselves being submissive. We become numb, robotic, apathetic, or detached and struggle to remain present in the room. Analysis of these reactions yields rich information, which hopefully encourages us to pause and contract and figure out how to move toward ethical attunement. We may recognize that we are triggered in the session and not know how best to cope in the moment. We may also not realize that we are triggered until after the session and have to develop a plan to address it during the next session. And we may recognize we are triggered in the moment, pause, contract, and do something different.

Matthew, a CCM group therapist, knew he was triggered in the moment but had no idea how to think about what was happening or how to respond. He presented his situation to his consultation group a few days later. He was co-leading a group of teenage sexual offenders and the group was in Stage One, second session.

At the end of the session, a 14-year-old ran over to Matthew and gave him a huge bear hug and while in his embrace, rubbed his groin area against Matthew's thigh and giggled. Matthew confided to his consultation group, "It freaked me out. I got really scared and just sort of pushed him away and turned around to get away from him. When Jess, my co-leader, asked me what happened, I couldn't talk. At first, I wondered if it actually really happened; was I imagining things or did this jerk actually hump my leg and laugh? And then I got really scared: I mean, I'm the adult here and I felt totally out of control. I need to do something the next time we meet, I just don't know what it is."

Matthew's consultation group worked together to help him figure out what happened to him when he was triggered and also to problem-solve his next step when he met with the group. Matthew acknowledged his flight response and was able to connect it back to some experiences he had as an adolescent. He was able to articulate what he hoped he could do the next time he was caught off guard by provocative behavior. Furthermore, Matthew developed a plan for the next session. He planned to meet with his co-leader before the group and also to talk with the boy with whom he had the encounter. Matthew said, "I will remind him about safety and how my sense was that he was not feeling safe in the group and that his acting out behavior was an indicator of his not feeling safe and I'll talk to him about ways he can monitor that and ways that I can be helpful."

Pam, a CCM couple therapist, did not recognize that she was triggered until after a particularly difficult session. She was working with a couple who triggered each other's interactional cycle of survival so fast that Pam had little time to interrupt their cycle before they barbed each other with meanness. She too felt like a punching bag when she tried to intervene or to get them to slow down long enough so that she could thoughtfully engage them in collaborating with her. After one particularly trying session, Pam's daughter called to ask for permission to drive home with one of her friends. Typically Pam would agree to her daughter's request, appreciative once again that she followed the rules and asked permission before getting into a friend's car. Instead, reacting from her stressful session, Pam barked at her daughter to take the bus and to stop interrupting her at work. On her drive home a few hours later, Pam had a moment to pause, contract, and think about her behavior. She recognized that she had responded negatively to her daughter because of how reactive she had been with the couple and how out of control she felt the sessions were going. She immediately called her daughter and apologized. She then spent the rest of the drive thinking about ways to be different with this couple and felt energized and ready to see them the next week.

Sharon, a CCM-trained caseworker, noticed that she was triggered in a meeting with a probation officer and a family, and was able to pause and do something different immediately in the meeting. The probation officer was challenging the father of his 16-year-old client for not being present enough in the boy's life. Sharon watched the father's jaw clench and knew he was ready to bolt. Sharon was immediately aware that she was also triggered as she started to feel hopeless and powerless. She paused and thought to herself, "Sharon, Dad is triggered and he is going to do something he always does, which is to react in a way that is not helpful to his son and their relationship. You can help him do something different here." Sharon turned to the dad and said, "I gotta tell you, Tony, I am really impressed with you right now. You are being challenged and you are staying right here. We both see the door and we both know you could walk right out of it now, but you are sitting here for your son. You never ever had anyone do this for you, but you are sitting here doing it for him. I am really impressed. I just had to say it, acknowledge it, and let you know that I am totally aware of how incredibly difficult this is for you. And yet you are doing it anyway." Tony visibly relaxed. As often (but not always) happens with this sort of intervention, the probation officer seemed to relax into a more engaged mindstate, said something positive about Tony's parenting, and the session continued.

Twelve-year-old Lyle was physically and sexually abused by his grandfather. Lyle was in family therapy with a CCM therapist and also saw an individual therapist. In family sessions, Lyle was cooperative, aware, engaged, and making terrific strides. In contrast, in his individual sessions he destroyed the toys, regularly bolted from the room, often refused to talk except to swear, and even hit the therapist. None of this behavior was displayed in family therapy. When the CCM therapist asked Lyle about his behavior in individual therapy, he said, "Lucy (the individual therapist) never tells me what she is feeling or thinking. She scares me. I think she is always against me, I think she is going to take me away from my parents. She always stays so calm, so quiet, I have no idea what is going on with her. She just keeps saying in a calm voice, 'Lyle what you are doing is not safe, you could hurt yourself. This is not safe behavior.' That makes it worse. I go crazy, my trauma mind is out of control."

We have learned from our clients that successful therapeutic relationships are characterized by active engagement from all participants with open minds, hearts, and spirits. Our collaborative relationships encourage familiarity with and increased access to engaged mindstates that empower clients to have influence over their own lives. Our caring relationships make them feel valued, and our road map provides them with a powerful way to engage life stresses in the future. A model that is informed by these concepts not only leads to ethically attuned therapists, it also leads to successful therapy.

Pause and Ponder: It can be overwhelming when realizing how much we have to attune to during an interaction with clients: what is going on inside of our body, mind, and brain, our thoughts and feelings; seeing how we are going to behave as a result, at the same time observing our clients' body language, breath, and behaviors; while listening to them on literal and metaphoric levels. All of this we must attend to at the same time. Therapy is a complex process needing a great deal of energy on the part of both clients and practitioners. Do you recognize when you become unaware in sessions and do you have resources that help you become ethically attuned in the present moment? Do you have a comprehensive energy management plan that helps your energy stay balanced in your professional and personal life? Do you have techniques of how to stay ethically attuned during sessions?

References

Figley, C. (Ed.) (1995). *Compassion fatigue: Coping with secondary traumatic stress disorder in those who treat the traumatized.* New York: Routledge.

Figley, C. (2002). *Compassion fatigue.* New York: Routledge.

Siegel, D. (2010). *Mindsight: The science of personal transformation.* New York: Bantam.

Siegel, D. (2012). Keynote address: The attuned therapist. *Psychotherapy Networker Conference,* March.

Wilson, J. P., & Lindy, J. D. (Eds.) (1994). *Countertransference in the treatment of PTSD.* New York: Guilford Press.

Wilson, J. P, & Thomas, R. B. (2004). *Empathy in the treatment of trauma and PTSD.* New York: Routledge.

Wilson, J. P., Friedman, M. J., & Lindy, J. D. (Eds.) (2001). *Treating psychological trauma and PTSD.* New York: Guilford Press.

Part II

Expanding Realities

The Collaborative Change Model

If something or someone doesn't work, it's in a state of grace, progress, evolution. It will attract love and empathy. If it does work, it has merely completed its job and is probably dead.

Solomon (2012, p. 42)

five
Stage One
Creating a Context
for Change

The Collaborative Change Model

The Collaborative Change Model (CCM) is an organizational blueprint designed to help clients and therapists have a successful therapeutic experience. As one client so aptly phrased it, "The Collaborative Change Model is the order of how to put my life back in order." Consider the metaphor: a hurricane or tornado destroys the building where you live and the goal is to rebuild after this traumatic event. What would happen if you went to rebuild without a blueprint? The blueprint is the order in which the building follows. It is the way the contractors and subcontractors communicate with one another. And you would not draw a blueprint that recreated the exact same dwelling. When rebuilding, you would create a structure that was stronger, without the vulnerabilities that contributed to the collapse of the building. This is exactly what needs to happen in the treatment of complex trauma. We follow a blueprint in order to communicate, to give us structure and predictability. We want to address the vulnerabilities and augment the strengths. We do this by following a blueprint of the model. This meta model divides treatment into three stages that correspond to three stages of each session. The model follows the cyclical phases of natural growth and evolution: the contraction/pause/cocoon phase is followed by an expansion/growth phase, which leads naturally into a consolidation phase. The therapeutic healing process happens in these three stages over time, each session includes the three stages, and within each session the same cycle recurs over and over again. This is the blueprint for therapy, both a visual map and a language that organizes the labor of everyone involved. The goal of the blueprint is to help all participants understand and envision the project and goals of the shared work and to help guide our clients into their own natural cycle of growth.

The blueprint is a useful metaphor to teach clients about the stages embedded in the change process or as shorthand to talk with colleagues about working together to rebuild clients' lives after a series of traumas. You might describe the process as follows: building construction begins with an architectural design, as all stakeholders create a vision collaboratively. Excavation begins after the plan is authorized, followed by pouring the foundation, laying the floor, building the walls, studs and frame, and then the roof. Before any specialty sub-contractors appear on the scene, this foundation and framework are created to build upon and everyone is cognizant of working from the same blueprint. Then specialty sub-contractors come in to plumb and wire. The final stage is the interior, when the house becomes livable. All involved are working off the same blueprint, so they share a common language and logical order.

The CCM is the blueprint of how change happens in recursive stages. *It is a man-made rendition of what happens in nature.* As every room in a house follows the blueprint for the entire structure, so every session follows the sequence of the stage model. Stage One is creating a context for change, Stage Two is challenging patterns and expanding realities, and Stage Three is consolidation. Every session will have three stages, which means during Stage One of the session, therapists create a context for change, therapists are challenging some patterns and including a psychoeducational component, and finally in the session therapists reground, helping clients center before ending the session, and engaging with their natural environment. As a CCM client exclaimed after her therapist had explained to her the stages and how each session would also have three stages, "I get it, there is a beginning, a middle, and end." Other clients have told us that we put words to their experiences which give meaning to how complex trauma has played out in their lives and we give words to the process of change. Therapy is no longer a mystery. It is not something being done to them, it is instead a process they fully understand and do together with practitioners as guides and partners.

While it would be lovely to write that these stages flow fluidly, anyone who has ever rebuilt a home or been on the journey of psychotherapy is well aware that there are fits and starts along the way. These fits and starts are part of the natural cycle of change. They are not mistakes, and should not be seen as setbacks or regressions. There is movement, there is pause, hesitation, contraction, recalibrating, there is regrounding, then there is movement again, followed by pause, regrounding, and movement. It is empowering and validating for all involved to understand this natural flow and to recognize that therapy is designed to follow the natural progression of change. Recognizing and respecting the nature of change supplies confidence, direction, hope, and possibility instead of dread, fear, and survival mindstate when there is a challenge.

With a blueprint, the therapeutic process may still be chaotic, but without a blueprint, therapy with trauma victims is not only chaotic but may actually be harmful. Creating a context for change (Stage One) is the part of the natural cycle of healing that is compared to cocooning and contraction. It focuses on the foundation, what created the problem, what the clients bring to therapy for fixing the problems, understanding and learning the interactional cycle of survival and the natural cycle of evolution, and designing the treatment. Challenging patterns and expanding realities (Stage Two) is the skill-building stage where the client is emerging with new skills and motivation for expansion vs. homeostasis. Consolidation (Stage Three) is where the client and therapist look into the future, whether it be the next day, the next week, or life after therapy, and plan how during times of difficulties they have the skills to go from survival cycles to evolving cycles.

The three stages of our model are embedded in each stage of therapy. Using the blueprint metaphor to build a home again, let's think about pouring the foundation as Stage One. A home is only as good as its foundation and therapy is only as good as the therapists' and clients' foundational creation of a context for change. The beauty of our organizational model is that the same steps that are used for pouring the foundation are the ones used for the finishing touches or the last stage of therapy, consolidation. If pouring the foundation was akin to Stage One, pouring the foundation also uses Stage Two and Stage Three concepts. So, for example, before the foundation is poured, a great deal of work is needed. Workers are skilled, safety precautions are put into place, knowledge of the land is sufficient, concrete is on the property, and equipment is ready to use. Then the work of pouring the foundation occurs, which is akin to Stage Two in therapy. The concrete has to dry, workers have to clean up and assess the situation for the next day's work, which is consolidating (Stage Three) the day's work. If while building the toilet doesn't fit the hole in the floor, the building process stops and the plumber and the builder must recalibrate to fit the toilet.

The identical organizational structure occurs for building walls, putting in the plumbing, and making the home a safe, livable, functional, and engaged place. To mix metaphors, again, you can see that the model is a fractal model. The parts of the whole and the stages of therapy share structure and function. We make those connections in therapy and will share many of them as we explore the concept in our three-stage model below.

All good trauma-informed treatment follows a sequence that has been eloquently articulated in Greenwald's (2007) fairytale of trauma therapy. He writes about a small town with a dragon and the town's desire to rid itself of the dragon by finding a hero. In Stage One, they find the hero and urge him to slay the dragon, but he does not have the desire, courage, or the skills to do the work. In Stage Two, the town finds him a place to work out, they hire a personal trainer, and encourage him along as he works hard, experiences both defeat and success, gets ready to slay the dragon and then, with a great deal of support, is successful. In Stage Three of the fairytale, the town's people discover why the dragon was attracted to their town to begin with and work constructively together to ensure that a dragon never returns. Our model follows the same sequence and we often tell our clients about Greenwald's fairytale when explaining how therapy works (see Appendix 4).

Pause and Ponder: The recursive nature of the CCM is the essential understanding in creating change. Take the time now and recognize in every session
how you and your clients need to pause, create the necessary context to change,
then think or try something new, expand, and then sit with the new awareness
or feeling or behavior. This sequence will repeat numerous times within sessions,
and throughout every stage of therapy. This recurring sequence occurs in all
forms of treatment in which change and healing are the goal. It is essential that
you understand the flow of this pattern in order to structure your experience
with the client to follow the cycle, to explain it to your clients, so that you and
they may recognize it in therapy and in their lives.

Stage One: Creating a Context for Change

In Stage One, whether it is the Stage One of therapy, the Stage One of a session, or
the Stage One of the change cycle within the session, we help clients move from
a context of trauma and homeostasis to a context of change. Stage One, then,
through the therapist's ethical attunement, helps clients begin to believe that the
therapeutic relationship can be helpful, provides hope, and organizes the process
of treatment planning. Stage One is the context for both clients and therapists to
understand what danger/threat is for the client, what triggers danger/threat, what
the trauma narrative is, and how it organizes symptoms and relationships. Stage
One also provides the groundwork for collaboration between therapists and clients in the therapeutic process and treatment goals.

In Stage One, we share our blueprint of therapy. We help clients understand that
therapeutic change is a process of moving them from survival cycles to evolving
cycles, and we explain this process as transparently as possible. We repeat these concepts as much as possible in all stages of therapy. The conversations about therapy
and the teaching of the model are very deliberate and overt conversations, collaboratively designing the face of therapy. Furthermore, throughout the course of therapy, we are observing and describing to clients what we see happening in the room,
between family members and between therapist and client. A CCM therapist is practicing the three stages of the growth cycle repeatedly during every session. So, for
example, it would be common to hear the following conversation in a first session:

CCM therapist: Give me a moment, I want to think about what you just
described to me.

Or

CCM therapist: I just observed something between you two; I need a moment
to describe to myself and then to you, my observation.

Then

CCM therapist: You probably noticed that I asked for a pause before I began to speak to you. Please let me explain that pause. As I explained to you, the process of therapy follows the natural cycle of all change and growth. And so in the pause, I created a mini cocoon where I made sure I tried my best to communicate using my entire engaged mind, not just the survival part of my brain. As I like to say, I will "pause and ponder" throughout the course of every session and many times I will ask you to do the same thing. You see the same three stages I described for therapy, we will be repeating in the session. This is how change happens. And so when I pause, I am basically choosing which path I want to take to communicate and interact with you most effectively.

In our experience, the foundational work of Stage One is crucial to the success of therapy, and is the most important phase of the evolving cycle. If you do not create a context for change with clients who have a history of complex trauma, they will experience therapeutic interventions from a survival mindstate and treatment runs the risk of being re-traumatizing. Paradoxically, Stage One seems to be the least respected stage of therapy. Psychotherapists see themselves as change agents, but they risk misalliance, premature termination, and re-traumatization if they do not honor the natural cycle of evolving and the importance of Stage One. Stage One is often rushed through or skipped entirely and this undoubtedly creates therapeutic failures. Pacing of treatment is crucial for success; that is why there is such an emphasis on structure and predictability.

We are trained to begin our therapy after a brief period of "joining" to move quickly into assessment, followed soon after by interventions to challenge unproductive behaviors, thoughts, and feelings. We teach skills to extinguish symptoms and create positive behavioral, cognitive, and emotional changes. This rapid movement toward challenge and change can, and often does, trigger a survival mindstate for our clients. It is stressful. It can be disorienting and threatening. Something is happening to them that is completely unexpected, and they do not understand. Lacking a detailed blueprint for the process of therapy, the therapist's actions may seem confusing, irrelevant, or critical. This stressful situation triggers survival mindstates in which it is virtually impossible to achieve therapeutic growth. All of our clients' energies are focused on surviving while in this state and change is not an option. Therapeutic techniques and interventions, then, are neutralized and become ineffective at best and re-traumatizing at worst.

When Stage One is rushed and undervalued, it is highly possible that clients will discontinue therapy, or become non-cooperative, running the risk of being labeled resistant, difficult, and/or personality disordered. Misalliances are common therapeutic failures. For example, Carmen and her 7-year-old son were referred to a CCM therapist after Child Protective Services was called to their home because of constant fighting heard by the neighbors. Carmen told the therapist that she had walked out on a previous therapist who told her that she had a personality disorder so she couldn't change. Actually, when Stage One is mishandled, clients with a history of complex trauma may simply stay in survival mindstate, in some version of fight, flight, or freeze. Practitioners may become frustrated, irritated, ashamed, hopeless, or helpless, and a negative cycle of interaction envelops the therapeutic context. When the blueprint for therapy follows the natural cycles of evolution, stress reactions are to be expected and can be managed collaboratively by creating a context for therapy and a context for change within each session. This stage of context creation might need to be repeated many, many, many times in a session and during the overall therapy. It is not client or practitioner failure, nor a regression, it simply is the natural cycle of evolving: pausing/cocooning/recognizing that pause and then gently expanding to new thoughts, behaviors, and feelings. When we look at growth and change in nature, we notice that the cycles are repeated over and over, a tree repeats the same cycle annually, the tide, the sun, the moon, daily. Growth and change is a repetitive cycle; that is why we practice the same thing over and over again, in order to keep growing and changing. We cannot improve in any area of our life without repetition, thus we repeat the cycles over and over again within the session and throughout treatment.

Stage One Core Concepts Chart

Creating Refuge

Assessing Vulnerabilities and Function of the Symptom

Assessing Resources

Exploring the Positive and Negative Consequences of Change

Understanding and Validating the Client's Denial, Availability, and Attachment

Setting Goals

Ongoing Acknowledgment

Creating a context for change has seven core activities in its structure: creating refuge; assessing vulnerabilities and the function of the symptom; assessing resources; exploring the positive and negative consequences of change; understanding and validating the client's denial, availability, and attachment; setting goals; and ongoing acknowledgment. These core concepts do not occur in a linear fashion, rather they happen concurrently. However, once again, this can be used as a checklist, as each of these seven activities must be accomplished in order to create a context for change. Goal setting could easily happen while refuge is being created. Refuge may be created while validating availability through positive and negative consequences for change. For purpose of delineation, each of these principles will be described separately. It is important to keep in mind that in many ways these tasks develop simultaneously, just as the five essential therapeutic elements, mentioned earlier, will happen concurrently. They can happen over moments and over sessions. Keeping in mind that the natural cycle of change (contract, expand, and consolidate) is a cycle with no beginning and end will help the reader to view and remember the concepts embedded in each stage. Although they will be discussed in a linear fashion, they will be implemented simultaneously (see Appendix 4).

For an audio file that explains the Collaborative Change Model and Stage One, please refer to the book's eResources site: www.routledgementalhealth.com/ 9780415510219.

Creating Refuge

Creating refuge is the process of helping clients feel safe and secure enough to change. In Stage One, clients are taught that safety has to come before evolving can take place. Similar to Siegel's four S's (seen, safe, soothe, and secure), refuge starts in context and is practiced internally and interpersonally. Creating refuge includes exploring safety, understanding the cultural and contextual variables that interfere with safety, multidirected partiality (Bozsormenyi-Nagy & Krasner, 1986), pretreatment planning, and an introductory discussion of mindfulness. Creating refuge means discovering the harnesses that are needed so that clients can risk being different. These harnesses are internal and interpersonal. Before we explore these harnesses with our clients, CCM therapists are encouraged to make sure that they are creating refuge for themselves in therapeutic communities, in their offices, and in themselves. Just as each client's safe space is idiosyncratic, the same is true for therapists. Doing well with clients with complex trauma histories requires that therapists be in supervision and/or consultation with other therapists so that they are always engaged in supportive and helpful environments. CCM therapists must experience safety, both physical and emotional, in their offices as well.

Jonathan, a CCM therapist we trained, pays attention to his breathing for two minutes before seeing every client, whereas Marie performs stretches. Kelly has a photo of her dog on her desk that she looks at during session, and Justin thinks about his partner and walking beside him on a beach. Steven has created an office space where he can sit anywhere and experience himself as calm, cool, and collected. When clients walk in for the first time, they often ask where they should sit and he suggests they sit wherever they feel comfortable. Susan, another CCM therapist in the same practice, has a particular chair that is hers and she instructs clients where to sit when they first arrive. Her chair has a pillow that her grandmother gave her and it reminds her of their relationship that inspires her warmth and creativity.

Once the CCM therapist has created refuge within, it is time to consider safety with our clients. We ask clients about their internal and interpersonal harnesses.

We often explore these harnesses experientially with clients, although this is case-specific and determined within the nature of the therapeutic relationship. If we think it might be helpful, we will ask clients to think about a time in their childhood when they felt safe and to draw that particular moment on a sheet of paper we provide for them. We let them know that this paper is theirs, that this paper is a symbol for them and not for anyone else, and that they can choose to share as much or as little as possible about the memory. Furthermore, we explain the intent of the experiential assignment. We explain that some people can find a memory and others are unable to remember a safe place. For some, that inability is because there is no memory of safety and for others it is because right now, in the present, the memory is unavailable. If the memory is not available, some are able to create the fantasy of one, but others are not.

We explain to clients the purpose of this exercise and are completely transparent about the need to create a context for change. Some of us are fortunate enough to have had experiences in our growth and development which prepared us in a safe way for an experience that was going to be difficult, but others of us were not so lucky. While development can happen in a context of danger, positive change is more likely nurtured in safety. Notice the importance of the reaction to the child who takes his first steps and falls, or the response to a child's first utterance, or to the importance of the environment in the narrative of a new couple falling in love. As family therapists, with many years of experience between us, we have both noticed a remarkable difference in childrearing strategies with our clients. Take as an example children entering school for the first time in early fall. Some children are given no preparation and others are coached in ritualized and nurturing environments to begin the school year. This organizational environment, which is further ritualized daily, creates a predictability and structure that enables children to feel safe. In Stage One we attempt to create this experience of safety within the context of the therapeutic relationship. This experience of safety is most readily internalized by the client when we are calm, centered, and grounded, when we are in control and experience agency and the ability to be competent. When we feel safe, if we sense danger, we sense that we are capable of coping well and feel supported by some other presence. Often there are people or animals or nature or a spiritual presence within us or near us that calms us and keeps us centered. There is a sense of balance and serenity.

Some clients experience safety in nature, some when they are alone, and some when they are with one person or many. Some feel safe with the sunlight, others appreciate the night. Some are running, some are sleeping, some are being cared for, some are caring for others, and some are alone. Clients have told us about ten-second moments and others have told us about safe decades. Some clients are able to draw a safe space, or think of one, and are comfortable not sharing that space with us. When we ask clients to think of a safe space, we explicitly say that we want this to be a moment for them to remember feeling safe, which is the importance of the exercise, not that they share that experience with us. The explanation goes something like this:

So, part of Stage One is creating refuge or safety in our therapy encounters and everyone is really different in terms of what makes them feel safe and how they define safety. Remember what we talked about; that I would end up knowing many things about you and that many times therapy might feel threatening, scary, or just plain uncomfortable. When there are moments that our time together is distressing, I want to be able, in the moment, to help you pause and take a breath, try to focus, and together we will to figure out what you need. What would be really helpful to me helping you is for me to know how we can facilitate a space that feels safe for you. So, what I would like you to do now is to take the paper and colored pencils I just gave you and to see if you can draw for yourself a time when you felt safe. Think about where you were, who was there or who was not there. If you were alone, what were you doing; if you were with other people, what were they doing? What was their energy like, what was the interaction between you like? This will be just for you, you don't have to show me the drawing, and you can write words or stick figures or colors or whatever you want—it is not about the picture and how good it is. But I find in putting your thoughts and feelings down on paper, they become more alive for us in the moment. And then we are going to talk about the important ingredients. So take a moment to yourself and give it a try.

Clients may ask for more clarification or resist this assignment. If they tell us they do not want to do it or that they never felt safe, we explore their thoughts and feelings about this. We explore with them what safety means to them, often we find that they think it simply means being happy or experiencing a lack of danger. In exploring safety, we sometimes find that clients experience danger everywhere and all of the time. This is an important discovery for then we already know that our clients spend a great deal of time in a trauma mindstate. We also realize that it may take a significant amount of time and skill to create the context for change.

For other clients, once they have completed this assignment, we ask them purposely if they would like to share some of the ingredients of their safe space that might be helpful to try and recreate in the therapy room. So, for example, if music is involved, would they consider bringing a CD to play on low when they come into therapy? There may be certain smells that are soothing for clients, which we encourage them to bring to therapy and even certain clothing or textures. Asking clients to share something about their safe space often leads to a discussion about personal space and boundaries, about our work styles, and about ways we may have to reorganize to provide more safety for them. We ask about the particular qualities of a person or people who contributed to their safety; behaviors, attitudes, and tone of voice, and we ask about what might have contributed to them feeling safe, seen, heard, and understood. We are transparent, sharing with the client the behaviors we have or do not have in common with some of their safe people. We also try to encourage clients to share with us, as we become better acquainted, what is happening, in the moment, that contributes to their sense of safety in sessions.

Another example of assessing safety in the professional relationship is having clients think about the characteristics of a person in their lives that they felt valued them. This intervention is a method to assess what clients need in the relationship with us in order to feel safe and it is also a means to discover what they value in themselves. By finding out what they value in themselves, we are determining some of the resources that they have that will contribute to their capacity to change.

> CCM practitioner: When you think back through your life, can you think of someone who you know valued you? How did you know they valued you? What did they do? What specifically did they say? How did they communicate their feelings for you?

The clients' answers will give us an awareness of how we are a good fit with them, what of our style will feel validating to them, and what we might be aware of that could create an invalidating context.

> Client: My grandmother valued me. She loved me for who I was. And I know this because she was calm, soothing, peaceful, and loving. She used few words, and her words were gentle. She baked and always had a nurturing sense about her, as if I deserved her love.
>
> CCM practitioner: Fantastic, just from that little bit of story, I have lots of thoughts I want to share with you. First: I want us to look around my office and for you to claim some items to you that look, feel, and smell nurturing so that we can know what will give you a sense of value and safety when you are here. And if ever you are feeling overwhelmed or not comforted or anxious etc., we will have ways right here in the office to recreate the safety. Remember when last week I talked about the cycle of change, and the cocooning, the pause and ponder? When you need to cocoon or pause, we will know what resources are right here in the room that will help you. Secondly your story gives me some ideas of what resources you have and what ones we might need to build upon, to help you be less reactive outside of this room. Finally, the description of your grandmother is calming. I want you to feel safe and cared for in our relationship, and much of how you describe your grandmother would not be words people have used to describe me. I want to be a validating relationship to you, so I will keep in mind to perhaps use fewer words, speak more softly, pace myself to not be overwhelming. I also hope you will tell me if my energy becomes overwhelming and invalidating. Stop me if I am too loud, too hyper, use too many words. And know that when I am enthusiastic and perhaps a bit over zealous, it is because I am excited, passionate, and motivated by the work we are doing together.

This simple intervention accomplishes many ingredients at once, creating refuge, assessing resources, exploring vulnerabilities, and creating opportunity for change immediately. It also encourages mindfulness, which is another strategy introduced in the exploration of safety. We introduce mindfulness strategies by explaining to the client how we use mindfulness, the different facets of mindfulness, and how mindfulness fits into the overall goals of creating new pathways. Mindfulness techniques are used to create refuge within the sessions with the intention that they will be used outside of the sessions as well.

Contextual Variables

Creating refuge involves exploring the nature of safety. It is also about attempting to create refuge from contextual variables that dehumanize our clients and leave them vulnerable to re-traumatizing events (Stone Fish & Harvey, 2005). Contextual variables include but are not limited to variables such as gender, age, religion, race, class, and sexual and gender identity. "To create such environments, therapists must become conduits of the intimate interaction. It is through our facilitation of these environments that families learn how to become therapeutic presences for each other" (Stone Fish & Harvey, 2005, p. 87). Discussing contextual variables and how they may interfere with clients experiencing safety with us is a way to begin setting the stage for intimate interactions.

We are actively curious as to how the sociopolitical culture both negatively and positively impacts our clients and want to make sure these influences do not negatively impact the positive development of therapeutic relationships. So, for example, when we train male therapists working in the trauma field, we urge them to recognize the power imbalance that occurs in therapy by the nature of their gender in the same way we urge white therapists to be cognizant of how their white privilege informs their therapeutic relationships. We are also curious about how clients feel powerless, damaged, out of control, or disconnected because of their sociopolitical contexts.

For example, in training a few years ago a CCM therapist was relating a disturbing client narrative in which a young boy, Antonio, had been sexually abused by a neighbor. Being a minor himself, the neighbor received a negligible punishment by the local court system. Although never sexually abused again, Antonio was re-traumatized regularly just by the neighbor's very presence in the area. One of the trainees raised her hand and said, "I totally blame your clients' parents. Why didn't they move out of that neighborhood immediately?" She continued to vent her anger at the parents without asking questions or being curious. The CCM therapist informed the trainee that Antonio was being raised by a single grandparent who had lived in the same house for over 40 years and had no relatives or resources to relocate or take other actions available to middle-class families in this situation. When we are not aware of the extreme limitations that context imposes on our clients and their choices, we do a disservice to them and can be re-traumatizing agents.

A CCM white male therapist was assigned to work with a heterosexual couple in which both partners were survivors of complex trauma. The husband was black and the wife was white. The couple had a history of physical violence and the husband had been repeatedly beaten as a teenager by white youth in his neighborhood. In Stage One, when the therapist discussed how to create a safe environment in therapy, he raised the issue of the effect of his whiteness on the therapeutic alliance. When the husband talked about some of his experiences and his lack of feeling safe, the therapist said, "I am going to have to be extra mindful in therapy about the ways you have been and continue to be hurt by people who look just like me. Because this is a dimension of me that has been hurtful to you, we start with a deficit and I hope we can find ways to work together to promote you feeling safe with me."

Part of creating this refuge is recognizing that all families are organized by racism, sexism, heterosexism, homophobia, sexism, ableism, classism, and other -isms because the family is an open system organized by its members and its various contexts and cultures. These -isms create conflict between family members that is often covert and insidious, and that must be addressed so that our clients can understand how to become refuges for each other.

A CCM therapist was working with a family that was attempting to reconcile the expulsion 20 years earlier of their teenage daughter Nicole after her mother had discovered that she had had sex with her girlfriend. Nicole had struggled through many lost years of homelessness, rage, sadness, and drug abuse. Her parents had mourned the loss of their daughter and regretted their actions. During one of the initial sessions the therapist met with the parents alone. Their pain was evident as they shared the guilt they were feeling for abandoning their child when they discovered she was a lesbian. The mother said, "I made a lot of mistakes as a parent, but this was the worst. I was so angry at her when I found out she was gay that I just lost it and my anger got the better of me. Somehow, I think, I thought it was my fault and I was going to be blamed for her turning gay." The guilt made it difficult for her to be receptive to hearing her daughter's painful experiences, which was necessary for them to understand her drug-abusing behavior. When the CCM therapist explored the effects of heterosexism and homophobia on the parents' decision to act in a way that went against their love and caring for their daughter, they were able to begin thinking about ways to act on their loving feelings. Creating refuge from the -isms that permeate our intimate relationships is a part of Stage One and creating safety.

Multidirected Partiality

Creating refuge also involves discussing with clients who is important to them and how they are going to be engaged in therapy. The systemic concept of therapeutic multidirected partiality (Boszormenyi-Nagy & Krasner, 1986) is useful here. While there are victims and perpetrators, every member of a client's context is worthy of care and consideration. Helping our clients develop a different understanding of their relationships, with the concomitant development from the guarded survival mindstate to the more receptive engaged mindstate is incomplete if therapy ignores those who are experienced as most threatening and triggering. It is our experience that, although uncomfortable for all parties, it is most beneficial to have them become part of the change process, figuratively and literally. If someone is partnered or married, has children, is still involved with their family of origin, has work situations that are triggering, or other intimate relationships that are important, we discuss, in Stage One, the possibility that any or all of these people may be part of the treatment at some point, because they are a part of the context for change.

While we believe that every person in a client's life is worthy of care, we are safety-conscious, and must always seek to determine the risk of harm to clients outside the therapy office. Part of creating a context for change is helping clients assess their current level of safety, internally as well as interpersonally. We ask about their current level of safety emotionally, psychologically, physically, sexually, financially, and spiritually. Frequently in Stage One, we must create safety commitment contracts that are continuously revisited. Not necessarily in a first session, and often done in individual sessions, we have a thorough discussion of safety inside of the home. A safety plan can be designed as casually or as detailed as the threat of harm demands. In many ways, the assessment phase and goal-setting may be conceptualized as designing an overall emotional, spiritual, and physical safety plan. The goal of therapy is for the clients to find refuge and safety in their lives. An overt safety plan is designed when there is imminent or past threat of physical or sexual violation; in cases of child abuse and neglect, child and/or adult sexual abuse, couples violence, elder abuse, or any other form of physical or sexual violence. If violence or the threat of violence emerges at any point in treatment, then safety immediately becomes the central issue. This is an important time for pausing, re-engaging, and exploring safety, then expanding by designing a safety plan, which is examined in each subsequent session.

Pause and Ponder: Consider these questions when thinking about creating refuge. What are your personalized ways that you create refuge for yourself? How do you discover what your clients consider to be safety in your office and in their lives? Can you think of ways you invite your clients to create refuge in the context where you work? Do you make the idea of sanctuary overt, no matter what age your client, or what type of client you are seeing? Are you aware of what attributes of yours your clients find refuge within? Similarly, are you aware of ways you may have triggered clients in the past? Do you have methods to determine what variables are necessary to create safety for each of your clients? Do you just assume that you are safe and that how you do treatment is validating? Do you have a violence safety assessment schema and can you write a safety plan? Do you have a collaborative concept of how to create a context of safety in the room to mindfully bring your clients back to sanctuary?

For an audio file that explains Creating Refuge and Five Essential Ingredients, please refer to the book's eResources site: www.routledgementalhealth. com/9780415510219.

Pretreatment Planning

Preparation is a necessary and significant part of any protocol, process, or experience. As we have compared the CCM to a blueprint for building a house, once you have the blueprint then you would make sure you communicated with the contractor and the subcontractor and that everyone understood the concept and had all the tools they needed to begin the building. Pretreatment planning includes the collaborative measures taken to build a team with professional and personal people involved in our clients' lives. For treatment to be a refuge in which clients move from survival mindstates to engaged mindstates, we incorporate anyone in their life orbit who may be able to facilitate the metamorphosis from a reactive to a responsive environment. We begin by reviewing past experiences with helping professionals. We ask about teachers, caseworkers, probation officers, physicians, nurses, psychotherapists, and others. We are interested in both the helpful and the unhelpful interactions and relationships, those that harness the natural cycle of growth as well as the aspects that inhibit growth and development, encouraging clients to remain stuck in their survival cycles. Thus, if we discover at the beginning of treatment that one of our clients had a positive relationship with a high-school teacher, we will attempt to determine as much as possible about the specific nature of that relationship in order to replicate the positives within therapy and in the clients' other contexts. Similarly, we will pay particular attention to relationships which have been violating and seek to understand the dynamics in those relationships and work with the client on how not to replicate the interactions in the therapy room and in outside relationships.

In pretreatment planning with a family that was trying to reconcile after sexual abuse charges split them apart ten years ago, conversing about helping professionals was very useful in creating a context for change. While the family disagreed on a number of concerns, they completely agreed that when the abuse was reported, the response from the professional community was incredibly disappointing. The parents had initially called the abuse hotline to report the actions of a babysitter. Rather than being supported, what they all remembered is a barrage of police, caseworkers, social workers, and psychotherapists who made them feel guilty, neglectful, abusive, and all around "scum of the earth." They all felt that the professionals split the family apart and made the various family members believe they lacked strengths or resources. The family never had any idea what was going to happen from one meeting to the next, who was going to be there, or who was on their side. They all agreed with the mother's assertion that it took the family two years to recover from the babysitter's sexual abuse and ten years to recover from the trauma of reporting the abuse. Pretreatment planning with this family, then, was focused on careful management of an atmosphere of collaboration and mutual respect.

Pretreatment planning sets the stage for working collaboratively with other professionals. When possible, we meet with or talk to other professionals in our clients' lives with our clients present to create a context for change. We introduce our ways of working, our expectation about realistic timelines for change, and our collaborative goals. We also discover their expectations for our clients and their work with them. We clarify roles so that duplication of services does not occur, and so that as many of the clients' needs are met as possible. Ideally, we share goals and meet periodically throughout the treatment process.

Pretreatment planning also considers clients' personal relationships with a special focus on an understanding of the nature of relationships that support engaged mindstates contrasted with those in which clients are caught in interactional cycles of survival. Many clients with a history of complex trauma have supportive relationships that are undervalued, under-recognized, and underutilized, particularly in the treatment context. We are often so focused on survival cycles and dangerous relationships that we forget to ask about the "angels" in our clients' lives. In an exit interview with a client who was asked about what helped her change, she said, "At the beginning of therapy, Susan asked about meaningful relationships in my life. I have a sister who is 10 years older than I am, who lives four hours away from me with her own family, but who has always been there for me. Susan encouraged me throughout therapy to rely on my sister in ways I hadn't done before and it made all the difference in the world. When things got really rough, Susan always asked if I had spoken to my sister about it and pretty soon it became second nature for me to call her and visit her. I now hope to be able to be that kind of person for her daughters, so it really helped for Susan to continue to remind me about the importance of support."

Thorough probing discussions of physical and psychological safety in personal relationships are of paramount importance and need to be discussed in pretreatment planning as well. Some clients with a history of complex trauma are involved in physically and/or psychologically abusive relationships when they enter therapy. Asking about safety and violence in all of our clients' relationships is important and needs to be done in individual sessions in a way that promotes self-disclosure. Practitioners have an ethical and legal obligation to report to the appropriate authorities if they believe that someone is in danger of suicide or homicide, or if they suspect child abuse, neglect, or sexual abuse. Clients need to be very clear about the duty to report prior to the first session so that we are transparent and collaborative and they are allowed to make informed decisions about self-disclosure. Even if clients have been involved with child protective services, or battering programs, the duty to report must still be discussed with everyone. Reporting laws are not consistent across state or even county lines, so it is imperative that each practitioner understand the rules where they practice.

Practitioners who are informed are mindful and engaged and protective of their own professional lives.

When assessing for violence, CCM practitioners ask directly about its use in a non-judgmental and discerning way. Some CCM therapists also have clients complete paper and pencil assessment instruments (such as the Revised Conflict Tactic Scale). While we recommend doing both, we acknowledge that this is not always possible. Most important is that questions about violence are asked in a way that promotes non-judgmental and safe practices. New research (Stith, McCollum, Amanor-Boadu, & Douglas, 2012) and our clinical experience indicate that all genders can be violent in intimate relationships, though violence has a different impact on the individuals in those relationships and on the gender dynamics. Creating a context for change involves contracting for no abuse, no violence, and no physical contact when frustrated or angry.

In Stage One, assessing for safety outside of the office must be done in individual sessions between the client and practitioner. Disclosing physical harm in the presence of another might be unsafe for the client and asking about violence in the company of others indicates that the therapist does not understand that her actions were dangerous, which would make a client rightfully doubt the therapist's ability to guide her on a safe journey. For example, in an individual session a CCM therapist might ask questions such as: "So when you and your partner have differences, how do you handle them? Give me an example of an argument you've had that has gotten out of control. Has there been any pushing or throwing, you know, any hitting or shoving or any physical ways you guys get with each other that feels bad? Do you ever get scared about somebody getting hurt? Have you or your partner hurt each other physically when angry or frustrated? Are you frightened? How does it usually end? What's been the worst way it has ended? Do you lose control when you are angry? Does your partner? How?" The same questions are asked about other relationships in the clients' lives and should include children, parents, siblings, grandparents, and others. CCM practitioners find their own ways of asking about abuse and violence. Most important is that it is asked and that clinicians make sure that they are working toward contracting for no abuse, no violence, and no physical contact when frustrated or angry. This no-violence contract is part of preplanning and continues to be monitored throughout therapy. (A sample of a no-violence contract can be found in Appendix 5.)

When couples present for couples therapy, we see them individually and conjointly in pretreatment planning. If we find that a client is involved in intimate partner violence (IPV), that is, violence between two adults who are in a couple relationship, we must make a decision when to see them conjointly. When it involves intimate partner violence, we follow Johnson and Ferraro's (2000; Johnson, 2006) typologies when considering seeing couples conjointly in therapy. They have identified four types of violence in couples (situational couple violence, intimate terrorism, violent resistance, and mutual violent control) (limited to heterosexual couples at this point) and suggest that conjoint couple sessions are contraindicated when there is violence perpetrated based in high levels of coercive control. Situational violence stemming from a lack of conflict resolution skills may respond to contracting in a conjoint format. Stith et al. (2012), in their comprehensive review of IPV, state: "For offenders who are violent within their family but are not generally violent or for those who are engaged in situational couple violence, systemic treatment may be called for. For those presenting with characterological violence or intimate terrorism or a history of violence outside the family, individual and gender-specific group treatments may be more appropriate because of safety concerns regarding the existence of more severe forms of violence and patterns of coercive control in those experiencing intimate terrorism" (p. 222).

The beauty of the CCM is that individual, couple, family, and group therapy are discussed in Stage One as options for treatment at different stages of change, so if violence makes it unsafe to see individuals together, the blueprint already accounts for individual treatment. Each individual is viewed as unique, and living in a unique set of life situations. We encounter humans who have experienced trauma and violence through innumerable avenues. If we are a teacher, we meet the child through the classroom, a probation officer through court, a community worker on the streets, a child care worker in the residential setting, and a therapist through a referral. During the pretreatment phase of creating a context for change, we need to understand the demands of the context in which we are establishing our relationship. Together we have to understand and then work to create an atmosphere that promotes and supports change. There might be many factors that impinge on a person's ability to engage in their growth cycle. In pretreatment planning, we need to familiarize ourselves with these factors.

We need to familiarize ourselves with:

1. Our clients' professional relationships in the past. Who was helpful? How? Why?
2. Our clients' professional relationships in the past. Who was not helpful? How? Why?
3. The expectation of each professional involved in the current situation. How can we best work together, have shared goals, and not overlap services?
4. Our clients' personal lives. Who is supportive? How may clients most fruitfully capitalize on this support?
5. Our clients' personal lives. With whom are they engaged in interactional cycles of survival?
6. If our clients are in danger. Begin the process of creating and implementing a no-violence contract.
7. Our ethical obligations about reporting laws. Make certain we are following them with complete transparency with our clients.

Practitioners need to be aware that exploration of the pretreatment variables is threatening, so that in-session behavior from clients may be from a survival mindstate. Recognition of this would be a time for the clinician to pause, and in the moment recreate safety through techniques that bring the client into the present. Then, when they are present, we can ask them what they are experiencing and how we can be helpful in keeping them engaged in the present. Pretreatment is not a time to challenge but a time to support resources and create a positive context for change.

Pretreatment introduces and demystifies the change process. Whatever the context in which we work, a CCM practitioner will explain to clients how the process is structured. If it is an investigation, we provide a detailed description of how the process will proceed and the roles of the various parties. If we are running a community group in a residential treatment facility, we explain the process of the group, how it will be conducted, and how it will be structured. If it is an initial evaluation, we examine the different steps of the intake protocol. If we are conducting a therapy session, we teach the clients about the three stages of therapy, and we teach them the sequence within a session. We talk about our style of therapy and what they can expect from us. For example, with children we might not explain the process using words like cycles and change, rather we might say something like, "Every time you come here we will spend a little time playing with whatever you pick from the toy shelf. And we will spend some time playing with your mom or dad. We might do some fun stretching or breathing exercises. We could draw or play or talk. And we end each time with clean up and adding pages to the story we will be writing together." The important part of this with any age group is creating a sense of predictability in the process.

We also encourage our clients, young and old, to keep a journal to use throughout the process. They use the journals to write down questions during the week, comments and thoughts that occur to them, to take notes during the sessions, to keep track of their homework, and to chronicle whatever aspects of the journey they choose. We introduce the journal in pretreatment planning and ask about it throughout the stages of treatment. For some clients, journaling is a lifeline and for others, an imposition.

Pretreatment planning is structured to familiarize the professional with what is involved in helping clients from a contextual standpoint: before meeting us, with whom has the client been involved, with what, where, and why? Pretreatment planning is also structured to familiarize clients with us and our process, to prevent as much as possible the perception that they are involved in a relationship in which they lack volition, where they are passive or unwitting recipients of processes being done to them. Pretreatment is a mirror of how therapy will progress. Clients understand the who, what, where, and why. Again, CCM treatment, unlike past violations, is collaborative, with mutual agreements and a spirit of working together.

Pause and Ponder: Pretreatment planning is a step rushed through or even omitted by many clinicians. When this step is missed, we might unintentionally be repeating errors of other clinicians. We might not be fully cognizant of the many and varied factors impinging on our clients' capacity for change. We might not know what has worked for them in the past and what internal and contextual variables may interfere with effective therapy. We might not know all of the players involved in the case. What are the expectations that the referring party has for us? What is our role in the legal or judicial aspects of the case? What releases for collaboration need to be signed? What needs to be orchestrated for case management? Expending time, energy, and attention during pretreatment will save time and reduce misunderstanding and interruptions as therapy progresses.

Assessing Vulnerabilities and the Function of the Symptoms

The third component to Stage One is assessing vulnerabilities and the function of the symptoms. We explore the idea that when people feel vulnerable, they act to feel powerful, in control, and/or to feel valued. We explore the link between vulnerabilities and symptoms. We hypothesize that the function of many symptoms is to help people feel powerful, in control, and valued. When individuals in survival mindstates feel fear and vulnerability, they act to feel powerful, in control, and valued. Because they act from survival mindstates, the reactions often become symptoms. The function of the symptom is to help with the fear and vulnerability, but symptoms end up not being helpful (which is why they are called symptoms).

We assess vulnerabilities individually, in the family, and in the sociopolitical contexts in which our clients live. Individually, we are curious about mind and body symptoms that make it difficult for clients to function. Flashbacks, states of disassociation, and nightmares are examples of symptoms, as are body aches and pains, anxiety, depression, and/or drug and alcohol use and abuse. Abusive behaviors toward others in the form of emotional, verbal, physical, and/or sexual maltreatment are assessed. Self-harm, eating disorders, and suicidality are also assessed in Stage One as symptoms used to help clients feel powerful, in control, and valued. Dissociative and hyperaroused states become traits (Perry, 1994) in some people with histories of trauma and we assess for these vulnerabilities in Stage One. Some clients enter therapy already acknowledging some survival mindstate functioning, whereas others experience feeling powerless, out of control and devalued but have no insight into how or why this occurs.

We explore vulnerabilities and the function of the symptom through a variety of interviews and written assessments. We look at the immediate cause for distress and its relation to the presenting problem for treatment. We want to understand the client's view of the problem and how it is impacting them and others in their lives. Furthermore, we use a variety of assessment tools and interview techniques when working with children. We have found the assessment and therapeutic techniques described in the book, *Paper Dolls and Paper Airplanes: Therapeutic Exercises for Sexually Traumatized Children* (Crisci, Lay, & Lowenstein, 1998) incredibly helpful in exploring vulnerabilities. The authors describe techniques that create refuge and challenge existing patterns while assessing both the vulnerabilities and resources of children.

We consider alcohol, drug abuse, and eating disorders in Stage One as potentially both a vulnerability and as a symptom which will have different functions for each individual. For example, eating disorders, while not always a reaction to complex trauma, can be an attempted solution to the experiential residuals of complex trauma. Janet understood her eating disorder as an attempt to feel powerful. She experienced herself as out of control, powerless, and disconnected, and as a teenager she stumbled across the fact that losing weight made her feel empowered and in control. It encouraged her parents to react; her mother paid more attention to her and her father seemed to stop sexualizing her because she became so thin she looked sickly and prepubescent. Similar to other symptoms, eating disorders were effective for a while for Janet and then became part of the problem. As she began to obsess about her weight and had difficulty controlling it, she felt powerless, out of control, and isolated.

Problematic use of alcohol, similar to eating disorders, often provides a slippery slope from helping to alleviate feelings of powerlessness and being out of control to being part of or the new central problem. Mind- and mood-altering substances distract from emotional pain and do temporarily help alleviate the pain of complex trauma. They can even allow clients to tolerate being in relationships that are traumatic. We may similarly conceptualize many symptomatic behaviors as self-sabotaging behaviors that work for a while, even a very long time, and may even continue to work in some ways for clients, which we and they need to understand. Usually, however, people enter into treatment because somehow the symptomatic behavior is not working anymore, either for the client or the people who are involved in the life of the client.

In a first session with Amy and Craig, for example, a CCM therapist asked about individual and couple dynamics and learned that alcohol played a big part in their arguments. "When we first got together," Amy said, "all we did was party. Drinking and drugging were the juice that spiced up our relationship and helped us to relax. We were both so uptight without it." In the ten years they were together, however, the partying began being problematic with violence and blackouts, car accidents, and missed days at work. Amy finally joined AA, became sober, and started individual therapy to heal sexual abuse wounds that she numbed with alcohol. Craig, however, was still drinking. He did not see his drinking as a problem, but Amy was convinced that the drinking allowed him to deny that he came from a problematic, alcoholic, and abusive family. Part of Stage One, assessing for vulnerabilities and function of symptoms, was working with Amy and Craig to help them decide the function of alcohol in their couple system and in their healing.

Couple and family relationships that are avoidant and/or chaotic are seen as vulnerabilities as well. Sometimes clients have people in their lives who are supportive and trustworthy, but most people with a history of complex trauma have not been able to surround themselves with supportive relationships. Vulnerabilities and the function of symptoms are often two sides of the same coin where relationships are concerned. When clients have been traumatized in intimate relationships they are likely to avoid or resist intimacy, so the function of the symptom ends up making them more vulnerable. Pushing people away or alienating them with one's behavior serves to increase vulnerability.

For example, a CCM therapist was working with a 30-year-old adult married male, Rich, who was traumatized at a very young age. When Rich was 4 years old, his mother found him in the bathroom masturbating and became extremely reactive. She picked him up, wrapped a towel around him, threw a pair of pants on him and a coat over him, and whisked him down to the priest to lecture Rich about the sin of masturbation. Instead, the priest sexually abused him. Whenever his mother was upset with Rich, over the years, she would take him to the priest for spiritual guidance, and again instead, the priest sexually abused him. Rich had memories of shame and humiliation throughout his childhood as his mother criticized him, he was sexually abused by someone who was supposed to help him, and he was bullied and beaten by classmates.

Rich was referred to therapy because at work he was extremely volatile with male employees and was reported for sexual harassment by a female employee. Although referred by his Employee Assistance Program at a job he enjoyed, he did not see anything wrong with his behavior. After his first session, the administrative assistant told the CCM therapist that Rich gave her what she considered a creepy look. At the end of the first session, as he was leaving the therapy office, Rich said, "Oh, now I get to go past that hot secretary." While this behavior is obnoxious, it was also problematic because he was married and acting out sexually with friends and acquaintances. He was feeling vulnerable upon beginning therapy, and the function of his symptoms was to make him feel powerful, in control, and valued for his sexual prowess. He had been stripped of these positive feelings as an abused and neglected boy, and the symptoms he had developed to help him feel better were now serious and problematic behaviors. In Stage One, the CCM therapist worked with Rich to understand his vulnerabilities and the function of his symptoms, and how sexualizing his relationships and his extreme volatility had become major problems in his life that needed adjustment. Part of Stage One work is acknowledging problematic behavior because healing will not occur before clients are both acquainted with their self-defeating behavior and recognize what is problematic about their behavior.

Rich's case is useful for discussing the complexities of assessment and the differing stages of our model. With one client, we can be in various stages for separate problems and with different relationships. The CCM therapist and Rich were able to work on understanding and acknowledging how his behavior with others was a serious problem in his life, and he was able to work on a beginning treatment plan that would have moved therapy toward Stage Two of challenging patterns and expanding realities. At this point he was not ready to consider his obsessive pornography use as a problem because it was still something that soothed him, made him feel powerful, connected, and in control. Furthermore, while he was willing to discuss his explosive behavior with his wife, he was not ready to acknowledge how his sexualizing behavior interfered with his marriage. So, while we were moving towards Stage Two work at his place of employment, we were still in Stage One in his personal life.

Treatment oscillates from Stage One to Stage Two to Stage Three in each session and often with each problem that clients bring to therapy. The CCM therapist and Rich spent a year in therapy, for example, before he was able to admit to sexual addiction and become able to address his sexualizing behavior with his wife. When clients do not let go of their symptoms, we must remember the stage model and recognize that some symptoms still serve a function of survival mindstate, which makes them feel powerful, valued, and/or in control. When symptoms persist, it is a wake-up call to the therapy team that we need more time in Stage One creating refuge so that clients feel safe enough to let go of symptoms. We can also recognize persistent behavior and a need for more Stage One work by how our therapeutic relationship is progressing. It is a therapeutic mistake to not pace the sessions collaboratively.

One day, a few months into treatment and two weeks after Rich acknowledged the function of his symptoms, the CCM therapist met him in the waiting room to take him back to her office. Rich was walking behind the therapist as she stopped to fill her water bottle at the water fountain before her office. Rich said, "Hey, your legs look great today." Before this had occurred, early in Stage One, when the CCM and Rich were discussing his vulnerabilities and function of his symptoms, the CCM therapist asked Rich how she would know he was sexualizing her. They had discussed how counterproductive that would be for their relationship and for his treatment and how useless she would become to his recovery. These were all Stage One conversations in terms of creating safety. As the CCM therapist sat down and closed the door, her expression mirrored the disgust she felt and at that moment Rich asked, "So, what's that look about?" The CCM therapist explained how negatively she experienced his behavior at the water cooler and they continued to discuss it until he was able to admit that he was in fact angry with the CCM therapist because he thought therapy was moving too quickly. He said he had experienced the therapist's encouragement to acknowledge his sexually offending behavior with his wife as challenging and unhelpful. While he was ready to move toward Stage Two in some individual attitudes and behaviors, he needed more time in Stage One before he was ready to work on certain aspects of his relationship with his wife.

Another way to assess vulnerabilities and strengths is the "Structural Session" (Trepper & Barrett, 1989), a very effective and dependable format to assess both vulnerabilities and resources. The structural session is an example of the creative interventions that can be designed to assess and intervene in the symptoms of trauma. We ask individuals, couples, and families to think about what they want their family to look like when they are finished with therapy. We point to the family variables on the vulnerability/resource handout (see Appendix 6) and ask families how they want their family or relationships to change and how they want them to stay the same. We often help families draw family maps. We ask the family about hierarchy, rules, roles, communication skills, adaptability, etc. We help them delineate areas of healthy functioning and those that still need work. We then draw with them (or after explanation, let them draw alone) their renditions of the different family structures in which their family cycles in and out. As we look at the pictures they have drawn, we ask questions about the family's resources and vulnerabilities expressed in each structure they have drawn. So, for example, a CCM therapist in Stage One presented the structural session to a family in the following way:

CCM therapist: We are going to use these pictures to talk about how your family is working well together and the ways it needs to change. So look at the first picture, see how the adults are on the top and then there is a dotted line and the kids are below? In your family who is on the top of the dotted line?

Dylan (10-year-old boy): My mom and my grandpa and my grandma are on the top. And when we visit dad he is on top.

Lisa (12-year-old girl): Steve (mom's boyfriend) and some of our aunts and uncles. Lots of people are in charge of us.

CCM therapist: Good point, it takes a village, have you ever heard that saying? It takes a lot of people to help a family, particularly after sexual abuse. So I agree there are a lot of people helping. That can be both good and bad. We will talk about that in a second. At the end of therapy we want the picture to look something like this, where mom is in charge, that dad, as his therapy goes and you are seeing him more, he will have his own picture at his house and there is a dotted line because there is good communication between the four of you. That grandma and grandpa will be helpful, maybe not as much as in charge as they are now and the roles and rules will be clear. It is not easy for any family to work together perfectly and sometimes now and even after therapy the roles change around. Like it is okay for Lisa to be in charge sometimes when she is babysitting, yet there still are rules. Now you all have paper and pencils. Everyone should draw what they think their family looked like when (whatever the problematic behavior is) was happening. What does the family feel like to you when there are problems? Draw that. And then we will look at everyone's family and talk about what needs to change so you can look like the first picture we talked about.

(See Appendix 6: Vulnerability/Resource Model.)

For an audio file that explains the Vulnerability/Resilience Assessment and the Description of the Structural/Vulnerability Drawing Intervention, please refer to the book's eResources site: www.routledgementalhealth.com/9780415510219.

Pause and Ponder: All humans live in three contexts: social political, familial, and internal. In each of these three contexts there are experiences that render people powerless, feeling out of control, devalued, and disconnected, potentially triggering the survival mindstate. Our clients are vulnerable to these triggers in every context.

We need to assess collaboratively and continually with our clients what variables in their lives render them vulnerable, and trigger them into a survival mindstate. What do they think, feel, and do as an attempt to regain power, control, value, and connection that in fact does not work for them? How are they doing a disservice to themselves and keeping themselves experiencing their world as dangerous?

Assessing Resources

Assessing resources in Stage One is as important as assessing vulnerabilities because clients' strengths are the cornerstone to the healing process and to Stage One completion. Resources are the non-symptomatic behaviors that we utilize to help regain power, control, and value. Although clients often enter therapy in despair with the firm belief that they are continually experiencing symptoms ("24/7," as one client glumly stated), they are not in fact always symptomatic. We explore resources in Stage One as both a way to work toward safety and a means to effect change. An awareness of the clients' resources will help create a context of change, while an awareness of their vulnerabilities will help design Stage Two interventions. For example, if a client is more prone to introversion, a skills-based psychotherapy group would be a Stage Two intervention. Clients prone to introversion might have difficulty in a psychotherapy group because they have to engage with other people, yet this inability to engage in social support may keep them stuck in survival mindstates.

A strength of the CCM is that the assessment of resources can be done flexibly in a variety of ways depending on the context of therapy, the therapists' model, and the clients' resources. Resources can be assessed formally or informally, quantitatively or qualitatively, and both in and out of therapy sessions. Psychological evaluations, psychiatric diagnoses, medical examinations, and personality assessments are all used by different psychotherapists who have incorporated the CCM into their practices. If your psychotherapy practice is part of a large and vibrant trauma-informed context and community, you may have multiple methods of assessing resources. If you practice alone with a limited amount of community support, your assessment may be limited to the therapeutic relationship. The CCM model stresses the importance of overtly working together with your clients to assess the resources they have at their disposal as they begin to engage in therapy.

Individual practitioners, furthermore, have their own ways of assessing resources. At the Center for Contextual Change we utilize the Trauma Symptom Inventory (TSI-2) (Briere, 1995; Briere & Elliott, 2003) in all three stages of treatment for an ongoing assessment of client progress and the model's effectiveness. When there are allegations of physical and/or sexual violence, there are a comprehensive series of evaluative tools rendered (see Appendix 7). Our understanding of offending behavior in the context of survival mindstates does not conflict with our conviction that acknowledgment and accountability are necessary for change and growth. Offenders of all ages will need to acknowledge, take responsibility for their violent behaviors, and commit to the process of change.

Most professionals have a particular method for how they choose to implement the assessment phase. One CCM therapist swears by the Myers Briggs Personality Inventory (Myers & McCaulley, 1985) when she assesses for resources. She has her clients take the inventory and then, in Stage One, she attempts to engage the dominant parts of her clients' personality to create a context for change and explores the non-dominant parts as she thinks about Stage Two interventions. An engaged mindstate is open to exploring all resources and we will discuss interventions for differing vulnerabilities and resources in Stage Two.

Vincent was a corporate lawyer who sexually abused his daughter, Amy, for several years until Amy told her mother and her mother called the police. Vincent was sent to jail and the family went into treatment. At the beginning of therapy, Vincent was in jail and his wife said she was planning to divorce him as soon as his sentence ended (which she never did). When he was released from jail, a court order stipulated that he could not move back home so he moved into an apartment a block away. While the family was in treatment, he ended up moving back into the home. Vincent stayed in treatment for five years and the mother and children were in treatment for a couple of those, coming in and out of treatment when necessary. Amy stayed in individual therapy with a CCM therapist for a number of years and met with her periodically during college when she hit some rough spots with boyfriends.

This family was interviewed ten years after they had finished treatment as part of the exit interviews that were conducted at the Center for Contextual Change to help build this collaborative stage model. Two sons were married and Amy was engaged at the time of the interview. She was also working on her Masters in Social Work. Vincent was asked and talked about what had helped him change. He said, "I had done some really bad things and part of being different was acknowledging them and asking for forgiveness, which my family gave me, even if I didn't deserve it. But I also think what helped was that our family had a lot of strengths that the therapist helped us use to put our family back together again. I remember our therapist saying that we were a family that didn't give up on each other and I remember that making such a difference when therapy and life got hard."

Amy, who had been in her late teens at the time of family therapy, was 27 years old when she was interviewed about the treatment. The interviewer asked Amy if she was ever afraid, worried, or anxious that her fiancé might end up abusing her or her children. Amy said she was not worried and the interviewer was curious about why she was so confident. Immediately, with a big smile on her face, Amy said she attributed her confidence to something her individual therapist and her mother had given her. She said, "My internship is with a domestic violence shelter. So many of my clients were sexually abused and when they told someone about it, no one believed them. My mother believed me and my therapist believed me, and they both constantly told me how strong and resourceful I was and am. So it just makes me realize that I have agency."

Resource assessment is similar to vulnerability assessment in that we are curious about individual, familial, and sociopolitical contexts that are resources for our clients. Individually, we ask about ways that clients have been able to experience being in control, powerful, and connected. We ask about psychiatric medication, and their opinion about its use. Sometimes clients report that medication is the only thing that they can count on to calm them down and feel in control and able to stay connected to friends and family. We believe it is vitally important to discuss our collaboration with the medical community and how useful it is to have a thorough psychiatric evaluation in circumstances surrounding medication. Clients have told us that they really appreciate this discussion in the beginning stage of therapy. They contrast this careful approach with previous therapists who have suggested a psychiatric evaluation in a middle stage of therapy, causing clients to wonder what they said or did to alarm the therapist, and whether their therapist believed they are "mentally ill."

Many of our clients, in their exit interviews, remember with surprise being asked about what individual resources they bring into therapy. Terry is a 45-year-old teacher whose earliest memories include being in a car accident in which his father drove into a tractor-trailer, killing his mother and younger brother. Terry developed such severe anxiety symptoms whenever a school shooting occurred in another community that his survival mindstate made it impossible for him to function in the classroom. He was interviewed after treatment about what he remembered being helpful:

> In the second or third interview, I had brought a cycling helmet into session because I was training for a half Ironman. My therapist asked me about the training and throughout therapy, which lasted about a year, she kept going back to something I said in that session about my confidence in my athletic abilities. Whenever I would feel defeated, fearful, anxious, or depressed, she would somehow bring it back to my confidence as an athlete, how I felt powerful and in control while biking and running and actually swimming as well. I guess I assumed therapy would be all about me opening up the past and learning new ways to focus on the present, but instead it felt like she was encouraging me to hold onto what was good and build different kinds of muscles as well.

We also ask clients to think about relationships they are in where they feel powerful, in control, valued, and connected. Clients may have some of these in their friendship network, extended family, and work or mentoring contexts. While there are many people in our clients' lives who have treated them horribly, there are often a few who have been heroes to them and who have enabled and encouraged their progress in life. In traditional therapy practice, it may be that there is less of a focus on beneficial relationships. An integral aspect of creating safety is bringing the safe people into the therapy, figuratively or in reality. When inquiring about relationships in which clients feel valued, we often find themes that these relationships have in common and they can be aspects of the therapeutic relationship that can be encouraged. So, for example, in Terry's case, when he was asked about safe relationships, he talked about friends and colleagues who shared his sense of humor. His therapist asked whether that was something the client wanted to bring into their relationship and they talked about the use of humor as a resilient but sometimes tricky response to traumatic events.

Sociopolitical contexts are also addressed in the beginning stages of therapy because many find comfort in community. However, treatment may lack this important resource if the therapist does not make a deliberate effort to ask. Rachel had been sexually abused by her Rabbi as an adolescent. She discussed how the Rabbi traumatized her, not only through his abuse, but because she could not walk into a temple, nor do anything associated with Judaism, because of the impact and memories of what he had done. The CCM therapist asked Rachel to think about ways her religious practice was a resource, in what ways she felt connected, in control, and powerful in relation to religion and her spiritual dimension, and how she could develop that now. Rachel located another synagogue, led by a progressive female Rabbi and developed community that she told her exit interviewer years later was a vital and important part of her healing context. Had the CCM therapist not been curious about sociopolitical resources, this may never have happened.

The CCM highlights the value of community as a resource for practitioners as well as clients. Working the model in our own lives means collaborating with other professionals and gathering as much support as possible. It also means discussing this aspect of our work with our clients. The CCM works in centers where everyone is trained in the model and also in clinical practices, university settings, group homes, and inpatient settings where a lone therapist is trained in the model. Most communities are filled with practitioners who are experts in areas that a particular therapist is not and it is the expectation that the CCM therapist consults with and refers clients to trauma-informed practitioners throughout the community, DBT groups, addiction specialists, AA groups, other self-help groups, EMDR trained therapists, psychiatrists, yoga instructors, nutritionists, etc.

As we determine clients' resources, we actively utilize these resources in designing the treatment plan. We understand that utilizing the clients' own methods of how they healthily and productively soothe themselves and how they already naturally and instinctually use their skills, abilities, and capacities to change will create a more effective and productive process of change and growth.

Pause and Ponder: Humans have natural resources that enable them to grow and change. These resources can be categorized in three categories: social political, familial, and internal resources. It is the responsibility of each clinician to discover with each client what those resources are. The clinician must work with clients to identify and examine those resources, and then utilize them in therapy to help clients change on a daily basis. Humans have resources in many areas; humor, creativity, relationships, courage, initiative, intuition, faith, to name a few. We need to examine how we, as a guide, discover our clients' resources and how to cultivate and use them in the process of change.

Exploring the Positive and Negative Consequences of Change

The fourth part of creating a context for change is discussing the positive and negative consequences of change. For every goal that is set in Stage One, implemented in Stage Two, and consolidated in Stage Three, it is important to keep the positive and negative consequences of change in the conversation. In Stage One, the concept is introduced as, simply, looking at the goal and exploring what would be positive if the goal was attained and the potential risks and negative consequences of attaining the goal. The client is advised that discussing both positive and negative aspects of change will be incorporated into clients' repertoire of skills when making later decisions in therapy.

When we discuss the positive and negative consequences of change for specific goals our clients are setting, we are helping them begin the process of using their engaged mindstate. Thinking about change can be a trigger into survival mindstates because change in the future is uncomfortable, unknown, and breeds uncertainty, which triggers fear and fires up the amygdala. When we are thoughtfully engaged in articulating some of the possibilities that the change process elicits, we engage clients in experiencing some control over a process in which they have felt powerless in the past. Being mindful and communicating, which are two of the important components to engaged mindstates, helps clients experience the possibility that they can indeed change and that their lives will improve.

In Stage One clients begin to understand that the symptoms they have been experiencing, which are incredibly painful, have their uses. They have come to recognize, for example, that anger outbursts keep them from getting hurt or that cutoff keeps them from disappointment. What they do not understand is how these negative consequences keep them stuck in survival mindstates and in interactional cycles of survival that keep them dissatisfied. Therapy, by its very nature, is intended to change clients' lives. In any journey we leave behind time, relationships, events, and objects that we may not be aware we will miss until we miss them. Preparing clients for what they will miss makes Stage Two easier when they come up against the negative consequence of embarking on the journey they are taking. Exploring the positive and negative consequences of change helps us move toward Stage Two.

We have worked with many clients with a history of complex trauma who are in intimate relationships that are clearly destructive. Although the clients recognize that it would be more prudent to discontinue, they are often unable to extricate themselves from the relationship. They are aware of an abundance of reasons why discontinuing the relationship is in their best interests. They are aware that they will feel good about themselves if they terminate the relationship, and possibly have done so, a few times. Family members and good friends exhort them to leave, arguing that they deserve better than this, that the person they are involved with is abusive, neglectful, not worthy of them, using them, and does not value them. The clients clearly understand the likely positive consequences of change. They know that "throwing the bum out" will please those who worry about them, free them to be available to meet someone who will treat them better, will probably be forward progress with their lives, will assist them in not feeling so badly about themselves, and will enable them to start living the life they had always imagined for themselves. It is much more difficult for them to contemplate the negative consequences of leaving the relationship, but absolutely necessary for the process of change to occur.

The negative consequences of leaving the relationship often keep clients mired in interactional cycles of survival. One negative consequence, for example, is fear of how the break up will affect the other. They may fear that partners will harm themselves, the client, or other loved ones, and wrestle with their sense of responsibility for this aggression. This is a negative consequence of change that must be addressed for clients to believe they have the ability to change their lives. This is a complicated dilemma because theories of personal empowerment state that we only have control over our own thoughts, feelings, and behavior. On the other hand, our traumatized clients know very well how other people have impacted if not completely dominated their thoughts, feeling, and behaviors. Stage One is about creating a context for safety so that dilemmas like these can be articulated, acknowledged, and thoroughly processed.

Discussing self-destructive behavior provides another opportunity to explore the positive and negative consequences of change. Clients may come to therapy ready to acknowledge that drug and/or alcohol abuse is starting to become problematic, but they are only rarely aware of negative consequences of discontinuing the problematic behavior they know so well. Drinking alcohol provides a ready social context and is a culturally accepted, convenient way to relax and forget about your problems. Abstaining completely or even reducing frequency or quantity of average consumption may very well result in relational consequences, including social awkwardness or even complete alienation. Discussing the negative consequences of change examines the specifics of how the to-be-discarded behaviors actually are coping mechanisms, and helps the client project what losses will be experienced when these are no longer utilized.

A CCM therapist saw Jim and Barb in therapy after Barb started to have panic attacks before interactions with her family of origin. She had been sexually abused by her stepfather and thought she had dealt with the trauma, only to have it resurface as she aged. Jim and Barb had a distant and troubled relationship, but their sex life was one consistent way they could connect. Barb was considering giving up drinking, and wondered if her pattern of drinking through her problems interfered with her recovery. While Jim was supportive of Barb, wanting to work on her panic attacks and her abuse, he was adamant that the alcohol was not a problem. "I don't want to give up our Friday nights at McGully's," Jim said. "It is something I look forward to all week long and if you give up drinking, this will have a major impact on our relaxation and social life. And what about sex, I don't think you've ever had sex without a drink in you. You aren't an alcoholic. I don't know why you need to ruin my life to save yours." The CCM therapist used this as an example of a negative consequence of change and cautioned the couple to consider all the variables in their Stage One discussions.

The intent behind this discussion is to acknowledge major behavioral patterns and minor ones. Each time a change is warranted, negative and positive consequences should be identified. So, for example, if a partner states that she wants to spend more time with her partner, she is encouraged to identify where she would have less time, and be mindful about what she would be losing. This discussion ensures that the change process, when it occurs, becomes something that the client implements with full awareness. When clients examine both the positive and negative consequences of certain behaviors and then realize that the advantages to changing outweigh the disadvantages, then they are ready to take the risk of the negative consequences. We often find, if we do not spend enough time discussing this part of Stage One, that we become more invested in the change process than the client.

The positive and negative exploration is used throughout all stages of treatment. It is an intervention that is used after a pause, when any new goal or behavior is being introduced, and explored, in each and every stage. In Stage Two, it is appropriate to explore the positive and negative consequences of introducing a new modality into the treatment. For example, what are the positive and negative consequences in introducing sensory experiencing exercises with a client who has been doing primarily cognitive behavioral therapy but during couples therapy has complained she feels neither pain nor pleasure during sexual relations? During consolidation of therapy, it is important to explore the positive and negative consequences of the therapy no longer being a regular active part of the client's life.

A person cannot explore the positive and negative consequences while in a survival mindstate. The very activity of exploring the consequences brings the clients into an engaged mindstate. We highlight this process as we engage in Stage One assessment. Many clients believe that they do not have access to moments in which they are calm, cool, and collected, and fully engaging their inner and outer resources. When we highlight the engaged mindstate moment in the treatment process, we remind clients that they are already engaged in behavior they would like to continue.

Pause and Ponder: There is always risk involved in change. No matter how much change is desired, there is the fear of the unknown, fear of the loss of comfortable patterns, fear of the unfamiliar, fear of the other shoe dropping. These fears will likely trigger anticipatory anxiety or even survival reactions, encouraging homeostasis so that our clients fear change, and appear resistant, when in fact they are simply being protective of themselves and others. Examining the negative consequences of change addresses these fears. Exploring both the positive and negative consequences for each goal and each potential change is an empowering process. Collaborative decision-making is the antithesis of complex trauma and is a tangible demonstration of our belief that it is the clients' opinion of their own life that is most valuable. It is a helpful process when creating new pathways for engaged mindstates. We all can actively integrate the idea of positive and negative consequences of change into our relationships.

Understanding and Validating the Client's Denial, Availability, and Attachment

The human brain has the ability to compartmentalize experiences, thoughts, and emotions so that humans can function. While this is a successful survival strategy, when our brains compartmentalize certain aspects of our experience, our engaged mind is less available. Earlier in the book we discussed the relationship between complex trauma and attachment. For example, children whose parents are not available for soothing try to avoid experiencing feelings that require soothing. So, again, while it is an adaptive survival tool, those feelings are compartmentalized and therefore unavailable. The feelings are there and clients react from them but they often do not have access to them in a way that is helpful. In our work with clients with a history of complex trauma we have witnessed how understanding the attachment styles of both the therapist and the client can be an important element in successful treatment. Attachment styles certainly play a significant role in the client's ability to attach to the therapeutic team and environment. Issues of attachment also impact what triggers the trauma mindstate. Attachment also influences clients' ability to assess material in their trauma narrative with respect to memories and relationships and how they access information about their role in relationships.

Attachment style affects our ability to process memory and understand responsibility in relationships. Clients who have attachment styles that tend to be avoidant, preoccupied, disorganized, insecure, or dismissive often have a difficult time being available. They have trouble taking responsibility for their behaviors or acknowledging the impact of their behavior on self and others. They also have difficulty acknowledging the impact of others' behaviors on them, or simply even remembering facts, or situations. Those with responsive caregivers have a mediating variable that is not present with clients whose attachment to caregivers is not secure. Responsive parenting facilitates the capacity to stay present in the moment and incorporate new information and access most aspects of their experience. This is the availability we explore in Stage One. Our experience of our relationship with the client helps us determine their availability to relationships and to cognitive material.

For example, when clients lose words when describing an experience, or dissociate during a session, we understand that at this moment certain parts of their brain are not available to them. Or when clients continually cancel sessions, show up late, or stonewall during sessions, we understand this to be part of their attachment style and their inability to be emotionally and/or cognitively available to the process. Traditionally, we have referred to these processes of not having emotional, intellectual, and physical experiences and material available as denial (personal communication with Cece Sykes, 1983; Barrett, Sykes, & Byrnes, 1986; Trepper & Barrett, 1986, 1989). Although initially conceptualized as a natural form of resistance, denial is now understood as a strategy formulated, consciously or unconsciously, while in a survival mindstate. The process of compartmentalizing and denying material is a technique for surviving unmanageable stress. The problem, of course, is that in a survival mindstate, all stress is perceived as unmanageable. The survival mind is singularly focused on the perceived threat and lacks access to mindfulness and thoughtfulness.

We discuss in Stage One of treatment the importance of mindfulness meditative practices with all of our clients and we attempt to refocus on mindfulness each and every time we experience either ourselves or our clients leaving the present and reacting as if there is a perceived threat in the moment. The survival mind does focus on the moment, yet not the self-and-relationship-engaged present moment. Instead in survival mindstate, threat makes it so that we do not have available an awareness of the facts, the impact, and/or our relationship to what is occurring. This lack of availability is another way to look at dissociation and denial. For our purposes, and to help it make more sense to our clients, we simply speak of what we have available to us in the real or perceived moment.

It seems counterintuitive to validate or reframe a part of behavior that we have learned in our training is a defense mechanism that keeps people from being honest with themselves and others. In fact, this unavailability seems to be alive and working in almost every situation of complex trauma. Part of creating a context for safety includes understanding the importance and the effects of unavailability in clients' lives. The unavailability exists intrapsychically and interpersonally. We experience it as therapists in the room with our clients, when they do not have an experience available to them or when we are aware they are no longer available in therapy or interactionally with family members.

Some clients engage in therapy to work on processing traumatic events, but many clients we encounter with complex trauma do not have a conscious awareness that these events had a devastating impact. This unawareness or intra/interpersonal unavailability is a signal that we are still in Stage One of either therapy or of the cycle of change. For example, a client may be in Stage Two in wanting to change the way she relates to her children but Stage One as to how it is that she is so angry all the time. Working with her, you may believe, from the symptoms she reports, that her childhood may have been challenging, but she tells you that her family of origin was perfect. Just the opposite occurs as well, where clients are able to acknowledge their traumatic childhoods but deny that this has anything to do with the types of problems they bring into therapy. In both these situations, Stage One is about understanding how the client presents and how that presentation makes sense in their lives. The lack of their awareness, their ability to attach, and their skills accompanied with the perceived threat in the environment which leaves the client unable to access facts, impact, and responsibility of past and current situations (personal communication with Cece Sykes, 1983).

For example, an adolescent was referred to therapy for being sexually aggressive with her peers. She is furious about the referral and denies the impact of her behavior on her classmates. She acknowledges that some bad things happened in her family when she was younger but is adamant that these events did not impact her. In Stage One, we are attempting to discover how her current behavior helps her feel powerful, in control, and valued. It is not our intent to process those bad things or to help her understand how those bad things may impact her current behavior. We believe that the lack of awareness has a useful purpose for her. Instead, our goal is to understand how she understands her current behavior. So, when she talks about how those bad things had no impact on her, we ask how she stayed so focused and in control when those bad things happened. We ask her how she managed to survive, what sorts of things she did to maintain power, control, and take care of herself. We may recognize that the current behaviors are a direct impact of those bad things, but in Stage One, we are aware that this is unavailable to her in order for her to not be constantly triggered into a further trauma state. This helps her maintain her dignity and must be kept intact until she is safe enough to acknowledge the impact. In addressing the denial and unavailability, it is another opportunity to use the tool of positive and negative consequences for change.

CCM practitioner: Pretend with me for a moment, what do you think would happen if you experienced your childhood as both perfect and not so perfect at the same time?

Or

CCM practitioner: You say you do not remember sexually abusing your daughter, you never say you didn't do it; you repetitively say that you do not remember. What do you think would happen to you, or your daughter or both of you, if you ever did remember?

CCM practitioner (a little later): Can you imagine anything positive happening for you or your daughter if you would remember? What do you think you would need from me in order to feel safe and strong enough to be able to remember what happened, as your daughter remembers what she believes happened to her?

Or

CCM practitioner: I hear you, you are saying that it was not you abusing your sister but that she was a willing participant in the sex and that she has as much responsibility as you do. Yet if you hear her, she says that she was afraid to say no to you and that you told her not to tell your parents. What would be the pros and what would be the cons of trying to put yourself in her shoes and try to understand how she saw the sexual contact?

When clients are able to acknowledge the effects of complex trauma and how their behavior is affected by it, and how their behaviors and feelings affect others, we can move to Stage Two for this particular behavior. It is paradoxical that one way to survive a threatening thought, feeling, or action, whether triggered externally or internally, is to avoid the facts of the trigger, the impact of the trigger, or taking responsibility. Yet it often occurs that, in order to survive a perceived threat, avoiding its existence allows us to survive. What happens, however, is that we become unavailable to the narrative of our lives or the narrative becomes unavailable to us. A therapist needs to expect these forms of denial, avoidance, or unavailability to be part of the trauma cycle. In Stage Two, it will be integrated into the change cycle.

For an audio file that explains Interventions for Working with Denial and Availability, please refer to the book's eResources site: www.routledgementalhealth.com/9780415510219.

Pause and Ponder: When in a survival mindstate it is a natural reaction to be unaware. We all lose sight of details, of the impact of our behavior on self and others, and/or we often do not recognize and acknowledge responsibility for our role in the sequence of events, i.e., how we have become a victim to maltreatment or a perpetrator of violation. We also become unavailable in our relationship to self and to others, which is an outcome of early and present attachments. This unavailability to self and others is often experienced by professionals as resistance. The unavailability of our clients triggers in us, the practitioners, feelings of inadequacy, frustration, helplessness, hopelessness, anger, defensiveness, in other words fight, flight, and freeze. We may then become unavailable to our clients. We need to recognize, accept, and emotionally hold ourselves and our clients while they work through and build pathways to avail themselves of all the resources necessary to change.

Setting Goals

Goals for treatment and life goals are articulated in Stage One. Although they are not stagnant, goals evolve as treatment does; setting goals helps to create a context for change. It is important to be as specific and as realistic as possible in setting goals and to focus on small steps in the process. Having small observable and manageable goals sets the stage for success and triggers engaged mindstates. When goals are met, we tend to feel powerful, in control, and valued. Our internal locus of control is stimulated and we experience the world around us as safe and manageable. Rather than being stuck in interactional cycles of survival, when we accomplish set goals, we are engaged in the evolving cycle of change.

There are client-specific idiosyncratic goals, and there are goals that are part of the CCM treatment model. Client-specific goals are based on the vulnerabilities and symptoms that clients present and their hope for the future. Remember that we believe that when people feel vulnerable, they act to feel powerful, in control, and/or valued. The function of most symptoms, then, in our model, is to help people feel powerful, in control, and valued. Unfortunately, the symptoms are problematic as they interfere with engaged mindstate behavior. Setting and then reaching specific idiosyncratic goals will help clients use their engaged mindstate when vulnerable, adding more options in their lives, and moving them toward the natural cycle of change. The part of the goals that are specific to the CCM treatment model are contracting, explaining the role of discomfort in the change process, expanding parts of the natural cycle of change, and exploring mindfulness-based practice.

Setting idiosyncratic goals can be tricky because many of the behaviors our clients use to enhance their feelings of control, power, and value are helpful in the short term but ultimately self-sabotaging. Furthermore, these behaviors may not initially be seen by the client as self-destructive, may be enjoyable on some level, and/or may provide inner satisfactions; i.e., they may not want to change in some important ways. This is where the collaborative nature of the CCM is very useful. In the process of setting goals, practitioners, team members, family members, and clients all have input into the goals of treatment in a supportive way. The client is at the center of goal setting and is supported while challenged to set goals that are realistic and useful to the client in moving from a survival to an engaged mindstate.

Molly was a 16-year-old survivor of childhood sexual abuse by a next-door neighbor, a 70-year-old convicted sex offender who somehow slipped through the judicial system and violated Molly and her younger sister. Molly was in family therapy with her single mother and her sister and during the goal-setting phase of Stage One, multiple goals were set with all individuals and with the family as a whole. The mother was very concerned about Molly's self-injurious rituals, but Molly was not willing to relinquish this behavior. Burning herself with cigarettes and cutting herself with a razor blade provided the only respite from searing guilt about failing to protect her sister from the neighbor. After insuring that Molly's behavior was not suicidal, the CCM practitioner, Molly, and her mother decided to set a goal of Molly and her mother learning to communicate about Molly's self-injurious behavior in a way that helped both of them.

Along with idiosyncratic goal setting, CCM practitioners explore the role of discomfort when setting goals with clients. Many clients with a history of complex trauma avoid discomfort since it typically leads to survival mindstate. They find themselves unequipped to deal with anxiety and other uncomfortable feelings, so it is important to set the stage for discomfort in setting goals. With Molly and her mother, the CCM practitioner said, "So one goal that the two of you agree on is that you want to be able to talk openly and honestly with each other, not just about Molly's cutting, but also about a whole host of other topics. You both agree that you haven't been able to do this before without one of you getting hurt or storming out. These conversations are uncomfortable, really uncomfortable. I will help you learn the skills you need so that you can have these conversations. They will still be uncomfortable, however, so the other thing I will teach you is how to soothe yourselves and each other when you are uncomfortable. Any new behavior is uncomfortable, but the only way we grow is by trying on new behavior. You both have learned that avoiding these conversations is not helpful, so we have to do something different and I will help you with it. I know how to do that."

Goals from outside contexts need to be integrated into the treatment goals. Over the years, we have discovered that many of our individuals and families with a history of complex trauma are "mandated" to be in treatment by someone or some institution. They may be mandated by the courts, the school, the hospital, the employer, the partner, the child, the parent, the list is endless. Someone, something is demanding that our clients change. Because of this demand, we feel a responsibility to integrate the goals of the referring party or referring demand. This might mean helping a parent find a new apartment, or creating strategies for organizing the home, if the Department of Child Protection has the goal of returning children. There may be court-ordered goals such as abstaining from substance use, or attending parenting classes in order to establish visitation. Frequently the goals of the outside contexts are in conflict with the clients' goals. Once again this requires the need for transparent conversation.

CCM therapist: I know by what you have been telling me the last few weeks that you do not feel you need to be here and looking at your own life and struggles. The court, based on your ex-wife and children's testimony, has referred you here, but you don't feel the need to work on any problem.

Client: Right! I just need to see my kids. This whole thing is ridiculous.

CCM therapist: I see that and yet, in order to see your kids, we have to explore what your kids were and are saying about their fear of seeing you right now. So would you agree that a goal of therapy would be for us to work collaboratively with your kids' therapist and figure out what is necessary to happen for you to see your kids?

Client: I don't need to work with anyone, this is all about my ex and her trying to punish me.

CCM therapist: This really irritates you? Infuriates you? Makes you sad? Disappoints? What would you say?

Client: Infuriates.

CCM therapist: And when you are infuriated, what do you do?

Client: Just say, forget it. I don't care.

CCM therapist: Remember how last week we talked about the brain and I gave you the picture. Do you have it, in your journal? Take it out and let's look at it.

The therapist and the client together looked at connecting his anger at the situation to the ideas of survival mind and through this pathway the father's and the court's goals of therapy were intertwined. Finding new ways to respond to his frustration helped him meet the goals of the court and at the same time benefit him and his children. The father learned a workable reality for the future, because remaining angry and withdrawn simply kept his situation stagnant.

The natural cycle of change is also explored in setting goals. We overtly articulate the natural cycle of contraction and expansion and we actually show clients how we are using it ourselves in treatment. Practitioners might, for example, talk about an idea they had about a client between sessions and acknowledge the natural cycle of change in that comment. A CCM therapist might say, "So, I thought about what we were talking about over the weekend and I had some more ideas about you and some questions about what you said last week that I did not ask you. I also want to make overt how what I just said is actually the natural cycle of change that I introduced a few sessions ago. When not in session, I had a moment to pause and be thoughtful about our last session. I contracted. In that contraction I realized that there was a big part of what we were talking about last week that I still do not have a handle on as it pertains to me being helpful to you. I want to have an expanded vision of you and me and our relationship. Does that make sense?"

Exploring mindfulness-based practice is also part of goal setting and is acknowledged from the start as generic to the CCM as well as to all good trauma-informed practice. Some of our clients have been introduced to these concepts, some have practiced mindfulness, and others are unaware of the benefits. We discuss the benefits as part of setting goals. With some clients we recommend readings, workshops, video blogs, or audiotapes, and with others we present the idea and help them figure out the best way for them to incorporate mindfulness into their lives. Mindfulness practice and techniques seem omnipresent when we look for them and we sometimes have to guide our clients to look and to see and experiment with reflection in a way that they have not done before. Mindfulness incorporates silence (a quieting of the mind) and reflection and is a skill that with practice can be learned. Mindfulness increases our capacity to remain present even with painful sensations and emotions. It decreases our reactivity to inner experiences and increases our capacity to react to externals with awareness and intention. When we strive toward nonjudgmental attitudes to our experiences, which mindfulness practice teaches, we are able to engage more comfortably with the process of change.

Jeremy, age 16, was seen by his school social worker who had training in the CCM. Jeremy lived in a high-crime neighborhood, had recently moved from a homeless shelter to a subsidized apartment with his disabled mother, and had begun meeting with a social worker because he wanted to go to college. He was having a hard time waking himself up to get to school on time, and once he was there, he had difficulty concentrating. He knew that if he did not change, he would fail high school and not even have a chance to attend college. In setting his goals, the CCM practitioner explained mindfulness this way: "So, Jeremy, one of your goals is waking yourself up to get to school on time. Right? And you said that you have no idea why some days you are able to get up and some days you aren't. Right? So one of the ways we can work on your goal is by getting you to be more aware of what happens when you get up and what happens when you don't. Right? Awareness is actually a skill that you can practice. You can learn how to practice awareness or mindfulness, doesn't really matter what it is called, and it will help you reach your goal. That is something we can explore in the coming sessions. Okay?"

Mindfulness practice engages us in the process of being aware of what we attend to and in creating a context for change; this is exactly what we are attempting to do. We are attempting to pay attention to the survival mindstate process and the interactional cycles of survival and how they are triggered. Once we understand how these processes work we can entertain the possibility of changing them.

Goal setting is an evolving process mirroring the cycle of change. Identifying that change is happening often creates the necessity to collaborate on the formation of new goals. We pause and contract and identify goals and then we expand as we identify new goals and a more complex vision of the future.

Pause and Ponder: Goals evolve throughout the stages of therapy. Goals are set for sessions, for stages, and for the overall process of change. Goals will address: the presenting symptoms, the function of the symptoms, and the integration of the referring party. Goals are present- as well as future-oriented. When creating the goals, remember to include the specifics about how the goals will be met, the skills necessary to meet the goals, the interventions utilized to teach and practice the skills, and the modalities used. Refer to the goals continually with clients, reminding them of the purpose of therapy, how we will accomplish the goals, and how we will know when the goals are met.

Introducing Acknowledgment

We believe that the role of acknowledgment is one of the most powerful and most underutilized interventions in therapy with complex trauma. Acknowledgment is the burgeoning recognition of how clients understand their symptoms, how they contribute to their problem cycles, increasing awareness of impact, facts, and responsibility, and clear statements about what they are committed to changing. Each acknowledgment in a session can easily be woven into the client's goals. So once again, just like the cycle of change and the stages of therapy, acknowledgments happen repeatedly during a session, and throughout the stages of treatment. When a client acknowledges a thought, a feeling, or a behavior during a session, it is the practitioner's responsibility to capture that moment and integrate it into the process of change.

Client: I just wish I knew how to handle my anger.

CCM therapist: Wishing that you knew how to handle your anger is a great start. Recognizing that you want that to change is incredibly important. Should we make that one of our goals?

Client: Sure, sounds like a good idea.

CCM therapist: Let me share with you some of my ideas of how we might learn some skills that will help you meet your goal.

Another example:

Client: I have absolutely no idea of how to handle my daughter's cutting. I just don't understand it! I am completely overwhelmed.

CCM therapist: You saying that and me knowing that is really helpful. I bet her cutting is triggering a lot for you, which makes it even harder to know what to do.

Client: That is for sure.

CCM therapist: You recognizing that gives me some ideas about the direction our sessions could go. You are acknowledging that you feel overwhelmed and you have acknowledged before that when you feel overwhelmed you retreat and, using your words, "go home and lick your wounds." You've also talked about wanting to be more involved in parenting her, so we can work on different things for you to do when you are overwhelmed instead of retreating.

Acknowledgment sessions signal the end of Stage One, and are the set-up for Stage Two. It seems as if, once people can acknowledge that what they have been doing is not working and that they have the power and control to change their behavior, we can move into Stage Two, which is the work of changing that behavior. Acknowledgment sessions are another example of the importance of an organized approach to treatment. They mark the delineation between stages when working on a specific goal.

Remember that a person can be in Stage One in one form of treatment and Stage Two in another. For example, a couple may work all the parts of Stage One and then acknowledge how they contribute to their interactional cycle of survival and clearly be ready to start making changes, which is Stage Two work. While in Stage Two, however, when they begin to struggle with communication and deeper intimacy, one partner or both may realize that there are some individual or family of origin issues that they must address and for those issues, we pause and reorganize, utilizing Stage One interventions. Refocusing on safety, goals, assessment of needs, and resources is not conceptualized as a regression or setback to Stage One. Rather, this oscillation is a simple and elegant part of the natural cycle of change, which includes pausing, regrouping, refocusing, and then moving into expansion. Like the blueprint for a house informs construction, we are forever running into unforeseen circumstances in which we must consult the blueprint, so that we can move forward in a constructive way that respects clients' needs for feeling valued, in control, and powerful.

Acknowledgment sessions can be formal or informal. Some of this depends on the practitioner's style and work environment, and some depends on the clients, their particular situation, and why they were referred for treatment. When practitioners work in formal environments where paperwork is completed at the end of Stage One, then acknowledgment sessions are more formal. Acknowledgment occurs and a treatment plan is designed which begins Stage Two. In some agencies, acknowledgments and a treatment plan are written and signed by both clients and practitioners, or even by the team that is working with the clients. In less formal settings, acknowledgments may not be formally documented but they nevertheless must occur for treatment to move to Stage Two.

When treatment is mandated by the judicial system, then the acknowledgment sessions tend to be more formal as well. Probation officers, caseworkers, and judges may want a formal statement not only that their clients are following through on treatment, but also that they have acknowledged problematic behavior and have established concrete goals toward working on change. When working with other professionals, the CCM practitioner can explain to all involved how Stage One sets the stage for helping clients reach treatment goals in Stage Two, so that everyone is working the model together.

Monique, age 32, had her son James, age 13, removed after James told the assistant principal of his middle school that his mother beat him with a broom after he told her he was gay. James was sent to a group home after the failure of an initial foster care placement. Monique was assigned parenting classes and seen in therapy by Simone, a CCM-trained practitioner. When Monique began treatment, she wanted James back home and blamed the school personnel, James, James's father, the foster care family, and her mother for James's removal. She agreed to parenting classes and to individual therapy because she was mandated, but did not believe that she had contributed in any way to having her child removed from her home. She felt completely powerless, devalued, and out of control. Following numerous conversations about safety, vulnerability, how the brain works, survival mindstates, and the positive and negative consequences of change, Monique began to feel safe enough to explore some of her own behavior. She acknowledged that she had an anger problem and that she lost control of herself when she was angry.

Many sessions ensued with Monique in which she was able to acknowledge her anger but continued to blame the people in her community for triggering her rage. Monique, Simone, and the caseworker, planned together to schedule family sessions as soon as all three adults believed that these meetings would be safe and productive. They all agreed that family therapy must wait until Monique acknowledged her behavior and its contribution to James's placement outside of her home. Monique left these pretreatment planning meetings furious with Simone and the caseworker for not working fast enough on her behalf to get James home and she blamed James and his biological father for causing her to be angry in the first place. While she acknowledged that she hit James with a broom and could have found a different way to discipline him, she blamed his "mouth" for causing her to hit him. She said, "He knew I was upset to begin with and he puts this gay thing in my face just to taunt me, to manipulate me, to get his own way like he always does. Then he gets the assistant principal to think I'm some prejudiced person, that I don't love my son no matter how he turns out and that I'm an abusive mother. He's got his father's mouth and slyness. I shouldn't have hit him so hard but he knew he was making me angry, so he deserved it."

Simone continued to explore Monique's understanding of her survival mindstate, her vulnerabilities, and her resources. Monique saw danger and disappointment everywhere and always responded to interpersonal stress with a fight response. She never felt in control in any relationship and even though she was learning in her parenting classes about hierarchy and responsibility, she was aware that her survival mindstate took over even when she was triggered by James. When she was alone, however, she was a consummate crafter. She was insatiably curious about some internet crafting sites and an avid contributor to online discussions about crafting products. Simone and Monique mapped Monique's interactional cycle of survival and with plenty of coaching and attention to detail, Simone and Monique learned together what Monique needed to be able to access through mindfulness in times of stress. Monique developed what she called a crafting mindstate and experimented with it in individual sessions with Simone in exceedingly successful ways.

Around this time, in a supervised visit that Monique had with James, she apologized for hitting him the night of their fight and he started to cry. The caseworker heard about the incident and called Monique to say that this was the acknowledgment she was waiting for and that she was ready to sign off on family therapy. Monique was clearly proud of herself and her progress in her next session with Simone. However, Monique was also confused by James's response, and understandably anxious about the prospect of family therapy with her son. Family therapy would start, of course, in Stage One, but individual therapy was ready to move to Stage Two. Monique said, "I understand now the difference between saying I have an anger problem and acknowledging that I have an anger problem. So James and I have a lot to work out and he has to learn that I am the parent and all that and we've got to work out visitations with his dad and all that other crap. That hasn't gone away. Stress will never go away. I and only I, though, am in control of how I handle it and I acknowledge that I shouldn't have lost control that way and it was my fault he got taken from my home."

In earlier iterations of the CCM, we referred to these as apology sessions. As we continued our research, we realized that change emerged after acknowledgment rather than forgiveness. Forgiveness is a complicated and very personal subject to each client and therapist. In fact, how one defines forgiveness is unique. Positive therapeutic change may occur without forgiveness, but not without acknowledgment. If forgiveness is important to the client and it becomes a goal to either forgive another or to be forgiven, then it is addressed as such, as a goal. Collaboratively we determine how we will address the goal of forgiveness. Forgiveness when using CCM to treat trauma is not a prerequisite for change; acknowledgment is, however. Acknowledgment is the acceptance and open admission that I have a problem and that I will address it. Acknowledgment involves taking responsibility and is a process integral to change.

Pause and Ponder: Acknowledgment is one of the most important processes in creating a context for change. As practitioners we must recognize in the moment when clients accept the existence of a thought, a feeling, and/or a behavior. We need to punctuate the acknowledgment and then utilize the acknowledgment in the steps of challenging and expanding. It is imperative for the practitioner to recognize the moment in the interaction when clients acknowledge any aspect of their survival mind. When they recognize their thoughts, feelings, or behaviors as problematic, as not coming from their engaged mindstate, as something they want to change, when a small success has occurred, etc. Use the acknowledgment for goal setting, designing interventions, teaching skills, and expanding the vision.

References

Barrett, M. J., Sykes, C., & Byrnes, W. (1986). A systemic model for the treatment of intra-family child sexual abuse. In M. J. Barrett & T. Trepper (Eds.) *Treating incest: A multiple systems perspective*. New York: Haworth Press.

Boszormenyi-Nagy, I., & Krasner, B. (1986). *Between give and take: A clinical guide to contextual therapy.* New York: Brunner/Mazel.

Briere, J. (1995). *Trauma Symptom Inventory (TSI).* Odessa, FL: Psychological Assessment Resources.

Briere, J., & Elliott, D. M. (2003). Prevalence and psychological sequelae of self-reported childhood physical and sexual abuse in a general population sample of men and women. *Child Abuse & Neglect, 27,* 1205–1222.

Crisci, G., Lay, M., & Lowenstein, L. (1998). *Paper dolls and paper airplanes: Therapeutic exercises for sexually traumatized children.* St. Paul, MN: Jist Publishing.

Greenwald, R. (2007). *EMDR: Within a phase model of trauma-informed treatment.* New York: Routledge.

Johnson, M. P. (2006). Conflict and control: Gender symmetry and asymmetry in domestic violence. *Violence Against Women, 12,* 1003–1018.

Johnson, M. P., & Ferraro, K. J. (2000). Research on domestic violence in the 1990s: Making distinctions. *Journal of Marriage and the Family, 62,* 948–963.

Myers, I. B., & McCaulley, M. H. (1985). *Manual: A guide to the development and use of the Myers-Briggs type indicator.* Mountain View, CA: Consulting Psychologists Press.

Perry, B. D. (1994). Neurobiological sequelae of childhood trauma: Posttraumatic stress disorders in children. In M. M. Murburg (Ed.) *Catecholamine function in posttraumatic stress disorder: Emerging concepts* (pp. 253–276). Washington, DC: American Psychiatric Press.

Solomon, A. (2012). *Far from the tree: Parents, children, and the search for identity.* New York: Scribner.

Stith, S. M., McCollum, E. E., Amanor-Boadu, Y., & Smith, D. (2012). Systemic perspectives on intimate partner violence treatment. *Journal of Marital and Family Therapy, 38,* 220–240.

Stone Fish, L., & Harvey, R. (2005). *Nurturing queer youth: Family therapy transformed.* New York: W.W. Norton & Co.

Trepper, T., & Barrett, M. J. (Eds.) (1986). *Treating incest: A multiple systems perspective.* NY: Haworth Press.

Trepper, T., & Barrett, M. J. (1989). *Systemic treatment of incest: A therapeutic handbook.* New York: Routledge.

six
Stage Two
Challenging Patterns and Expanding Realities

Clients who have experienced complex trauma present to helping professionals in different ways. Some clients are overt about traumatic events that they believe have impacted their lives before coming for help and some present with psychological aches and pains, discovering much later in the treatment process that their difficulties make sense given the context of their traumatic relationships. Some clients come as individuals and others as couples or families. Some present initially with great motivation and compliance and others resist help and fend off the practitioner. Some clients come to outpatient treatment following discharge from recovery programs, eating disorder units, psychiatric hospitals, wilderness experiences, individual, couple, or family therapy experiences, and some have never walked into a treatment facility before. Regardless of where they start, Stage Two occurs when the context for change has been set, goals are agreed upon, and acknowledgment has occurred so that the natural cycle of evolving is supported and the change process has already begun. Stage Two includes the ongoing work of psychotherapy.

Creating a Context for Stage Two

Once goals are set and a context for change has been established, we begin the process of challenging patterns and expanding alternatives. We may envision Stage One as discovery and exploration of well-worn survival pathways and the explanation that treatment involves learning and practicing how to create new pathways. Stage Two, then, is the practice of walking down different paths. Or continuing our building metaphor, Stage Two is after the foundation is poured and the studs are up, we are ready to begin the wiring, the plumbing, the walls, the windows, and the rest of the interior. As in all parts of the CCM, Stage Two is not a linear process so that we may be in Stage Two for one goal while still in Stage One for another goal. Certain family members can be in Stage Two while others are in Stage One. Furthermore, Stage Two processes may trigger clients and cause too much discomfort for them, so we cycle through Stage One until challenging patterns can be accomplished without triggering a trauma response.

It must be remembered that the cycle of change is recursive, repeating over and over again in every session and every stage. If we review child development as a comparison, there are linear stages of growth, yet these stages do not emerge in a step-by-step orderly flow. There are spurts and stops, repeating and practicing milestones as necessary. These repetitions of the milestones are a natural process that all individuals and families practice in order to achieve mastery. The same process occurs in our CCM. As we challenge patterns and expand alternatives, there is always a need to pause and cocoon and then re-engage in expansion. Then a change is consolidated and we can move on, although the change may have to be re-examined along the way.

Given the recursive nature of change and the stages, each stage of the model has the three stages embedded in all the stages. Creating the context for Stage Two means the client and therapist agree upon the goals. There is agreement of what skills will be learned and how they will be taught. There is an understanding of the possible interventions that may be utilized and there is a thorough understanding of and transparency regarding the mechanisms of the process of change.

Stage Two Core Concepts Chart

Collaborative Exploration of Differential Trauma-Informed Interventions

Expanding the Refuge and Context for Change

Challenging Vulnerabilities and the Function of the Symptoms

Expanding Resources

Challenging and Expanding Availability

Accomplishing Goals

Ongoing Acknowledgment

Collaborative Exploration of Differential Trauma-Informed Interventions

In Stage Two, CCM practitioners work with clients and their collaborative contexts to determine which interventions and techniques are going to be used to help clients move from survival mindstates to engaged mindstates. The treatment team (which includes clients, of course) has a thorough understanding of the clients' vulnerabilities and how their symptoms function to keep them surviving and a thorough understanding of their individual and contextual resources. The positive and negative consequences of change have been explored, availability has been conceptualized, and the concept of acknowledgment and personal responsibility has been introduced. Furthermore, goals have been set so that everyone is working toward them together, and clients and therapists are monitoring the natural cycle of change, readying for evolution.

There are a number of techniques and intervention strategies that have been shown to be effective with clients who have a history of complex trauma (e.g., EDMR, CBT, DBT, Somatic Experiential Therapy (SET), mindfulness yoga) and the beauty of the CCM is that when practitioners work collaboratively, they can be conduits between clients and their communities to guide clients toward intervention strategies that are a custom fit. The intervention strategies are based on the blueprint of goals that the therapist and clients have worked on in Stage One and a corresponding fit between client vulnerabilities with the client, CCM practitioner, and community resources. The following are some guidelines to consider when thinking about differential trauma-informed interventions:

1. An acceptance that there is not one modality or theoretical model that works for all clients. Humans are not cookies, hence there are no cookie-cutter approaches.
2. Interventions and modalities should be chosen based on the collaboratively set goals of the clients.
3. Interventions should utilize clients' natural resources for change.
4. New skills are taught through modalities which facilitate the evolving of vulnerabilities into resources.
5. Modalities are realistically available to the client by the current practitioner or the community.

The fractal nature of our model is important to highlight here for the reader, our clients, and the community in which we work. When we refer clients to other therapeutic resources, we may be in Stage Two of the model, but the new relationship is in Stage One. We encourage clients to be mindful of the necessity of creating a context for change in the new relationship. We explore with them what may interfere with their using new resources productively and check back continuously about how the referral is being used, integrating that new knowledge into our therapeutic relationship.

Differential trauma-informed interventions depend on the major goals that have been articulated in Stage One. For example, Cheryl and Keith, both in their mid-thirties, had decided on two major goals in Stage One. They wanted to work as a couple to improve their conflict resolution skills and individually Cheryl chose to work on emotional regulation and family of origin exploration, while Keith wanted to work on anger management. In Stage One, a CCM therapist had seen them in individual and couples therapy as they struggled to stay together following Keith's admission of infidelity. They had been together as a couple for eight years and both had children from previous relationships. Two months before starting therapy, Keith announced that he had been sexual with Cheryl's sister-in-law the previous Christmas and a few other times since then. He felt guilty about the affair and wanted the air cleared so their relationship could be repaired. He took some responsibility for his affair but also blamed Cheryl because she was not warm enough for him and was too wrapped up in the stress of caring for her children to attend to his needs. The CCM therapist also learned that when they argued they tended to become violent with each other and that Keith had pushed Cheryl on numerous occasions and thrown her to the floor. In Stage One, when CCM therapists learn of violence that is current, it is addressed directly so that refuge can be created. Cheryl and Keith signed a no-violence contract (see Appendix 5) and a safety plan was created. Cheryl learned in Stage One that whenever she was angry with Keith or he was angry with her, she went immediately into a survival mind-state because it triggered her memories of violence she had witnessed between her mother and father, and her father and her brother. Keith had learned that he had anger management problems when he felt threatened and that impulse control had always been a problem for him.

Part of the Stage One safety plan was for Cheryl to go to her mother's house (parents were separated) or contact the local women's shelter if she felt the signs of danger. If Keith believed he was going to lose control, he had a brother he could call and he could leave the house and take a break, as long as he let Cheryl know where he was going. The interactional cycle of survival explored in Stage One went something like this: Cheryl would have a bad day at work because she felt panicked that Keith was lying to her and was continuing the affair he had with her sister-in-law. She would arrive home angry and irritable while at the same time seeking reassurance from Keith that he was trustworthy. Rather than reassurance, Cheryl's behavior triggered his fear that she was always going to be "this way," in his mind, cold and distant and trying to push him away. This threatened his sense of safety in the relationship and he would appear contemptuous, become moody and impulsive, all of which triggered Cheryl's survival mind and feeling out of control, devalued, and lonely. A few months into therapy, Cheryl contacted the women's shelter because she felt she was in danger and then took her two daughters to her mother's home where she felt safe. This was a turning point in the couple's relationship because Cheryl was able to sense danger and react from an engaged mindstate, and Keith finally acknowledged that his behavior was unacceptable.

In an individual session with Cheryl around this time, she said, "When Keith was yelling at me in the kitchen, I realized that normally I would disassociate and watch us screaming at each other as if I were above it all. I felt nothing, no fear, no rage, no danger. I was just acting out a script of a raving lunatic who was completely out of control. But this time in the kitchen, it was different. Probably because we had been talking about this stupid dance we do with each other in therapy the week before, but this time, I realized that my survival mindstate was totally triggered and I felt fear for the very first time. It was like I was watching myself and I was in myself. I knew, again, probably for the very first time, really knew, that this was not good and had to stop so I got the hell out of there and called the shelter."

One of the goals that Cheryl had articulated in Stage One was working on family of origin issues that triggered her survival mind. She had started to have flashbacks of her father's rages and wanted to work on letting those go. Her CCM therapist was trained as a family therapist and worked closely with an EMDR-trained therapist in the community. Cheryl saw both therapists simultaneously while in Stage Two of the model. Keith was referred to an anger management group that was connected to the women's shelter, which used a CBT model to help men challenge the cognitive distortions that facilitate aggressive behavior toward women. The CCM therapist worked with both Cheryl and Keith on communication skills. This is an example of the use of differential trauma-informed interventions in Stage Two. The CCM therapist used the couple's goals to determine which interventions to use and the couple's and the therapist's resources to determine who was going to do what. Cheryl and Keith, the shelter, Cheryl's mother, the anger management group leader, the EMDR-trained therapist, and the CCM therapist all became part of the treatment team.

Another example of differential trauma-informed interventions in Stage Two occurred in a residential high school for adolescents. One of the social workers at the high school was trained in the CCM and was working with her teenage clients using the model. Jesse was one of her clients and they were moving into Stage Two of treatment, having successfully determined goals for therapy. Jesse was an 18-year-old whose parents reacted to the news of her rape at a party by blaming her because they had forbidden her from attending. She responded with a severe depression and attempted suicide by taking a handful of her mother's sleeping pills. Jointly the family decided Jesse could no longer live at home and she was sent away for the remainder of high school. While gaining distance from her high school and her family had a number of benefits for Jesse, she still suffered from a plethora of somatic symptoms that felt uncontrollable and scary. She was highly anxious, periodically feared she was having a heart attack, and had aches and pains that convinced her she was minutes away from being diagnosed with terminal cancer. One of the goals she had talked about in Stage One was having a better relationship with her body. The CCM therapist knew of a trauma-informed yoga instructor in the town next to the residential high school that Jesse attended. She was able to elicit help from her supervisor, who asked the director of the program if they could offer a class with this instructor. Jesse remained in therapy with the CCM therapist and enrolled in the yoga class. The therapist helped Jesse talk with the yoga instructor about her traumatic experiences and how her somatic symptoms were preventing her from moving forward in her life.

It is obvious that in order to have the most effective outcome, the treatment of relational complex trauma includes multiple modalities and theoretical constructs, and this can be costly and time consuming. In Stage One when planning the treatment and during Stage Two when implementing it, it is imperative to overtly communicate with funding sources and with clients in order to establish the most cost-effective and treatment-efficient plan. Practitioners must organize the treatment with health insurance policies, governmental referral agencies, contracts, and/or grants. Clients cannot be expected, nor is it wise, to be participating in numerous sessions a week unless the program is an Intensive Outpatient Program (IOP) or an Inpatient/Residential Program. The organization of sessions and modalities, whether inpatient or outpatient, is designed collaboratively with professionals and clients, according to the needs of the clients as well as the availability of resources.

Pause and Ponder: Exploring the differential trauma-informed therapies entails using techniques, interventions, and modalities that address the immediate and most significant therapeutic goals, utilizing the current resources of the client and the community. As therapy develops and the goals shift and change, the introduction of new interventions, techniques, and modalities expand the resources for the client, allowing them to venture into new skill areas. Exploring the differential trauma-informed therapies is the process of integrating both cognitive behavioral approaches and body–mind sensory approaches, all of which are necessary in creating new pathways. The decision to introduce and then the order in which the modalities/interventions are introduced are dependent on the availability of internal, community, and familial resources.

Expanding the Refuge and Context for Change

Stage Two categories correspond to both Stage One and Stage Three categories. So, while in Stage One we create refuge, in Stage Two we challenge isolation and overinvolvement if and when necessary. Isolation and overinvolvement, while seemingly opposite experiences, have some of the same roots. Survival mindstates may trigger our clients toward both or either of these poles and leave them without balanced social support. If, in Stage One, clients have expressed an interest in having different relationships with family members, friends, and/or co-workers, Stage Two is where this work is done. The authors of this book are trained and practicing marriage and family therapists, so we do this work with our clients. Other CCM therapists are not trained in relational work and collaborate with systems-oriented therapists for the relational work.

Family of origin sessions are common Stage Two therapeutic interventions. We often find that a great deal of therapeutic work is accomplished in the planning stages of family of origin sessions, even before the family walks into the therapist's office. A CCM therapist was seeing Amy, a woman in her late twenties who had not been in contact with her father and two of her brothers for the last five years. When she began to have memories of sexual abuse, she severed all contact with the male members of her family. Just thinking of them all in the same room with her triggered her survival mindstate and yet meeting with and beginning a dialogue with them was a goal of hers for Stage Two. The planning that went into how to keep her safe before, during, and after family sessions was rivaled by the panic that riveted her entire family of origin when Amy told them she wanted a family session. This Stage One planning paid off when family therapy sessions occurred in Stage Two.

Family of origin work with adults takes many forms. It can be as simple as the planning of letter writing, conversations, or visits which describe how the relationship might change. Family of origin work is also accomplished in family dialogue sessions, which are designed to follow a mediation format rather than therapy. Family dialogue is a facilitated conversation mediated by a CCM therapist between adult family members, which discusses how their relationships will look from the present day forward, not focusing on the past. This is a very solution-focused present-day dialogue that may only occur after adult survivors have developed new pathways from survival mindstate to engaged mindstate.

The Family Dialogue Project was developed to create conversations in families in which difficult conversations are being avoided or have created a great deal of conflict. For example, family dialogue is often used for conversations about disputed allegations of sexual abuse, or difficult conversations about a family member's behaviors while under the influence of alcohol. The Family Dialogue Project was created to facilitate communication and conflict resolution around issues that might be considered irreconcilable differences, which might have resulted in a "cutting off" of significant relationships. The family dialogue follows the CCM, where during individual sessions with all parties an assessment is made about the possibility of détente. Are the parties willing to participate, are they open to relationship change, what are the strengths in the relationships, the positive and negative consequences of the process, and where might the communication break down? The family dialogue assumes that each party has their reality of the situation and it is the job of the practitioner/mediator to help the family create a third reality that provides a possible bridge into the future (Barrett, 2003).

When children and adolescents live in a disruptive, traumatic context, or they witness abuses and violations, or they have been victims of abuse themselves, we encourage family therapy as a modality of treatment. We believe that it is clinically responsible to begin with individual, couple, and family therapy as multiple modalities of treatment from Stage One and continue in family therapy through all the stages of the model.

The Williams family is an example of this type of treatment. Michelle, age 48, and Jim Williams, age 50, were referred to a CCM therapist after they had filed a PINS (Person in Need of Supervision) report on their 16-year-old son, Christopher. Michelle made the initial phone call for an evaluation and therapy for Christopher, who had recently been expelled from school for inappropriate sexual behavior in the girls' locker room. The CCM therapist was a family therapist who asked to see Michelle and Jim first to gather information and begin creating a context for change. Christopher was referred to a trauma-informed attachment-focused individual therapist who became part of the CCM treatment team. In the initial session with Michelle and Jim, the CCM family therapist gathered information about the present situation and about the historical context of their family. Michele and Jim adopted Christopher as an infant following numerous miscarriages and failed fertility treatments. Christopher was born to a teenage mother in Texas who wanted her baby raised by a Christian. Four months after Christopher arrived, Michelle discovered she was pregnant and nine months later delivered Cynthia.

Christopher's childhood, according to both parents, was unremarkable. He was quiet and compliant. He did well in school and excelled at sports. He did not have much use for his sister but had a few good friends and was close to two male cousins on Jim's side. Things started to change during adolescence. The first indication that Christopher was troubled came when his parents discovered that Christopher was stealing from them. Michelle was stripping his bed and found one of Jim's watches underneath his mattress. When they confronted Christopher about it, he denied he had stolen it and his parents grounded him for six weeks, three for stealing and the other three for lying. He became belligerent and they stopped being able to get through to him. His temper became uncontrollable and the grounding meaningless. Recently, both parents had been concerned for their safety because Christopher had become violent. He pushed Jim during a fight and broke some of his sister's furniture. Six months prior to presentation for therapy, he was suspended from school for a day for sexting his girlfriend during math class. The precipitating incident for this therapy occurred the previous week when he went into the girls' locker room to have sex with the same girlfriend and they were both expelled. No one in the Williams family had ever been to psychotherapy before.

An essential element of Stage One work of creating refuge for the Williams family involved helping them see psychotherapy as a way to help their family be a safe place for everyone again. In the initial sessions, the CCM therapist met with the parents and the entire family together, as well as different subsystems. She was open and upfront about her agenda of helping everyone want to work on their relationships and work on them with her. She explained the collaborative nature of the CCM, explained how psychotherapy works, and encouraged everyone to ask her questions about the process. Everyone was feeling powerless, disconnected, and not valued and no one, except for Christopher, wanted to be in psychotherapy. Furthermore, the parents were not even sure they wanted Christopher to remain in their family. The CCM therapist acknowledged how unsafe they felt with Christopher in their home and facilitated a discussion of what they would need from each other to feel safe enough to remain as a family. Each of the Williams members agreed to feeling isolated and this was something they all wanted to change.

Before the CCM therapist and the Williams family were ready to move into Stage Two, a discussion about using mindfulness techniques to improve impulse control was held during a dialogue of vulnerabilities. The CCM therapist explained the amygdala's function when under stress, which helped explain Christopher's difficulty with his emotional regulation. Christopher described the intense frustration he experienced when he was embroiled in an argument with his parents and he felt as though he was going to explode but his parents forbade him from leaving the room. The family and the therapist discussed how their long-term goal was to create a stable context for change with the family so that they could work on communication dynamics, which would lead to less isolation. In the meantime, and as a short-term goal, they all agreed to make special efforts not to argue at home, to leave any intense discussions for the therapy office, and if they did find a conversation escalating that Christopher would be allowed to excuse himself and go into his bedroom to cool off.

When the family and CCM therapist were ready to challenge isolation in Stage Two, they engaged in difficult dialogues (Stone Fish & Harvey, 2005) about their relationships. Christopher had disclosed information to his individual therapist that was deemed important to share with his family and in Stage Two the parents declared that they were receptive to hearing and trying to accept whatever it was Christopher wanted to share. Christopher discussed finding his uncle (Jim's brother) hanging in their garage when Christopher was 12. It was a devastating situation for everyone and the family did the best they could to cope with it. However, no one ever asked Christopher about how he was processing the situation, having been the first on the scene. Christopher was able to share his experience in the family therapy sessions while his parents and sister listened, cried, and shared some of theirs as well. The watch that Michelle had found under Christopher's bed was his uncle's watch and his intention was not to steal from his parents but to have something close to him when he slept that reminded him of his uncle. Christopher told his parents that his individual therapist suggested that perhaps he was more sensitive about the loss because he was adopted. This was the first time the family openly acknowledged the adoption and this discussion broadened into conversations about grief, loss, and love.

Pause and Ponder: In Stage Two we are working with clients to expand their definition of refuge and expand the variables that provide a safe context for change. We explore ways to expand their "safety net," utilizing new resources and new relationships, and exploring new contexts that will continue to promote an engaged mindstate. We expand the modalities and put more emphasis on the challenges and the possibilities they have in the future. We suggest that you might ask yourself, do you have collaborative relationships with colleagues? Can you explore the possible solutions to problematic situations?

Challenging Vulnerabilities and the Function of the Symptoms

When clients are able to acknowledge that their symptoms serve a function that has been helpful but now causes more trouble than support, this signals they are ready for a Stage Two conversation. The key to success in challenging long-standing patterns is using resources in balance with vulnerabilities. The CCM therapist reminds clients about the cycle of change, reviewing the necessity of pausing or contracting and then entering into the vulnerability, pain, or traumatic experience in a dance that is balanced, as smooth as possible, and oscillating. Somatic experiencing-trained therapists refer to this process as pendulation (Levine & Kline, 2011). Clients have become acquainted with and then explored both their vulnerabilities and their resources during Stage One. In Stage Two, they expand the use and usefulness of their resources in order to evolve their response when vulnerable from a survival mindstate to an engaged mindstate, and improve their ability to make wise decisions when their system is stressed.

It is typically during Stage Two that clients explore the story of their traumatic experiences, also called their trauma narrative, in detail in individual, couple, family, and/or group therapy. We conceptualize the trauma narrative as a structured way to "tell the story" of their traumatic experiences in a way in which clients feel powerful, in control, and valued in the telling of the story. The story is told to an ethically attuned practitioner in a way that helps clients make meaning of the events that transpired. The details of the narrative are carefully explored and as the individual and/or family members are triggered by the story, the practitioner helps clients practice the skills they have learned in order to engage their whole brain so that they can respond to the story in an engaged rather than survival mindstate. The use of other trauma-informed models to help work through the narrative (e.g., EMDR, SET, imagery, IFS) can provide highly successful models for new responses to be actualized. The trauma narrative is told in a way that the story and the pacing are under the control of the participants.

Brian, a survivor of sexual abuse in the foster care system, developed panic attacks in his early thirties. He awoke in the middle of the night following an intense argument with his boyfriend Arthur, fearing he was having a heart attack. Arthur rushed him to the hospital where the panic attack was diagnosed and his heart was determined to be healthy. The argument was about commitment; Arthur wanted it and Brian was frightened. In Stage One, Brian learned about the survival mindstate and his cycle of interaction and began to understand how conversations about commitment and intimacy triggered his vulnerability. He had been practicing mindfulness techniques since college and expressed surprise and frustration at the hold his past continued to have on him. The panic attacks functioned to keep the focus off his fear of commitment but he was ready to challenge them and evolve. Brian's goals for Stage Two were to address the panic attacks and then participate in couples therapy with Arthur and work on their communication.

The CCM therapist who was working with Brian was also trained in SET (Levine, 2010) and in Stage Two worked with Brian on trauma processing of his foster care experience, especially the sexual abuse. Brian was able to release a great deal of the energy his body held from the immobility of his traumatic experiences through the pendulum of an alternating focus on his resources and his traumatic experiences. Somatically, he stored his trauma in his chest, which explained to Brian why he worried about his heart. At this time, Brian and Arthur began Stage One couples therapy, while Brian and his CCM therapist worked an additional six sessions on trauma processing. Arthur contracted with Brian and the CCM therapist to delay commitment conversations and sat in on two of Brian's individual somatic reprocessing sessions.

When the couple was ready to move into Stage Two with the goal of working toward communicating about difficult topics in a way that did not lead to heated conflict, the CCM therapist educated Brian and Arthur about some communication techniques. She said, "Let me explain it to you before we try it out. When one person talks, you will try to stay focused on one idea and one idea only. Then the person who is listening will repeat back that one idea and only that idea and the conversation will not move from that idea until the person who initiated the conversation believes that the other really and truly understood what was being said. The reason that we do this is so that we begin the process of listening in a way in which we can really be heard. Oftentimes we get so caught up in trying to be heard ourselves that we forget to listen and don't attend enough to what is being said. We will take turns doing this so each person has a turn to experience feeling understood and then we will talk about the process." Brian and Arthur worked diligently on changing the challenging patterns embedded within their interactional cycle that they no longer wanted to perpetuate.

Pause and Ponder: At times throughout clients' lives they have been vulnerable to becoming powerless, out of control, devalued, and disconnected in each context in which they live; social/political, family, and internal. Their symptoms have helped them regain and maintain power, control, value, and connection. In Stage Two we challenge them that they no longer need the symptoms and that they can be vulnerable without an instinctual reaction from a survival mindstate. We understand the power of awareness that in the sessions and outside the sessions we work with the clients to be aware that they may be vulnerable to entering their trauma/survival cycles and to be able to recognize when they are in a survival cycle.

Expanding Resources

In Stage One we assess individual, relational, and sociopolitical resources and in Stage Two we begin the process of expanding them. Clients have learned about how avoidance has contributed to survival mindstates and are challenged in this stage of therapy to engage in parts of themselves and their contexts where they have been devalued, powerless, and felt out of control. The intent behind expanding resources is to help clients recognize that they have choices. For example, it may be that a client may never be an artist but challenging herself to color her feelings or experiences expands her mind and creates opportunities. Furthermore, an introvert may never become an extrovert, but avoiding relationships because it is more comfortable to find solace in one's own ideas may result in a lack of social support for being in an engaged mindstate. In Stage One, we mapped available resources and addressed goals and in Stage Two, we challenge clients to expand their resources.

There are multiple resources within ourselves, our relationships, and our communities that are untapped and useful in Stage Two work on challenging patterns and expanding alternatives. Individually, we have affective, cognitive, and behavioral resources that are not engaged. Mindfulness techniques, meditation rituals, yoga, exercise, finding and enjoying beauty, allowing oneself 15 seconds more pleasure each day, are all resources most of us can access. Relational resources include making efforts to rejuvenate our relationships, reconnecting with family and friends with whom we have lost contact and who are a source of comfort, and in general committing to spending more time with those we enjoy. We can also find resources in relationships we previously avoided because they were unmanageable in our survival mindstates. Our communities have limitless possibilities. AA groups, religious gatherings, libraries, nature preserves, a softball league, even going inpatient for a stint of intensive psychotherapeutic opportunity are all resources that are helpful in Stage Two work.

When Wendy, age 42, was interviewed at treatment termination, she remembered when her CCM therapist Jeannie gently seeded the idea that at some point it would be very helpful to have Wendy and her mother in the same room for a few Stage Two therapy sessions. Wendy said, "I remember Jeannie asking me about my relationship with my mother at the beginning of therapy and thinking to myself, 'What does this have to do with what is happening now?', only to realize much later in the therapy process that my relationship with my mother was pretty central to my feeling better. "

Wendy had survived years of neglect and the witnessing of physical and sexual abuse between her mother and multiple men by avoiding access to any feeling or sensation and by avoiding her mother. She self-mutilated in high school and had been hospitalized for an eating disorder as a young adult and had gone through multiple therapists who she charmed into believing she was being helped. When the pediatrician of her 13-year-old daughter shared concerns that the daughter was developing an eating disorder and was eying razor blades in her father's medicine cabinet, Wendy called a CCM therapist for an appointment. In Stage One, the family was seen in therapy and multiple goals were established for each member of the family including Wendy. Wendy recognized her survival mindstate, which she believed she lived in 90 percent of the time, and agreed to work on becoming more engaged with her full self in Stage Two. She also agreed to have a few sessions of family therapy with her mother.

As Wendy became more aware of how avoiding discomfort and keeping her mother at arm's length were taking a great toll on her own life and on her relationship with her children, she came to the conclusion that she needed to work on expanding her resources by engaging her mother. She found the courage to ask her mother into a therapy session and they were seen together three times. Jeannie coached Wendy on how best to invite her mother to join her in therapy. Rather than confronting her mother with anger, disappointment, and resentment, Wendy made it clear that she was attempting to elicit her mother's helpfulness. Difficult dialogues were facilitated in therapy and Wendy was able to view her mother as the loving but limited woman she actually was. Wendy was able to rationally identify the support and guidance she had failed to receive from her mother during very important developmental milestones. Wendy shared certain aspects of these sessions in therapy with her own daughter, acknowledging what she had failed to give her daughter and committing to be different. The unintended consequence of expanding this resource was that Wendy's children developed loving relationships with their grandmother who had been kept away by the rift between Wendy and her mother. This relationship became a very important resource to Wendy's daughter, who adored her grandmother.

For an audio file that explains Build a Better Day, please refer to the book's eResources site: www.routledgementalhealth.com/9780415510219.

Pause and Ponder: Expanding resources in Stage Two is simply that. We think about ways we can help our clients use their current resources and challenge them to utilize them to a greater extent. We have our clients move out of their comfort zone to build a better day.

Challenging and Expanding Availability

Practitioners seem to struggle with finding methods that are supportive and validating but that also challenge limits in a client's emotional and cognitive availability. We often hear professional helpers of all types, including psychotherapists, teachers, counselors, social workers, child care staff, nursing staff, medical staff, etc. speaking of "breaking down denial." The energy and the meaning implicit in the words "breaking down" are threatening and thus run a very large possibility of triggering a client's survival mindstate.

Clients' unavailability often triggers the therapist's reactive survival state. As helpers we may feel that our value is dependent on how quickly and easily clients change and respond to us. It is as if our worth is equal to the clients' speed and process of change. In fact, one of the major ingredients consistently correlated with therapeutic progress is the connection and value that both clients and practitioners experience. If our clients are struggling and unaware of the facts of their narrative, the impact of the narrative on self and others, and do not acknowledge their own and others' responsibilities in their interactional cycles of survival, it not only is difficult to change, it often creates feelings of inadequacy for the practitioner. Challenging a client's availability, whether to relationships or to information, is best accomplished not with a "push through" or "break down" process, but rather with emotional holding, understanding of the client's survival mindstate, and empathy for their interactional cycles of survival and their attempts to feel powerful, in control, and valued.

Recognition that none of us exist in a fully engaged, completely mindful, aware, and present state of being assists us in patiently expecting that clients cycle in and out of their ability to be available. Not being available has protective elements for the client, as we learned in Chapter 5, and so it is necessary to be strategic about how we work *with* the clients to help them be more available. We must learn to work with whatever resources the clients have available and bring to therapy. We continue to create a context where they choose to be more and more present and to bring more and more to the treatment process.

For an audio file that explains a Guided Imagery for Professionals for Working with Denial and Availability, please refer to the book's website: www.routledgementalhealth.com/books/details/9780415510219/

Pause and Ponder: Our clients need to be available to themselves cognitively, in body, heart, and soul, in order to change. We need our clients available to us so that we can facilitate change. We understandably desire that our clients change in order to feel "a job well done," so we have a tendency to push clients to be available or to explore certain matters before they are ready. We must be accepting and at the same time gently challenging of the pace which works best for each client. We have often said, "Change is like good comedy: timing is everything."

Accomplishing Goals

In Stage Two, clients are working on accomplishing the goals they established in Stage One. The goals center around idiosyncratic issues, engaged mindstates, harnessing the natural cycle of change, and mindfulness-based practice. Idiosyncratic issues with clients with complex trauma, as stated before, are usually based in survival mindstate symptoms that they have used in the past to help them feel more powerful, in control, or valued. Part of goal setting in Stage One is the exploration of how vulnerabilities lead to symptoms and what the expected outcomes are if clients harness the natural cycle of change and symptoms dissipate. They have been introduced to how survival mindstates and engaged mindstates differ and about how discomfort is sometimes a necessary step in the change process.

Clients usually are working on multiple goals so that it is natural to be in Stage One addressing one goal and in Stage Two working on another. Sometimes Stage Two work stimulates the recognition of other goals and different forms of treatment are discussed and implemented. In the CCM, all new forms of treatment should follow the stage model, so creating a context for change occurs before challenging patterns, which is all followed and solidified with a consolidation phase. When goals are accomplished in Stage Two, they are consolidated in Stage Three.

Liz, age 31, and Eddie, age 30, accomplished an important goal they had set for themselves in Stage One of treatment. They had been married for five years and one important goal for Stage Two was to improve their sex life. Liz was a survivor of repeated childhood sexual abuse and Eddie had two alcoholic parents and thought of himself as the hero child. He had been patient with Liz for the first four years of their marriage about their impaired sexual life because he knew about her history of sexual trauma and believed his patient and loving ways could fix her. When she continued to inhibit sexuality in their relationship, Eddie had an affair with a co-worker. In Stage One, he terminated the affair and re-committed to the relationship and Liz committed to improving the sexual relationship with Eddie. They were both working in individual therapy with different therapists collaborating in working the CCM. Liz's therapist was EMDR-trained and Eddie's therapist specialized in families with addictions.

When Liz and Eddie had successfully completed the entirety of Stage One, the CCM couple therapist believed that they were ready to move to Stage Two. The therapist reviewed their resources and vulnerabilities and introduced Sensate Focus (Masters & Johnson, 1970) exercises in the following way:

> I am going to give you an exercise called Sensate Focus and I am going to explain fully why I am giving it to you and why I think it is so important for both of you. The relational dynamic we explored in Stage One that you both acknowledged you wanted to change was that you guys would be getting along, feeling loving and connected, then somehow one of you would smell sex in the air. Then the cycle began, I'll start with you Eddie, but we all know your cycle is a circle with no punctuation. Eddie, you felt close to Liz and wanted to pursue her sexually. This desire, that you believed only Liz could help you with, made you feel powerless, devalued, and out of control, and in your survival mind, you'd pick a fight with Liz. None of this you shared with Liz and you acknowledged that this was to punish her for rejecting you and to punish yourself for not being able to do what you were put on this planet to do, which was to cure your loved ones. Liz, Eddie's hostility triggered your

survival mindstate and you would freeze and detach in a panic, feeling damaged and fearful of Eddie's hostility and how it reminded you of your stepdad and the sexual abuse. You merged the past and present and projected the helplessness you felt in the past with a feeling of helplessness in the present and retreated from Eddie. None of this you shared with Eddie and you acknowledged that this was to punish Eddie for pursuing you and to punish yourself by not allowing you to actually experience the sexual pleasure that you used to feel with Eddie. And on and on until you retreated to your corners for weeks or months until you cooled off and then felt intimate and threatened and the interactional cycle of survival began again.

In survival minds you guys got nowhere and you both have acknowledged that. You are working towards engaged mindstates where you are internally and interpersonally present. And you are both willing to sit in discomfort a little bit longer than before, pausing and then expanding to the challenge of giving and receiving pleasure. So, here is what I want you to do: I want you each to pick a time this week and we will work out the details in here, time, place, how long, what is going to get in your way of doing it, etc., but I am going to ask each of you to pick a day and time that is totally and completely for you and your pleasure.

This first session is not sexual, so no touching any sexual body parts. So the person receiving pleasure only and completely thinks about what gives you pleasure and asks for it and lovingly receives it. Do you see why this is important? I want each of you to have a time this week where you feel valued, in control, and powerful.

Liz and Eddie were able to accomplish their goal of improving their sex life. Their goal was embedded in changing their interactional cycle of survival through encouraging engaged mindstates when they were experiencing unmanageable stress. While the nature of their specific survival mindstates and their interactional cycle of survival are idiosyncratic, the process of them achieving their goals has much in common with many clients who engage in treatment with CCM practitioners. The natural cycle of change helps clients, once they are embedded in therapeutic relationships in which they experience safety, to move from survival mindstates to engaged mindstates and achieve their goals.

Sidney was referred from Domestic Court for physical violence toward his spouse, Harriet. In Stage One his cycles were assessed and it became clear what triggered his violent behaviors and the function of these behaviors. A no-violence contract was signed, his wife began individual therapy, and both of them began group therapy separately, one for perpetrators and the other for victims of partner violence. They were each referred to internal family systems (IFS) therapists for the individual work (Goulding & Schwartz, 1995; Schwartz, 1997). We have found IFS to be a very effective model for the integration of mind, body, and cognition when working individually with clients. Sidney and Harriet through their IFS work identified their different parts that would be triggered and then built upon the leadership of the self to help organize and create new patterns, thoughts, feelings, and behaviors. They then brought their knowledge and skills from their individual work into their couples therapy that began in Stage Two.

> *Pause and Ponder: In the course of treatment, a great many goals will be created, discussed, and achieved. Goals are a significant element of the foundation in which the rebuilding occurs. The goals will keep us on task, will direct the type of intervention, will determine the pace of the treatment plan, and will signal the movement into the next stage. Being aware of the treatment goals can be compared to continually looking at the blueprint to assure that we are not forgetting any of the necessary processes or changing the plan while creating change.*

Ongoing Acknowledgment

In Stage Two clients are working hard to tolerate discomfort and achieve their goals, and are learning a great deal about themselves and the people with whom they are in a relationship. Ongoing acknowledgment is the part of Stage Two where clients hold themselves accountable internally and interpersonally. This process typically generates considerable discomfort, which clients have learned is part of an engaged mindstate. When we acknowledge not only how we have been victimized but also how we have hurt others and we accept responsibility for our roles in interactional cycles of survival, it is intensely painful and deeply cleansing. Ongoing acknowledgment epitomizes the validity of the statement "the truth will set you free."

When we discuss ongoing acknowledgment with clients, we talk about the difference between shame and guilt. We think of shame as a feeling that that does not help us grow and develop. Shame is typically instilled by others who blame or interpret our actions based on something other than our own behavior. So, for example, if I am physically abused as a child, as an adult, I might have a great deal of shame about being a victim of such abuse. I may wonder if I really tried hard enough to stop it, or what I did to deserve it, or just spend a great deal of mental energy with self-loathing thoughts because of the shame of the act itself. Shame often muzzles us and encourages being stuck in survival mindstates, preventing us from acknowledging the truth about our lives and how painful some experiences have been and continue to be in our lives.

Guilt, on the other hand, is something we feel when we have behaved against our own integrity. So, for example, if I physically abused a child, guilt can actually be a cleansing experience which leads me to acknowledge wrongdoing and attempt to make amends. While experiencing guilt is painful, if acknowledged, it can lead to change and growth and a fuller more engaged self. If I can acknowledge that I hurt another, I can choose not to do it again. If I cannot tolerate the discomfort of such acknowledgment, I am doomed to recreate interactional cycles of survival that keep me stuck and unevolved. Ongoing acknowledgment is a Stage Two task because discomfort is difficult. Clients have developed tools to tolerate the discomfort in Stage One and they are enveloped in therapeutic relationships, which help cushion the pain.

Jim and Cindy, both 38 years old, initiated couple therapy with a CCM therapist after Cindy threatened to seek a divorce if their relationship did not improve. In Stage One, they agreed to work on a number of couple dynamics, including their contentious relationship with Jim's parents. Jim was devoted to his parents who lived just a few blocks away and Cindy disliked both of them and especially Jim's relationship with them. In the course of Stage One Cindy said, "I know Jim feels really bad for his parents because Jamie (Jim's only sister) hasn't spoken to them in five years, so he feels like he is the only one they have. Jamie confronted Jim's dad for sexually abusing her when she was a teenager and his dad denied all charges and Jim's mom got mad at Jamie for causing Jim's dad to have heart problems. Jim, being Jim, didn't take anyone's side but this just contributes to how dead he is. He is a walking zombie and I blame his parents." Jim felt caught between a rock and a hard place. He wanted to be a good son and a good husband, but he had no idea how to please both his parents and his wife.

Ongoing acknowledgment for Jim at this point entailed working on the ways in which his childhood and adolescence left him wounded. He was sorely neglected as a child and he witnessed multiple disturbing incidents of abuse between his father and mother and his father and sister. He began, in Stage Two, to acknowledge that his past had an impact on how his behavior in the marriage with Cindy. He entered into the marriage in survival mindstate, a man believing that emotion equaled weakness and certain that he was a logical, controlled person. Once he was able to acknowledge that experiencing affect was an important part of using his whole mind, the sadness he felt when thinking about his childhood was easier for him to tolerate. Furthermore, he became more compassionate with Cindy when she needed him to be, which made it easier for her to be understanding of his need to be a good son. We have found that when clients acknowledge their own vulnerability, helplessness, and powerlessness, it is easier for them to comfort others, who invariably wish to reciprocate. Jim's ongoing acknowledgment included awareness of how he had been hurt as a child. Healing also occurs when clients acknowledge how they have been hurtful to others.

Jody, age 42, presented to a CCM therapist, following a recent discharge from an inpatient psychiatric facility after attempting suicide by overdosing on prescribed sedatives. Stage One was a long slow process of trust and skill-building in individual, couple, and family therapy. Jody was taking antidepressant medication, attending couples therapy, participating in a DBT group, and practicing mindfulness-based yoga. One of the goals set for Stage Two was to work on improving communication between Jody and her two daughters, Haley, age 12, and Hannah, age 10. Both daughters had a great deal that they wanted to say to their mother but feared she was too fragile to tolerate their anger and disappointment. In Stage One therapy, the girls shared many incidents of neglect and severe punishment that occurred in their home before their mother was hospitalized. They were locked in their bedrooms many afternoons after school when their mother complained of a headache. When their father arrived home from work, Jody blamed the girls for things they knew their mother had done. Most hurtful, however, was that they both believed that their mother's suicidal attempt and ideas sprang from her belief that they were too overwhelming for her to handle. They had chosen not to disclose the truth about their mother's behavior to their father, as both girls felt he was too preoccupied with work and his concerns about Jody to be very interested or useful to them.

A family session was arranged to help the girls talk with their mother about their experiences. When the CCM therapist asked Jody and the girls if they were open and ready to begin, all agreed they were ready. With fits and starts, Haley was finally able to talk with her mother about her experiences while Hannah held her sister's hand and cried. The CCM therapist sat close to both Haley and Jody, observing their verbal and nonverbal behavior and prompting them to help them return again and again to an engaged mindstate while conversing in this difficult dialogue. Jim, Jody's husband and the girls' father, sat next to Jody and periodically touched her back.

Haley: The thing of it is mom, when Hannah and I got off the bus, we never knew who was going to be home, you or crazy you.

Jody: I tried to warn you.

Haley: I know but . . .

CCM therapist: Haley, were you done explaining what it was like getting off the bus? (Haley shakes her head) I didn't think so. Jody, can you practice your breathing and continue to pay attention or do you need to take a break?

Jody: Nice catch doc. I am taking a breath. OK, sweetheart, please continue. I am able to hear you.

Haley: So we tried really hard (she starts to cry) to be good girls. We really did mom. We didn't complain a lot and we kept a lot of our own problems from you because we knew you were stressed. We kept the dog quiet when you had a headache and when Hannah was sick, I got the garbage can for her, remember? And we both do really well in school and we try really really hard to be good. All we ever do is try. And then you go and take all those pills anyway. It's like nothing we ever did was good enough. You tried to kill yourself mom and we couldn't stop you. No matter what we did, we couldn't stop you. We tried, we really really tried. How do you think that made us feel? (Everyone is crying now and there is a long pause.)

CCM therapist: Great job girls. Haley that was incredibly brave of you and Hannah, you are such a good sister, holding Haley's hand. And Jody, you were able to listen, and stay fully engaged and be there for the girls so they could share their hearts. Great job.

Jody (walks over to the couch that Haley and Hannah were sharing and takes their hands into her own): Girls, you are my everything. I tried to kill myself thinking at the time you all would be better off without me. I was in so much pain and I was delusional. I am so sorry that I put you in this situation. You both tried really hard, you are good girls. There was nothing you could have done differently that would have made a difference. You do not deserve this. This is my fault. I was in too much pain to see the way I was hurting you both. I wasn't being a very good mother.

Hannah: Mom, yes you were, don't say that. We love you.

CCM therapist: Hannah, your mother can acknowledge her behavior and soothe herself. That is not your responsibility. She is the mother and you are the daughter. She is strong enough to admit that she hurt you. What a gift.

At this point in the conversation, Jody, Haley, and Hannah all started to giggle and the therapist smiled and asked what was funny. Jim explained that when the girls were little and toilet training, someone used the phrase, "what a gift" when one of them made a bowel movement. Now the phrase was code for needing to use the restroom. While Jim was explaining this light-hearted piece of family history, Jody sat between her daughters and hugged them. They returned her hugs with warmth. Jody said, "I am so happy that you told me what you were thinking. I hope this is the beginning of you letting me know more about how these past few years have been for you. And the doctor is right. I am the mother. I am learning to soothe myself and I will try really hard to keep acknowledging all the ways I hurt you. And then we can get back on track. Okay?"

Ongoing acknowledgment, like all the parts of Stage Two, generates fresh behavioral sequences that evolve into healthy new cycles of interaction that perpetuate engaged mindstates. When we have options for how to respond to stressful situations, we feel a greater sense of power and control, and value ourselves more. When Jody, for example, experienced herself as someone who could be helpful to her daughters by acknowledging ways in which she had unintentionally hurt them, she felt, for the first time in a very long time, that she was being a good mother. In the consolidation phase at the end of the family session, they discussed ways to capitalize outside of therapy on what they were able to accomplish in the office. The girls committed to sharing with their mother a little more about their problems at school and with friends and Jody committed to practice her self-soothing techniques in the face of discomfort.

When we acknowledge what we did and what we can do differently, our daily life changes. We recognize that Stage Two is drawing to consolidation and we are moving together to Stage Three of treatment when the acknowledgment expands. Stage Two is the ongoing practice and repetition to make neurological, cognitive, and behavioral changes. As it is clear in the title of Stage Two, the work is about a repetitive challenging of patterns and a repetitive practicing of growth cycles. When our clients come to session reporting what went well during the week and what were their struggles, when they report how they handled their struggles rather than "saving to talk about it in session," and when they plan how they will handle it differently next time, when they report what they learned from the struggles during the week, when all of this is acknowledged we are clear it is time to move to Stage Three.

> *Pause and Ponder: All acknowledgments, no matter if within a session, within a stage, or within therapy as a whole, are indications that expansion is about to take place, or is taking place, or has taken place. Whether it is the end of a contraction in a session, where the client pauses, breathes, and then returns to the present, or an acknowledgment of a behavior that must change, or an acknowledgment of less dependence on the therapist, it is expansion and an indication that what will come next is recognition and consolidation.*

References

Barrett, M. J. (2003). Constructing the third reality: How to move from conflict to coexistence. *Psychotherapy Networker, 27* (4).

Goulding, R., & Schwartz, R. C. (1995). *The mosaic mind: Empowering the tormented selves of child abuse survivors.* New York: W. W. Norton & Co.

Levine, P. A. (2010). *In an unspoken voice: How the body releases trauma and restores goodness.* Berkeley, CA: North Atlantic Books.

Levine, P. A., & Kline, M. (2011). Use of somatic experiencing principles as a PTSD prevention tool for children and teens during the acute stress phase following an overwhelming event. In Ardino, V. (Ed.) *Post-traumatic syndromes in childhood and adolescence: A handbook of research and practice* (pp. 275–295). New York: Wiley.

Masters, W. H., & Johnson, V. E. (1970). *Human sexual inadequacy.* New York: Bantam Books.

Schwartz, R. C. (1997). *Internal family systems therapy.* New York: Guilford Press.

Stone Fish, L., & Harvey, R. (2005). *Nurturing queer youth: Family therapy transformed.* New York: W.W. Norton & Co.

seven
Stage Three
Consolidation

Coming together is a beginning, staying together is progress, and working together is success.

Henry Ford

The last stage of the CCM is consolidation. In this final phase of the model, which means the final phase of the moment, of the experience in the session, the session, the stage of treatment, or the treatment itself, therapists work with clients to cement the change or the experience that just happened and to move on to the next. Consolidation is really the integration of new ways of being. The clients integrate what they learn into what they will continue to be. The act of consolidating is the union or uniting of systems, of variables, of experiences. In our model it means connecting the moments, the experience, the interventions, and the changes that have taken place in the present, over the course of the session, over the course of the stage of treatment, and over the therapy as a whole. As is certainly clear by now, the cycle of change happens multiple times within a session. Beginning with a pause through breath, mindfulness, understanding, awareness, then moving into exploring possible responses, and then choosing a response, to finally a momentary exhale where we assess what just happened: What am I thinking? How do I feel? If it was an interactional experience, what is the other person thinking and how does the other feel? Was what just happened effective? Do I want to repeat it? Can I move on? Consolidation is the time in space in which integration occurs.

Consolidation, whether within a session or as a review of the entire course of treatment, occurs when practitioners reinforce clients' resources and abilities, retrospectively highlight changes, and explore future possibilities. In consolidation, the interaction between the client and practitioner is different, almost as if the practitioner is a consultant on the clients' project. The interactions might be phrased as questions such as: "What do you see different in your response? When you responded rather than reacted, how were you able to do that and how have you capitalized on it this week?" The answers during a consolidation moment, session, or therapy are focused on summarizing what has occurred and the process underlying the clients' choice of direction. As in the other CCM stages, consolidation provides an opportunity for practitioners to be creative and to design interventions according to their own theoretical model, their own style, and their own level of practice.

Stage Three Core Concepts Chart

Nurturing Environments

Engaging Vulnerabilities

Integrating Resources

Choosing Engaged Mind

Engaged Acknowledgment

Incorporating Success

Nurturing Environments

At the end of a session when practitioners tell clients that they saw improvement in their clients' lives, the practitioner is enhancing the nurturing environment and consolidating treatment. At the end of treatment when clients talk of the ways they have integrated what they learned into their lives, they are expressing how their lives have been nurtured through treatment and they are consolidating treatment. When clients terminate treatment, they have evolved in such a way that the therapeutic environment that was previously external in the form of treatment providers and experiences is now internalized. One CCM client, in his exit interview, explained it this way: "I realized I didn't need to keep coming to therapy when the model was tattooed like a third eye on my forehead."

Consolidation for the end of a session occurs when clients are asked how they are feeling at this moment, whether they are ready to end, and if they are in the emotional space to leave the room. Are they clear what their homework is and how they will accomplish it? Are they looking forward to practicing their skills? Did the session give them hope? What are the learning points, the take-aways from today's session? The consolidation for treatment as a whole mirrors the individual session consolidation.

In another exit interview a client talked about the great extent that the CCM informed her parenting. She said, "I grew up in a really chaotic family. I didn't understand it then, but I understand now that it was partially because of my mom's drug addiction and my dad's gambling problems. I knew there was something wrong, but I didn't really understand how the chaos affected me until I was in therapy. I had known about how the abuse ruined a lot of my intimate relationships, but I hadn't realized how much of an impact the chaos had until I saw something different in therapy. The most important thing I learned in therapy was about how to monitor my own life so I didn't recreate the chaos. So now with my kids, I am predictable and I consolidate. When I get home from work I find out about their days. I ask them what they learned in school and they have to tell me something. At bedtime, every night, I spend at least ten minutes with each kid and we go over what happened during the day and sometimes what they want to get done the next day. It's what I was missing growing up and I don't think I would have known to do it if I didn't have the experience of therapy." This is a specific example of how the CCM experience was internalized so that learning was generalized and thereby helped to create order and structure in a client's life.

Another client shared how they are aware all day long, every day, how so many experiences are truly cycles of change: phone calls, getting dressed, the sleep cycle, making a bed, the rising and setting of the sun and moon. Everything seems to be designed around the same blueprint of growth and change.

Engaging Vulnerabilities

Life is difficult and even when treatment is successful, life will continue to be challenging. When we struggle, we experience discomfort and sometimes other more intense and negative sensations. Our survival mindstate will be triggered regularly, we will still have rage, sadness, and relational difficulties. In consolidation we experience the discomfort amid the totality of our reactions and we access our new resources to support an engaged mindstate through the difficult experience. In the final stage of treatment clients often talk about ways they have coped with stressful life events in new ways. Rather than reacting from a survival mindstate, clients are able to acknowledge the stress, experience their vulnerability in the specific circumstance, "feel the feelings," and also engage in mindful thinking about response options.

Sharon, age 40, was sexually abused by her stepfather from the ages of 9 to 15. She did not disclose to her mother until she discovered she was pregnant. Her mother called the police, shamed Sharon, helped arrange an abortion, and divorced her stepfather. He was incarcerated and when he was released from prison nine years later, her mother remarried him. By then, Sharon had moved across the country and had limited contact with anyone in her family. She had made amends with her mother over the phone, but had not seen her stepfather since their remarriage. She had spent many years in CCM therapy, went to AA meetings twice a week, and taught mindfulness-based yoga in addition to her full time job as a nursing home health care worker. She was in a loving and supportive relationship with a girlfriend and was helping raise her girlfriend's daughter who adored her. She was in the process of terminating therapy, seeing her therapist every other week and discussing her progress, when she received a call from her stepfather informing her that her mother had died.

Sharon asked her therapist if she could have appointments on two consecutive days so that she could process this news and make a decision about what would be in her best interest to do about the funeral. When she arrived for the first of these two appointments, it was clear to her that she was feeling vulnerable and she knew what she needed to do to take care of herself. Sharon wanted to use the therapy sessions as a safe haven to experience her grief, sadness, and relief, and to review her decisions about the funeral. She and her girlfriend had spent a great deal of time discussing whether or not Sharon would attend the funeral and whether, if Sharon attended, the girlfriend should accompany her. They ultimately decided together that it would be best if Sharon went alone and stay with a cousin who had always been loving and supportive. Sharon acknowledged feeling supported by her girlfriend in a way she had never felt before. Sharon cried about her mother and was tremendously grateful for the life she was living and how she was handling this stressful situation. Sharon was able to engage her vulnerability because she felt powerful, in control, and valuable.

Integrating Resources

In Stage Three, clients are able to integrate the resources that are available to them in times of calm and in times of discomfort. When clients have generalized their new ways of behaving in an engaged mindstate and report in session about the generalization of skills as opposed to using therapy to make new changes, it is time for practitioners and clients to discuss reducing the frequency of sessions. For some clients a discussion of reducing therapy sessions elicits new challenges and sometimes clients experience gratitude and relief, since the therapist's raising this topic is another tangible sign of their progress. For others, it is a combination of both.

Consolidating gains made in therapy by integrating resources is often an idiosyncratic and creative process for clients and their practitioners. Some clients have lifelong relationships with their practitioners. Part of integrating resources is knowing that the treatment team is omnipresent. Clients may never recontact the team and yet are comforted by the knowledge that they are available. For others, graduation from treatment is an integration of resources because it implies the ability to function independently.

Both authors have families with whom we have been in a treatment relationship for over two decades. One such family began as a mandated case of child abuse. At the beginning of treatment, one of the family members was a 9-year-old girl. At the time of writing this book, she is a 29-year-old mother of a 3-year-old. Over the course of these 20 years, she has been in and out of the relationship with her treatment team. Once she scheduled an appointment just so that she could introduce her boyfriend to the therapist. Sometimes she arrives for a checkup, sometimes she wishes to process a particularly challenging situation, and sometimes she feels the need to engage in conversation with someone who knows her, and values her. Part of consolidation for this client is integrating the resource of the importance of this therapeutic space in her life.

Some clients consolidate external support into internal resources and are grateful to leave this chapter of their lives behind. For example, Chris, 32, was raised in a variety of foster homes and had multiple caseworkers, social workers, and probation officers through his teen and early adult years. As a young adult, he became involved with a CCM-trained school social worker at a local community college where he had enrolled in a tech class. With the help of a faculty mentor and working the CCM with his social worker, he graduated from college and was hired by a local engineering firm. Consolidation for Chris involved believing he could actually control his own fate. Once he learned that he had agency and that he could choose to be involved with social service agencies as opposed to being dependent on them, he was ready to terminate. He had the tools he needed to manage his life, a job he enjoyed, and a small and supportive friendship network. At one point, at the end of treatment, he said, "I only regret that my mother never learned how to manage her abuse. If she could have learned some of the skills I did, she, me, and my brother would have been a lot better off. But, then again, I wouldn't be the guy I am today, and I'm comfortable with him, so I guess it all worked out in the end."

Choosing Engaged Mind

Consolidation entails realizing that you have a variety of choices when under stress and that one of those choices is to pause, ponder, and evolve into action that leads to engaged mindstates. Clients notice that they are more engaged and that they and their family members are more available. When we see this happen in therapy, we acknowledge it in the consolidation part of the session. In the final stage of the CCM, we reinforce these choices. For example, a CCM therapist was seeing a family where Lou, the father, had physically abused his wife as well as his daughter. He had a volatile temper. In a family session, during Stage Two, Lou clearly went into a survival mindstate after his teenage daughter exploded at him, saying, "You are such a loser, I don't think I can stand living with you and mom another second. You make no sense, and I can't stand the sight of you." Lou reacted. He jumped out of his chair and walked toward his daughter. The therapist also stood and calmly, with the most soothing voice she could muster, said, "Lou, I need a drink of water. Come with me and let's get both of us a drink."

This intervention was an attempt to help Lou pause and engage his full brain. Changing location, removing him from his trigger, drinking a refreshing glass of water, verbally interacting with someone who valued him, all of this and more, began his change cycle. Outside of the room, at the water cooler, because he was in Stage Two of therapy, he was able to challenge his own patterns. He said, "I know

I just flashed into my survival mind, I did want to hit her. I don't think I would have hit her—probably she or her mother would have stopped me, or I would have stopped myself. But I am really glad you were here to show me a different way to interrupt that cycle." The therapist said, "I am glad I got to see it in action, and I am impressed with how easily you interrupted the cycle with just a bit of my coaching. These are all really great things, great progress. In your individual session we can talk more about how you can pause the trauma cycle, recognize what is happening in your body, and make engaged choices. Now, I would like to go back and try to finish this conversation differently with your daughter, using the communication skills that you both know. Do your feel like you are ready to go back in, stay in engaged mind, and try to talk with your daughter?"

Lou said he was ready. The therapist asked if there was something she could do to help him in the moment jump into a new pathway. Lou asked that she remind him to breathe. She agreed. The therapist said, "Okay, let's go back in, and when we get into the room, I am going to check in with your wife and daughter, and see where they are and if they are ready to re-engage in conversation so we can all do it differently." The conversation that ensued was calm and directed and actually led to problem-solving around the differing needs of each family member. At the end of the session, the therapist used the conversation at the water cooler as an example of consolidation. She said, "Lou, you chose an engaged mind. You experienced threat and you chose to go with me and get refreshed. You were so available to yourself and to me in the moment. You knew what you needed from me to help you stay engaged and then you stayed connected and engaged throughout the rest of the session. You consolidated the gains we had been talking about and it created a context for the conversation that ensued."

In the final stage of treatment we reinforce the growth that has occurred in developing engaged mindstates, highlight the changes we have witnessed, and plan for the future. Therapists and clients discuss future crises that are naturally stressful but don't have to be traumatic, and how clients can consciously plan to use the therapy skills they have integrated with the next stressful event. One of the recurring themes articulated in consolidation is that when clients communicate in engaged mindstates, using their full brains and knowing how to calm themselves down when they feel threatened, they are more likely to feel powerful, in control, and valued. They begin to recognize that the skills they have learned in therapy transfer into relationships with themselves and others that reinforce their engaged mindstates.

Engaged Acknowledgment

When clients with a history of complex trauma act from an engaged mindstate, they acknowledge that they have had traumatic experiences that impacted them. These experiences were traumatic and the environments they were in often re-traumatized them. They were exposed to experiences that overwhelmed them and they were not held, or seen, or soothed. They did not learn, then, how to hold, see, or soothe themselves or others. Clients with a history of complex trauma who change and grow in therapy learn how to manage stressful situations so that they are not overwhelming. They learn to hold, see, and soothe themselves and others, and they learn to discern stress and discomfort from danger. They may have first responses that are based in reactivity from their histories and they learn to breathe and engage the full brain before they respond.

Joanne was in Stage Three of her treatment and was acknowledging the work that still needed to be done as she continued to work toward responding from an engaged mindstate. She told a story about rushing. She said, "When I am not anxiously running around like a chicken with her head cut off, I can respond well to any situation that might be stressful. When I am distressed, my mind plays tricks on me. So I was rushing to pick up one of my kids the other day and I saw a flying monkey in the trees. I mean, the monkey was really there. Now, obviously, there was no monkey but it freaked me out. I went right to survival mind and knew this was it, I was going psychotic. But right away I used what I learned from mindfulness training. I took a few deep breaths and I told myself that this kind of stuff must happen all the time to Steven King and plenty of science fiction writers. I am not crazy, I am creative. And, I am in a rush which makes me anxious which makes my mind play tricks on me. I reminded myself I had plenty of time to pick Chris up and, if I was late, it would not be the end of the world and I could apologize to Chris and he would understand. It felt great. I was really proud of myself."

Ongoing acknowledgment includes appreciation for the journey of change, how far we have come, and how others have helped. A CCM therapist saw a client in a local grocery store who she had seen in therapy almost ten years ago. The client did not acknowledge the therapist, but they made eye contact. A week later, the therapist received a letter from the client. In the letter, the client wrote that seeing the therapist at the grocery store reminded him that he had never fully acknowledged how helpful the therapist was to his life and relationships. He wrote that the therapist had worked with his partner and him during the most difficult time in their lives. He wrote: "You helped us acknowledge the hurt we had caused each other and the hurt that had been done to us. I hope we also took the time to acknowledge how helpful you were and continue to be in our lives. Periodically we bring you up in conversation when life gets tough. We think about coming in to see you and sometimes we think about some of the funny things you said or the look on your face when we were irreverent. You made a difference in our and our children's and their children's lives. Thank you."

Incorporating Success

The natural cycle of change never ends and working from an engaged mindstate requires constant practice. Part of the final phase of therapy is working with clients on how they are going to incorporate the successes they have achieved into the rest of their life cycle development and how they are going to continue to practice engaging their full brain when challenges await. One of the wonderful things about having a successful experience in reaching a goal is that the experience of success is something you have under your belt. Almost everything we do for the first time is easier the second time.

Both clients and practitioners have discussed incorporating the successes they have achieved with the model. Many CCM therapists have proudly discussed how the model has helped them feel as though their work with clients with complex trauma is enhanced. Practitioners discuss how helpful knowledge of the brain has been to their work and how the evolving cycle of change is useful. They also discuss how collaborating with their clients and their colleagues has had a tremendous impact. Lastly, they have shared how comforting a predictable model of treatment is to their work and to their lives.

We too have had a great deal of success working with the model and are grateful to our colleagues and clients who have helped us incorporate each success into the next. We have been working with clients with a history of complex trauma for many years. Our work has been greatly enhanced by our understanding of interpersonal neurobiology that we did not have when we first started working with clients. Being able to explain to clients how it is that they are stuck and how they can rewire has been beneficial to our work. Many of our clients have shared with us how important this understanding has been for them.

We have received a great deal of positive feedback about how helpful our three-stage model is for work with clients with a history of complex trauma. Practitioners have shared that once they started using the model, they find themselves comforted by its predictability. One trainee said, "I have been working with traumatized clients for a very long time and used to get really frustrated at what I thought was resistance on their part. I had no idea what else to do at that point except to repeat the same thing I had been doing. Now I know that when I experience resistance, it is just a message that I need to go back to Stage One. Safety is so necessary and I hadn't realized it to such an extent until I started practicing the model. I have so many more options now and I am grateful for that."

Working the CCM has changed the way we think about change. This is the true meaning of consolidation. Now that the model has been internalized, it becomes a frame for much of the way we see the world. We recently read a story about restorative justice and thought that this was a story about the model. Baliga (Tullis, 2013), a survivor of child sexual abuse, realized that she needed to heal her wounds and, especially, calm her rage at her victimization, before she started law school. She traveled to India where she was told horrific stories from people who had experienced unspeakable trauma and yet had been able to forgive their perpetrators. Baliga was far from being able to consider forgiveness and was feeling even more lost and confused when someone mentioned that she should write to the Dalai Lama and seek his advice. She wrote that she knew her anger was killing her, but she wanted to work with people who had been traumatized and knew her anger motivated her work. Rather than write her back, the Dalai Lama invited her to meet with him, privately, for an hour.

The Dalai Lama gave Baliga two pieces of advice. He told her to meditate and to try and be one with her enemy. Baliga laughed and said the second was impossible. She said that she was planning to attend law school with the goal of locking up her enemy, and that she had no interest in opening her heart to them. It was at this point that the Dalai Lama patted her on her knee and with kindly acceptance said something like, "Okay, then just meditate." Baliga, in the telling of the story, comes to a great revelation in her meditative practice about forgiving her father, which changes how she sees the world and helps her work for restorative justice. To us, however, the story is about the intuitive wisdom of our model. The Dalai Lama recognized that Baliga was in Stage One and grounded her there. It is a profound example of the way we see how the CCM transcends treatment modalities and can inform all of our interactions.

For an audio file that explains Consolidation, please refer to the book's eResources site: www.routledgementalhealth.com/9780415510219.

Pause and Ponder: In thinking about consolidation, we think about the harnessing of all the moments that have preceded the current moment and using the information to be in the present and prepare for the future. It is taking the time to ponder where we came from, where we are now, and how we want to imagine the possibilities for the future. It could be future moments: walking to the bus, starting new relationships, new jobs, speaking differently, aging, giving birth, being without therapy—imagining the future possibilities and understanding how to integrate the past, the present, into the future.

In this moment, take the time to consolidate the experience of reading the book. What are the feelings? What are the thoughts: what still needs clarifying, what needs to be reviewed, what can be shared, what is integrated? What are the new beliefs and behaviors that are now in your repertoire? What needs to be practiced, what needs to be learned? What changes have happened from reading the book: what has been affirmed, confirmed, and what does the future hold for you in your work with clients with complex trauma?

It is not the strongest of the species that survives, nor the most intelligent that survives. It is the one that is the most adaptable to change.

Charles Darwin

Reference

Tullis, P. (2013). Can forgiveness play a role in criminal justice? *New York Times Magazine,* January 4.

Appendix 1
User-Friendly Diagram of the Brain

A simple, understandable way to think about our brain is to see it in three sections. We are thinking of it this way, not as neuroscientists, rather to help us plan how we are going to create new pathways.

Together, through what we learn, experience, and practice, we will be able to create new pathways. Each and every time we repeat a thought, a feeling, an experience, and/or a behavior, that helps move us toward our goals.

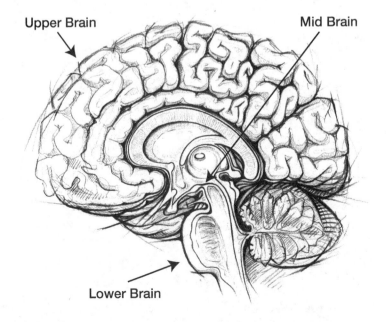

Upper Brain

Mid Brain

Lower Brain

The Lower Brain (the brainstem or hindbrain): This is where our survival instinctual behaviors and functions exist. It is at the base of the brain. It regulates our fight, flight, and freeze responses and autonomic functions such as digestion, heart rate, hunger, and breathing. It also manages our impulses and serves other reactive and protective functions.

The Mid Brain (the limbic brain): This regulates emotion and motivation as well as learning and memory. This part of our brain provides us with greater flexibility of behavior and integrates messages from both inside and outside the body. This is where we process nurturing, fear, social bonding, joy, stress, and other emotions. Information on where and how our body remembers is stored here.

The Upper Brain (the forebrain): This section regulates our executive functioning (planning, self awareness, and analysis that involves thought and feeling). The forebrain is where we experience logic, empathy, compassion, creativity, self-regulation, attention, and problem solving. The forebrain uses both left and right hemispheres and attempts to integrate information from the mid and lower brain to help us plan.

We want to build pathways between all parts of the brain to intersect and strengthen our engaged mindstate and to build pathways between our engaged mindstate and the engaged mindstates of others.

Appendix 2
Communication Skills

Skills for the Talker

1. CREATE YOUR POSITIVE INTENTION.
2. Use "I" statements.
3. Avoid the word "You" whenever possible.
4. Don't use the word "But."
5. State feelings.
6. Request a behavioral want.
7. State positives for the relationship.
8. Remember to breathe.

Skills for the Listener

1. Do not plan your rebuttal while listening.
2. Summarize what you heard, not word for word. Put into your own words what you heard.
3. Check in to see if you heard it correctly.
4. Wait for a response and further clarification.
5. Repeat Skills 2, 3, and 4.
6. Ask clarifying questions. Be curious, repeating skills in the process.
7. See if your partner is ready to switch roles.
8. Avoid the word "But."
9. Remember to breathe.

Appendix 3
Vulnerability/Survivor Worksheet

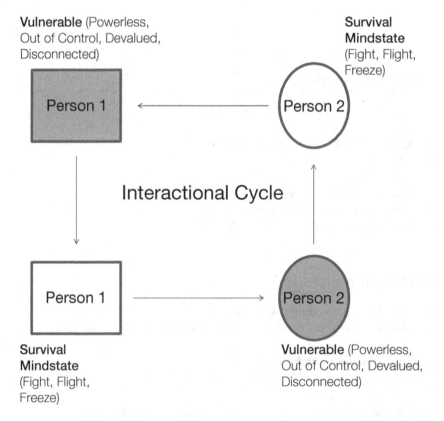

Vulnerable (Powerless, Out of Control, Devalued, Disconnected)

Survival Mindstate (Fight, Flight, Freeze)

Person 1 ← Person 2

Interactional Cycle

Person 1 → Person 2

Survival Mindstate (Fight, Flight, Freeze)

Vulnerable (Powerless, Out of Control, Devalued, Disconnected)

When person 1 is vulnerable they move to either survival mindstate or engaged mindstate, which will trigger either a vulnerable or a resourceful reaction in person 2. Our job is to help them identify these cycles and help them respond to vulnerability in self and in other from their engaged mindstate.

Appendix 4
Handout Explaining CCM

Collaborative Change Model: Collaborative Stages of Treatment

This outline is designed to familiarize you with how the CCM works. Although it is written in outline form, it doesn't happen in a step-by-step process. Change happens in a cyclical process—so all these ideas happen simultaneously, spontaneously, and repetitively throughout therapy. We believe that change is a collaborative process where you and your therapy team are co-creators of the change and co-collaborators in the process. Use these ideas as a touchstone and refer back to this outline frequently, with your therapists, so that you are fully aware of the cycle of change, where you are, where you have been, and where you are going. Please ask any and all questions you might have.

Stage One: Creating a Context for Change

A. Creating a safe relationship—What do we all need to make the relationship between us and the process of therapy a refuge?

Safety both inside and outside of the office

1. What CCM is all about: model, cycles, therapy, sessions
2. What brought you to treatment?
3. Do you have an idea of what successful therapy would be like, or how you want your life to be as a result of therapy?

B. Pretreatment planning and treatment planning—What has happened before our meeting? What professionals are involved? What helped? What didn't? Family members and community members involved?

    1. Refuge/sanctuary—Inside the office: defining, creating, building
    2. Safety—Outside the office: for all in the home—Emotional, physical, sexual, spiritual

C. Assessment—Getting to know you and how you grow and change

    1. Resources/resilience factors—How do you learn? How do you grow? What do you find helpful? How do you think you change?
    2. Vulnerability factors—What triggers you feeling powerless, devalued, disconnected, and out of control? And what do you do or not do to regain: power, value, connection and control?

D. Goal setting—What are your goals? What do you think others would say are goals for you? Creating a meaningful vision of the future
E. Positive and negative consequences of change
F. Introduction and explanation of possible interventions to reduce symptoms—Collaboration on what might work best and understanding the process of change
G. Acknowledgement—Agreeing on what needs to change and the process, roles, and commitment for all involved

Stage Two: Challenging Patterns and Expanding Realities

A. Patterns and cycles identified and mutually agreed

    1. Review of Stage One
    2. Identify old patterns/cycles and how they will be challenged, in and out of sessions
    3. Expanding realities—shifting in thoughts, feelings, and behaviors—Through different modalities
    4. Organizing and structuring the different modalities

B. Alternate realities and behaviors mutually explored

    1. In and out of session tasks and enactments—Mindfulness, cognitive, body-integrated, interpersonal
    2. Negative behavior cycle and or vulnerability/survivor cycle
    3. Alternatives—Modalities. Individual, family, couple, group
    4. Interpersonal—Skill-based interventions
    5. Symptom reduction—Interventions

C. Acknowledgement sessions—Progress in meeting goals for a vision of future

Stage Three: Consolidation

A. Punctuate changes

   1. Lifestyle changes
   2. Integrating changes

B. Relapse prevention/looking at future problem areas—Designing a plan
C. Acknowledgement: Change—Changes
D. Honoring the therapeutic relationship

Appendix 5
Sample No-Violence Contract

Physical, emotional, sexual, and/or spiritual violence is extremely harmful to all relationships. We are committing toward a Non-Violent Relationship and Family. Participation in physically and emotionally aggressive behavior on the part of one or both partners (or family members) results in numerous negative consequences. Some of these effects include: loss of trust, loss of respect for self and partner (or family member), emotional and physical pain, lack of intimacy, legal complications and less time spent together. Interpersonal violence interferes with life and with the possibilities for growth. Interpersonal violence makes it impossible to have a healthy and happy life.

For these reasons, I/we are making a commitment, both written and verbal, to stop all violence in our relationship and in our home.

By violence we mean harming or threatening to harm your partner or family member, either physically or emotionally. I _____ agree not to inflict any damage physically or sexually on any person, particularly in my family, or on myself. This includes no hitting, kicking, biting, throwing objects, scratching, pushing, shoving, restraining or excessive yelling, belittling, threatening or name calling. I will not destroy any property of mine or of anyone else.

When I feel powerless, out of control, and devalued, I am vulnerable to becoming violent or aggressive. The following experiences trigger my vulnerabilities toward anger and aggression:

_____

_____

_____

_____

I can tell when I am triggered toward anger, aggression, and violence when:

_____

_____

_____

_____

_____

_____

I agree to practice the following skills as a means to prevent my violence:

_____

_____

_____

_____

When I feel as though I may become violent in spite of my skills, I agree to the following plan (to be filled in by client with appropriate strategies determined in therapy session):

_____

_____

_____

_____

_____

I also agree on the method which my spouse has chosen as a way to protect her/himself in the case where I threaten violence by action or word. Her/his actions of protection will not cause me to threaten or be further violent.

If I become violent at any time, defined by the conditions above, I then agree to do one or more of the following (examples might be to pay restitution, to call the police, to move out, to be hospitalized):

_____

_____

_____

_____

_____

I am signing this of my own free will.

Signature _____   Date _____

Signature _____

Witness _____

Appendix 6
Vulnerability/Resource Handout

Vulnerability/Resource Model

SOCIAL/POLITICAL CONTEXTS

Community   Gender   Economic   Cultural

Religious   Special Needs   Racial

Sexual Orientation   Media   Education   Sex   Age

FAMILIAL CONTEXTS

Hierarchy   Attachment   Communication Patterns

Style   Rules   Peers   Roles

Adaptability   Boundaries

Transgenerational Patterns

INDIVIDUAL CONTEXT

Physiological/Biological/Neurological Patterns

Dissociation Continuum

Vulnerability/Survivor Cycle

Coping Mechanisms

Impulse Control

Special Needs

Mental Health

Temperament

Intelligence

Addictions

POWER ATTACHMENT CONTROL

Adapted from Trepper, T., & Barrett, M.J. (1989). *Systemic treatment of incest: A therapeutic handbook.* New York: Brunner/Mazel.

Appendix 7
List of Evaluative Tools

Adult and Youth Assessment Tools
Compiled and used by: Mark Brenzinger, Psy.D.
Licensed Clinical-Forensic Psychologist
www.PsychologicalRiskServices.com

Psychosexual Risk Assessment

Address the potential risk for sexual abuse/violence to others and identify if a client would benefit from participating in a psychotherapeutic treatment program to address sexual deviance, as well as other relevant treatment interventions (e.g., substance abuse/dependence, anger management or expression, psychiatric evaluation, and/or individual counseling) and safety planning.

Psychosexual Test Battery/Protocol

- Record review (e.g., criminal background, police/child protective investigation reports, past/current medical/mental health treatment providers, when available and accessible)
- Collateral information (e.g., legal guardian, past/current treatment providers, when available and accessible)

For Adult Males (Appropriate Substitutions Made for Adult Females)

Standardized psychological tests that address the following:

- Mental status (e.g., Cognistat, Mini-Mental Status Examination)
- Cognitive functioning (e.g., Shipley-2, The Wechsler Adult Intelligence Scale—4th Ed.)

- Psychopathology (e.g., Personality Assessment Inventory, Minnesota Multiphasic Personality Inventory—2nd Ed., Millon Clinical Multiaxial Inventory—3rd Ed.)
- Alcohol and illicit substance use (e.g., Substance Abuse Subtle Screening Inventory—3rd Ed.)
- Measure of sexual interest/preference (Multiphasic Sex Inventory—2nd Ed., Abel Assessment of Sexual Interest—2nd Ed.)
- Application of appropriate actuarial measures/structured professional judgment guides (e.g., Static-99R, Stable-2007, Acute-2007, Risk for Sexual Violence Protocol)
- Clinical, diagnostic, and forensic interview

For Adolescent Males Ages 12+ (Appropriate Substitutions Made for Adolescent Females)

Standardized psychological tests that address the following:

- Mental status (e.g., Mini-Mental Status Examination)
- Cognitive functioning (e.g., Shipley-2, Wechsler Intelligence Scale for Children—4th Ed.)
- Psychopathology (Adolescent Psychopathology Scale, Personality Assessment Inventory—Adolescent)
- Alcohol and illicit substance use (e.g., Substance Abuse Subtle Screening Inventory—Adolescent)
- Measure of sexual interest/preference (Multiphasic Sex Inventory—2nd Ed., Abel Assessment of Sexual Interest—2nd Ed.)
- Application of appropriate structured professional judgment guides (e.g., The Estimate of Risk of Adolescent Sexual Offense Recidivism, The Juvenile Sex Offender Assessment Protocol—II)
- Clinical, diagnostic, and forensic interview

Violence Risk Potential Assessment

Address the potential risk for violence (domestic/intimate partner, workplace, and/or general) to others and identify if a client would benefit from participating in a psychotherapeutic treatment program to address interpersonal violence, as well as other relevant treatment interventions (e.g., anger management or expression, domestic violence, substance abuse/dependence, psychiatric evaluation, and/or individual counseling) and safety planning.

Violence Risk Potential Test Battery/Protocol

- Record review (e.g., criminal background, police/child protective investigation reports, workplace incident reports, past/current medical/mental health treatment providers, when available and accessible)
- Collateral information (e.g., employment supervisors, legal guardian, past/current treatment providers, when available and accessible)

For Adult Males (Appropriate Substitutions Made for Adult Females)

Standardized psychological tests that address the following:

- Mental status (e.g., Cognistat, Mini-Mental Status Examination)
- Cognitive functioning (e.g., Shipley-2, The Wechsler Adult Intelligence Scale—4th Ed.)
- Psychopathology (e.g., Personality Assessment Inventory, Minnesota Multiphasic Personality Inventory—2nd Ed., Millon Clinical Multiaxial Inventory—3rd Ed.)
- Alcohol and illicit substance use (e.g., Substance Abuse Subtle Screening Inventory—3rd Ed.)
- Anger management and expression (e.g., Anger Disorder Scale, State-Trait Anger Expression Inventory—2nd Ed.)
- Application of appropriate structured professional judgment guides (e.g., Workplace Assessment of Violence Risk, Historical-Clinical-Risk–20—3rd Ed., Spousal Assault Risk Assessment, Stalking Assessment and Management, Structured Assessment of Protective Factors)
- Clinical, diagnostic, and forensic interview

For Adolescent Males Ages 12+ (Appropriate Substitutions Made for Adolescent Females)

Standardized psychological tests that address the following:

- Mental status (e.g., Mini-Mental Status Examination)
- Cognitive functioning (e.g., Shipley-2, Wechsler Intelligence Scale for Children—4th Ed.)
- Psychopathology (Adolescent Psychopathology Scale, Personality Assessment Inventory—Adolescent)
- Alcohol and illicit substance use (e.g., Substance Abuse Subtle Screening Inventory—Adolescent)

- Anger management and expression (e.g., State-Trait Anger Expression Inventory— 2nd Ed.)
- Application of appropriate structured professional judgment guides (e.g., Structured Assessment of Violence Risk in Youth)
- Clinical, diagnostic, and forensic interview

Child Assessment Tools

TSCC: www4.parinc.com/Products/Product.aspx?Productid=TSCC.

TSCYC: www4.parinc.com/Products/Product.aspx?ProductID=TSCYC.

UCLA PTSD: www.istss.org/UCLAPosttraumaticStressDisorderReactionIndex.htm.

Beck Depression: www.pearsonassessments.com/HAIWEB/Cultures/en-us/Product detail.htm?Pid=015–8018–370.

ConnersADHD: www.pearsonassessments.com/HAIWEB/Cultures/en-us/Product detail.htm?Pid=Conners_3.

Index

Note: 'f' after a page number indicates a figure.